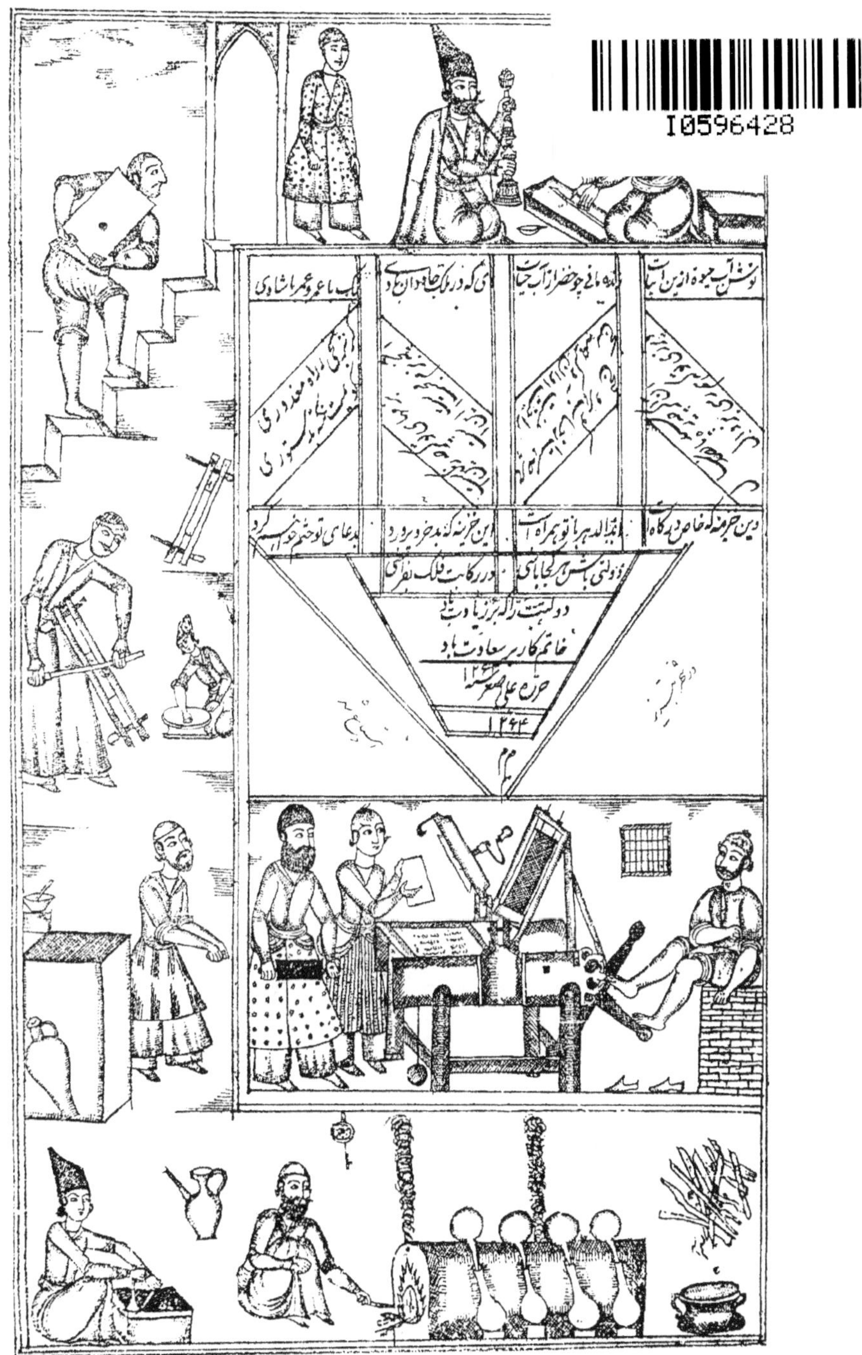

Illustration of nineteenth-century printing-press economy, from *Khamse* 1264/1847 (Tabriz, Iran).

Source: Illustration is kindly provided by Dr Ulrich Marzolph from his Archive of Illustrations in Persian Lithographed Books.

LITERARY MODERNITY BETWEEN THE MIDDLE EAST AND EUROPE

Only recently has the field of comparative literature begun to more seriously regard the study of modern Middle Eastern literatures. Yet, despite increasing interest in the field of such work, currently few academic studies concerning the comparative study of modern Persian, Arabic, and other regional literatures are available. This book aims to fill a gap not only in the often-Eurocentric field of comparative literature but also to impact upon the prevalent mono-linguistic framework in the study of modern Middle Eastern literatures.

The book examines the effect of circulations between Arabic, Persian, and English literatures in the nineteenth century and their interrelations with specific reference to modernity and social value. In opposition to the still predominant national-literature framework for literary study, it is the thesis of this book that the defining transformation to literary practice during this period may be best considered to have emerged from "transactional" texts—texts engendered through and emergent from travel or other intercultural contacts or through translation and circulation, and, that the modernity of these texts is a result of transformation in the social value of literature in these societies.

This highly researched book provides an essential read for students and scholars of comparative literature, cultural studies, and Middle Eastern Studies.

Kamran Rastegar is Lecturer in Arabic and Persian at the University of Edinburgh. He researches cultural history, postcolonial studies, and the cinemas of Iran and the Arab world.

ROUTLEDGE STUDIES IN MIDDLE EASTERN LITERATURES

Routledge Studies in Middle Eastern Literatures is a monograph series devoted to aspects of the literatures of the Near and Middle East and North Africa both modern and pre-modern. It is hoped that the provision of such a forum will lead to a greater emphasis on the comparative study of the literatures of this area, although studies devoted to one literary or linguistic region are warmly encouraged. It is the editors' objective to foster the comparative and multi-disciplinary investigation of the written and oral literary products of this area.

1. SHEHERAZADE THROUGH THE LOOKING GLASS
Eva Sallis

2.THE PALESTINIAN NOVEL
Ibrahim Taha

3. OF DISHES AND DISCOURSE
Geert Jan van Gelder

4. MEDIEVAL ARABIC PRAISE POETRY
Beatrice Gruendler

5. MAKING THE GREAT BOOK OF SONGS
Hilary Kilpatrick

6. THE NOVEL AND THE RURAL IMAGINARY IN EGYPT, 1880–1985
Samah Selim

7. IBN ABI TAHIR TAYFUR AND ARABIC WRITERLY CULTURE
A ninth-century bookman in Baghdad
Shawkat M. Toorawa

8. RELIGIOUS PERSPECTIVES IN MODERN MUSLIM AND JEWISH LITERATURES
Edited by Glenda Abramson and Hilary Kilpatrick

9. ARABIC POETRY
Trajectories of modernity and tradition
Muhsin J. al-Musawi

10. MEDIEVAL ANDALUSIAN COURTLY CULTURE IN THE MEDITERRANEAN
Three ladies and a lover
Cynthia Robinson

11. WRITING AND REPRESENTATION IN MEDIEVAL ISLAM
Muslim Horizons
Julia Bray

12. NATIONALISM, ISLAM AND WORLD LITERATURE
Sites of confluence in the writings of Mahmūd al-Masadī
Mohamed-Salah Omri

13. THE ORAL AND THE WRITTEN IN EARLY ISLAM
Gregor Schoeler
Translated by Uwe Vagelpohl
Edited by James Montgomery

14. LITERATURE, JOURNALISM AND THE AVANT-GARDE
Intersection in Egypt
Elisabeth Kendall

15. THE THOUSAND AND ONE NIGHTS
Space, travel and transformation
Richard van Leeuwen

16. ARAB CULTURE AND THE NOVEL
Genre, identity, and agency in Egyptian fiction
Muhammad Siddiq

17. LITERARY MODERNITY BETWEEN THE MIDDLE EAST AND EUROPE
Textual transactions in nineteenth-century Arabic, English, and Persian literatures
Kamran Rastegar

LITERARY MODERNITY BETWEEN THE MIDDLE EAST AND EUROPE

Textual transactions in nineteenth-century Arabic, English, and Persian literatures

Kamran Rastegar

LONDON AND NEW YORK

First published 2007
by Routledge
2 Park Square, Milton Park, Abingdon, Oxon OX14 4RN

Simultaneously published in the USA and Canada
by Routledge
270 Madison Ave, New York, NY 10016

Routledge is an imprint of the Taylor & Francis Group, an informa business

Typeset in Times New Roman by
Newgen Imaging Systems (P) Ltd, Chennai, India

British Library Cataloguing in Publication Data
A catalogue record for this book is available
from the British Library

Library of Congress Cataloging in Publication Data
A catalog record for this book has been requested

ISBN10: 0–415–42565–4 (hbk)
ISBN10: 0–203–93978–6 (ebk)

ISBN13: 978–0–415–42565–0 (hbk)
ISBN13: 978-0-415-59744-9 (pb)
ISBN13: 978–0–203–93978–9 (ebk)

FOR ANNEMARIE

قُلْنَا: فَمَا تَقُولُ فِي ٱلْمُحْدَثِينَ مِنَ ٱلشُعَراء و ٱلْمُتَقَدِّمِينَ مِنْهُم. قَالَ: ٱلْمُتَقَدِّمُونَ أشْرَفُ لَفْظاً. و أكْثَرُ مِنَ ٱلْمَعَاني حَظّاً. و ٱلْمُتَأَخِرُونَ ألطَفُ صُنْعاً و أَرَقُّ نَسْجاً.

We said: What is thy opinion of the modern and the ancient poets? He answered: “The language of the ancients is nobler and their themes more delightful, whereas the conceits of the moderns are more refined and their style more elegant.”

(*The Maqamat of Badi' al-Zaman al-Hamadani*)

CONTENTS

ACKNOWLEDGMENTS

The themes explored in this work arose principally from research carried out during the year I spent researching in Cairo, where the staff at the Dar al-Kutub, and librarians at the library of the American University in Cairo kindly facilitated my access to materials in their archives. Also, at Cairo University, Professor al-Saba'i Muhammad al-Saba'i provided kind assistance to my research. In Iran, my work was greatly facilitated by a number of individuals: Mr Akbar Afsari and Dr Jahangir Raf'at helped to locate textual materials, and offered generous and valuable advice. Alireza Mashayekh also offered useful assistance in locating difficult-to-access periodicals around the city. Staff at the Kitabkhanih-yi Melli-yi Iran and at the archives of the Mu'assissih-yi Mutaliat-i Tarikh-i Mu'aser-i Iran were also exceptionally helpful. In addition, I must thank the inimitable author Mahmoud Dowlatabadi for his inspiring and engaging conversations on a wide range of literary matters. At those times when I was unable to travel to Iran, my aunt Tahereh Rastegar sent or personally brought books to me that were invaluable to my research.

I must first acknowledge Magda al-Nowaihi's important role in inspiring my profound interest in modern Arabic literature, while I was her student at Columbia University. Her approaches have continued to inspire me in this work long after her passing away. For support and advice during the conceptualization of this project, I must acknowledge both Hamid Dabashi and Muhsin al-Musawi. Ammiel Alcalay and Elliott Colla both helped in shaping this project through their friendship, as well as through insightful comments on my work that often opened my eyes to unexpected vistas, as well as by reassuring me through their examples that academic life can accommodate both originality and humanity. Gauri Viswanathan initiated my interest in themes explored in this work and kindly provided insightful comments to early drafts of two chapters. Nader Sohrabi was a kind reader and commentator on the dissertation that this book is based upon. I am thankful for Roger Allen's careful and thoughtful reading of the manuscript of this book, which resulted in many very helpful comments and suggestions. Of course, any shortcomings in the work as it is are entirely my own.

Institutional support in the form of a Fulbright Fellowship in Egypt in 2001–2002, and dissertation completion funding from the Columbia University provided important assistance to my research and writing. I am grateful to my colleagues at the University of Edinburgh for their encouragement and accommodation of this project during the 2005–2006 academic year, in particular Carole Hillenbrand, Andrew Newman, and Yasir Suleiman. Also at Edinburgh, Ayman Shihadeh provided very helpful suggestions on matters relating to translation. I am thankful to Brown University's Department of Comparative Literature for providing an inspiring and pleasurable setting for the early revisions of this work by hosting me as a visiting scholar in 2004–2005. Portions of Chapters 2 and 3 have appeared in an article published by the *Journal of Arabic Literature*. I am grateful to Koninklijke Brill N.V. for permission to reprint this material. I am also thankful to Ulrich Marzolph for generously making available the image that appears as the frontispiece to the book.

It is my aspiration that this work will serve as a testament to the inspiration I have gained from my parents Asghar and Faye Rastegar, as its completion would have been impossible without their support and care. My final acknowledgment of debt—the most profound, and thus the least sufficient in expression—goes to Annemarie Jacir, who has been my partner, intellectual companion, and deepest inspiration through the years this book has taken to write.

Kamran Rastegar
Edinburgh 2007

NOTE ON TRANSLITERATION

Transliteration of Arabic and Persian in this work has been carried out here in accordance to the guidelines of the *International Journal of Middle East Studies* (IJMES), modified to preclude the use of any diacritic marks. The letter *'ayn* is designated by the [‘] and the *hamza* is transliterated as [’].

Part 1

LITERARY HISTORY AND COMPARATIVE LITERATURE

The Middle East and Europe

INTRODUCTION

Writing in 1834, an anonymous literary critic offered the following thesis to explain the ascendance of a new form in English literature called the novel: "This species of composition belongs to modern literature. It is probably of oriental origin" ("On Novel Writing," p. 196). This statement displays a surprising clarity in identifying what is at this time a rather new subject for study and evaluation, namely modern literature, and the manner in which a "species of composition" known as the novel can be linked to it. The second sentence of this statement is even more provocative, proposing a foreign origin for the novel form. Our critic next offers a hypothesis for the origin of this category of literature, identifying a single text as its best exemplar:

> *The Arabian Nights* are said to contain true pictures of eastern opinions, life, and manners, while the tales are wrought up with exquisite skill, with great exuberance of imagination, yet with remarkable felicity of style; and the perfection to which these beautiful creations had been brought, when those nations first became known to Europeans, shows that it had long been practiced.
>
> (Ibid., p. 196)

As a statement, this is a rather common evaluation of the *Nights* for the time. By the middle of the nineteenth century, the *Nights* edition prepared by E.G. Lane would crescendo the perception that this text offers veritable representations of immutable social and historical qualities (usually termed "manners") of the orient. A list of comments made by other critics to this effect over the course of the nineteenth century—most often using phrases as florid as "true pictures and 'exuberance of imagination' "—would fill many pages, so much so that these claims were to reify the notion of the text serving ethnographic, even empirical uses. Yet, our aforementioned critic is primarily interested in the marriage of this value of the *Nights* only insofar as it is related to a modern literary form, the novel. For it is only by the early- to mid-nineteenth century that the novel becomes widely recognized as a serious object of analysis for English literary critics.

To be certain, the anachronistic appropriation of the *Nights* into the field of the novel was a move that invited some controversy, nonetheless it was widespread by the mid-nineteenth century. For example, the *Arabian Nights* and its variants could be commonly found in booksellers' advertisements in periodicals under the heading of "novels." Yet, the claim of the critic cited above goes much farther than the more facile categorization of the *Nights* as a novel so as to inscribe its place in the period's print economy. Here, the *Nights* is identified as representative of the proverbial source-waters of the novel. Our critic presumes a remarkable consonance within the two phrases in the claim: "This species of composition belongs to modern literature. It is probably of oriental origin." The conception of this literary genre as being intrinsically "modern" is itself a subject for later generations to contend with, but the claim of the form's probable "oriental origin" brings a new origin-myth into the category of "literary modernity." Simply stated, what does it mean to link the ascendant mode of the modern European literary imagination to the orient?

I have begun with the issue of the novel to highlight what may be the most fundamental ambition of this study—to rethink the landscape of nineteenth-century literary production in what we still term "the Middle East" and "the West," by sidestepping the limits of both the novel and the nation. This project instead argues that before the full deployment of nationalist discourse, the destiny of literary production was not yet foretold within the history of any specific narrative form. Thus, this project aims to produce a literary history of this period that sharpens the focus of the varied engagements with modernity within Arabic, English, and Persian-speaking societies, engagements that did not view modernity as prefiguring the nationalist discourses that were to emerge as dominant by the end of the nineteenth century. In one sense, the novel has served as a marker for the social and intellectual movements that came to coalesce around nationalist discourses. By disentangling the intellectual history of this period from the teleological reading of developments in nineteenth-century prose writing as culminating in the novel, we can also begin to view this history outside of the evaluative criteria of nationalism. One way to embark is by proposing that the telos of modernity itself is and has been a highly contested one, with neither nationalism nor the novel prewritten as its meridian in either the political or literary registers. By relegating both novel and nation to margins of its narrative, the literary history here proposed focuses on the issues that both of the former repress: interlinguistic subjectivities, ambiguous imaginative geographies, and dynamic shifts in cultural register. These phenomena, while often rooted in premodern cultural and inter-cultural relations, are markers of the episodes of contingent modernities represented by many nineteenth-century literary productions.

By highlighting the above three areas, I will be proposing a reading of the category of modernity that is predicated on uniquely modern innovations—both literary and cultural as well as political—that challenge the perception of modernity and nationalism as coterminating. Where nationalist modernities have emphasized a return to linguistic purity, empowering the conceptions of territorial and geographic boundaries, and, perhaps most importantly, the codification of cultural fields with defined values by which all cultural production is marked, many of the works I will be highlighting in this book can be read as representative of what might best be termed as contingent modernities. Furthermore, this project presents a historical perspective mapping a rough trajectory over the course of the long nineteenth century—one that follows a transformation from experimental and synthesizing literary forms to the codification of new "universal" forms and genres that came to recalibrate the boundaries of social valuation of literature.

In this work I will assess transformations to the practice and consumption of literature in both Middle Eastern and European societies during the nineteenth century, an endeavor arising from rather simple questions: Over the course of the nineteenth century, did exchanges between Middle Eastern and European literatures enable innovations in both literary form and function in these literatures? Or is the process of transformation of literature during this period—what may be termed the emergence of literary modernity—best understood as having unfolded primarily due to factors *internal* to specific languages such as Arabic, Persian or English?

These questions derive from the limitations of considering certain nineteenth-century works through a novel-centered literary–historical perspective. For example, when considering the *Arabian Nights* in its English, Arabic, and Persian incarnations during this period, the tensions between the category of "modern literature" and "of oriental origin" spills over the limitations of such a literary history. Tracing the complex chain of transregional and interlinguistic exchanges involved in the production, reception, and circulation of a text such as the *Arabian Nights* would certainly challenge the predominant mono-social or monolinguistic model often used in assessing the "rise" of the novel as the culminative modern literary form. Our critic may be onto something when proposing that texts that are marked by a history of circulation between distinct social and cultural arenas may be quite significant in the emergence of the modern category of "literature" for both European and Middle Eastern societies. Yet, in the intervening years, the unchallenged dominance of the national-literature model for the study of modern literary work has to a great extent obfuscated the significant interactions between these and other literatures during the course of the nineteenth century. This point brings into question certain commonly held beliefs on this period's transformations in literary practice and consumption, and the "emergence" of literary modernity in general.

It is widely accepted that only recently has the field of comparative literature begun to regard more seriously the study of modern non-European, and among these Middle Eastern, literatures as falling within its purview. Yet, despite increasing interest within the field for such work, arguably no academic studies concerning the comparative study of modern Persian, Arabic, and other regional literatures are currently available. Those studies that adopt what may be called the "East–West" framework, comparing European and non-European literatures along an axis drawn on a centre–periphery model, are more common, but even these approaches are rather rare. This book responds to interests not only in the often-Eurocentric field of comparative literature, but also to the impact upon the mono-linguistic frameworks prevalent in the study of modern Middle Eastern literatures. It does so by examining the effect of social and cultural interactions between Arabic and Persian literatures in the nineteenth century on innovations in these literatures, as well as considering the role of European literatures—in particular, English literature—in these transformations, no less than the measurable effect of Arabic and Persian literary works on English literature. The questions raised above delve directly into the limits of the predominant modes of literary study in both comparative literature and area studies.

In addition, even within the fields of modern Arabic and Persian literatures, the period of the nineteenth century has received rather insufficient attention, often factoring simply as a precursor to the discussions of ascendant forms such as the modernist novel or short story. Thus, studies of nineteenth-century Arabic and Persian literary works have too often valued these texts only in accordance with their assimilation into the trajectories of novelistic writing as well as their legitimacy within frameworks of nationalist discourse. This predicament may be termed the *nationalist–novelist paradigm* of literary criticism. In opposition to this limiting paradigm, we may enquire to what extent the defining transformations to literary practice during this period may best be considered to have emerged as a result of *textual transactions*—resulting in the creation of texts engendered through and emergent from translation, appropriation and circulation of textual materials across cultural boundaries, and how these transactions brought about transformations in the social function of literature in these societies. These transformations resulted in the emergence of arenas for the autonomy of literary production from previous forms of legitimation and value. I will propose the term *literary transaction* to discuss how interlinguistic exchanges of texts served to innovate literary practice and to alter the predominant systems of legitimation and evaluation of literature.

Textual transactions mark the encounters and exchanges between social fields with different cultural value systems. In these encounters, and through these exchanges, the revaluation of a text is calculated in consideration of the various costs of the encounter. The concept of textual transactions may be most easily articulated around the economy of translation. As Tejaswini Niranjana notes, "translation studies . . . seems to be by and large unaware that an attempt should be made to account for the relationships between 'unequal' languages . . . Its notions of text, author and meaning are based on an unproblematic, naively representational theory of language . . . [resulting from] the refusal to consider questions of power and historicity" (Tejaswini, *Siting Translation*, pp. 48–9).

It is for this reason that the second part of this study is devoted to the translations of *Alf layla wa layla* as the *Arabian Nights* or as *Hizar u yik shab* (as it was rendered in Persian). By approaching *Alf layla wa layla* as a transactional text, its translation is understood to not simply have implications within the fields of linguistics and aesthetics, but also is situated within social and cultural histories of the cultures and societies that consumed the text. While work has been done to advance our understanding of the material circumstances around the development of nineteenth-century Arabic and Persian editions of the *Nights*, few studies have addressed the question of what social value these modern editions were thought to hold for their various readerships. What is at stake in these questions is a more rigorous understanding of how *Alf layla wa layla* came to find a position of increasing cultural value for nineteenth- and twentieth-century readerships in the English-, Arabic-, and Persian-speaking societies of the world. The transformation of the value of the text over the course of this period illuminates the changing social role of literary practice and consumption in these societies.

By foregrounding texts that are to a great extent formed through their circulation between social and linguistic arenas, we may posit that textual transaction is an important catalyst of the development of categories of modern literature. The effect of these transformations may be termed—with reference to Pierre Bourdieu's theory of cultural capital—the emergence of an *autonomous field of literary production*; a field no longer deriving legitimacy either from sacred or theological utility, nor from accordance to a sovereign's pleasure, but from an entirely self-sufficient system of values and legitimization. This book follows the emergence of autonomous areas for literature as a cultural product over the course of the nineteenth century, and shows that literary transactions were key to the development of autonomous systems of value for writing.

The first chapter of this book outlines how, over the course of the nineteenth century, Arabic, Persian, and English literatures were each marked by innovating and transformative stages that arose very specifically through interlinguistic exchanges between these literatures. The relations of these literatures during this period is read through the history of the intensification of the British colonial project, and the very different social effects of colonialism within these societies. The theory of literary transaction is discussed with reference to these three literary traditions, and is related to discussions within the field of translation studies. A literature review shows the precedents for this study, as well as identifying gaps both in the fields of comparative literature and Middle Eastern studies in addressing these questions.

In Part 2 of this study, comprising two chapters, I examine how the book productions of the *Alf layla wa layla* in Arabic, English, and Persian editions emerged from a constellation of textual transactions, enabled through colonial institutions, to circulate within various readerships (themselves rife with anxieties over the social value of the text). The effect of these literary transactions is examined, with a focus on how they were to legitimize the emergence of autonomous fields of English, Persian, and Arabic literary production. Reconsidering the historical conditions surrounding the production of printed book editions of this text in each language, I use a comparative framework to show the interrelations between them. Through this framework, I conclude that the specific historical circumstances of each edition evince the manner in which political and ideological concerns played critical roles in the social value accorded to the text during the time of its production and afterward.

Specifically, in Chapter 2, I focus on English criticism of the *Nights* through outlining the framework of an important debate between critics who emphasized religious or moralist values as central to the idea of literature, and those who highlighted the utilitarian aspects of public consumption of the text—most often identifying the value of the text for the colonial project. Chapter 3 follows the history of the production of printed Arabic editions of *Alf layla wa layla*—from its appearance within colonial educational facilities in India, to the landmark publication of the 1835 Bulaq edition, which inaugurated the text as a benchmark for Arabic book production, and heralded a re-appropriation of the text by nineteenth-century Arab intellectuals. To examine this, I present readings of the work of Arab critics and intellectuals who re-evaluated *Alf layla wa layla* in the late nineteenth century, often in reaction to engagements they had with European criticism of the text. This chapter then follows critical discourse on the Arab editions of the text through the end of the century, as debates over moral and ethical concerns related to the text, and the wider acknowledgment of women's roles as part of the reading public led to the abridgment and editing of later editions in line with Victorian English editions. The history of the Persian translation of the text in the provincial court of Tabriz during the 1840s is also situated within the cultural policies of the city's reformist governor, as a work carried out by an innovating religious cleric within the court. By reflecting this history against an early twentieth-century essay by the Iranian Minister of Education addressing the value of *Hizar u yik shab* within an emerging nationalist agenda for Persian literature, this analysis shows the tenuous relation of the mythic nationalist imagination to the actual material circumstances for the initial production of the modern text within Iran. These two chapters examine how the transactions of *Alf layla wa layla* between these languages resulted in a new estimation of its value for the text among its various readerships. Through this study I propose that these developments are closely linked to the emergence of a largely autonomous category of secular literature outside of religious or monarchical systems of legitimization.

Part 3 of *Literary Modernity Between the Middle East and Europe* focuses on the themes of travel and translation as significant dimensions to understanding the innovating potential of transactionary texts. In Chapter 4, I present an overview of the travelogue genre in Arabic and Persian during the nineteenth century, focusing on changes from religious and monarchical authorization for travel writing to a more subjective and autonomous mode of writing. In particular I discuss the travelogues of Hajj Sayyah, Rifa'a Rafi' al-Tahtawi, and Mirza Salih Shirazi, as close readings of these texts trace both subtle and more explicit transformations in travel writing in Arabic and Persian during this period. The transactionary aspect of this form of writing—given its "translation" of foreign spaces, manners, and texts—is shown to be a catalyst for innovations in the genre during this period. Through close readings of these texts I show how central travelogues were to the innovation of narrative prose writing, and to the reconfiguration of social values for the act of writing. Hajj Sayyah, in particular, set developmental themes—in the form of narratives of personal development through the experience of travel—into the transactional framework of his travelogue.

I turn to the enigmatic Levantine Ahmad Faris al-Shidyaq in Chapter 5, presenting his book *al-Saq 'ala al-Saq* as a further step into the subjective sphere of travel writing. However, in opposition to the developmental themes at the heart of Hajj Sayyah's work, Shidyaq's experiment hearkens to a form of modern imagination that refuses a codifiable identity, or a developmental model of personal narrative. Through a comparison with the Iranian reformist author and publisher Mirza Malkum Khan, I explore how the question of religious conversion enabled as well as confounded the assumption of modern subjective positions for intellectuals in the Islamic world, even when residing in Europe.

Chapter 6 includes examinations of the seminal fictional travelogues of Egypt's Muhammad al-Muwaylihi (*Hadith 'Isa ibn Hisham*, or *The Story of Isa ibn Hisham*), and Iran's Zayn al-'Abedin Maraqihi (*Safarnamih-yi Ibrahim Bayg*, or *The Travels of Ibrahim Bayg*)—both from the 1890s—showing how textual transactions in these late nineteenth-century works enabled investigations of the nature of subjectivity as well as of the institutional transformations of Iranian and Egyptian societies. Yet the appellation of each as an early example of novelistic writing has led to fairly limited engagements with these texts—in many cases only leading to discussions of how each text was a "failed novel."

The final chapter presents a study of the English fictional travel narrative of James Morier's *Hajji Baba Ispahani* (1826) itself a transactionary text for English readerships, which underwent significant re-estimation through its translation into Persian in the last decades of the century. Its publication on the eve of the Iranian Constitutional Revolution propelled its paradoxical reception among Persian-language readerships as an "anti-colonial" text, despite or perhaps enabled by confusion in both English and Iranian contexts over the identity of the author and the translator of the text. I argue that while the readerships of *Hajji Baba* were differently constituted in the British and Iranian contexts, there are affinities between the prevalent discourses of each readership that allowed for its migration through the act of translation. Complicated by misrecognition, the writing of *Hajji Baba* was initially as overdetermined as its readership was unrecognizable—produced through textual transactions, it played a catalyzing role in the innovation of the social role and value of literature in both England and Iran.

I conclude by positioning this study among larger questions currently subject to debate in the academic humanities, especially concerning methodologies for studying non-European literatures and cultures. These questions point to the need to reinvigorate the philological sciences—while considering the problematic history of philology within the colonial and postcolonial academy—for a more critical and rigorous study of modern literatures, and in particular the literary history of the nineteenth century. It does so by referencing a call for a return to philological study made by Edward Said in the lectures contained in *Humanism and Democratic Criticism*. Arguing that the questions of this study—tracing, for example, the development of transactionary texts, and the autonomy of the field of literary production in the nineteenth century—can be best approached through a philological methodology, this conclusion attempts to articulate a brief outline of the methodology of critical philology. Through this form of philological study, the field of comparative literature may be able to address critical questions between diverse literatures such as Arabic, English, and Persian concerning fundamental assumptions about the nature of literary modernity.

In this work I have elected to develop a range of critical portraits so as to illuminate the central assertions presented in the first chapter. In doing so, I have had to be less inclusive than some readers will feel is necessary—in my mind, the selectivity allowed for greater depth in my analysis. Nonetheless, there are certain geographic, temporal, and textual gaps that were unavoidable for a variety of reasons. In the discussions on nineteenth-century Arabic literature, the reader will note an absence of anything beyond a cursory mention of work from North Africa; similarly, when speaking of Persian literature, little substantive discussion in this text concerns the subcontinent's contributions during the period discussed; the examples from English literature are both limited and, in the case of Morier's work, very non-canonical. In this sense, I would like to warn the reader that the methodology of this study is somewhat less than systematic, and the scope less than encyclopedic. Indeed, the purpose of these omissions largely reflects the difficulty involved in choosing only a handful of the many available texts as case studies for a study such as this. It is my hope that the reader will not be quick to judge the merit of the discussions initiated here simply by what may be termed gaps, and instead will be generous enough to judge the applicability of the questions raised to the geographic areas, periods, and authors that have necessarily fallen outside the scope of the present work.

1

THE LITERARY ABACUS

Transactions in nineteenth-century Arabic, English, and Persian literatures

> The essence of this is that modernity should be a creative vision, or it will be no more than a fashion. Fashion grows old from the moment it is born, while creativity is ageless. Therefore not all modernity is creativity but creativity is eternally modern.
>
> (Adonis, *An Introduction to Arab Poetics*)

> We are touching here upon the radical impulse that stands behind all genuine modernity when it is not merely a descriptive synonym for the contemporaneous or for a passing fashion.
>
> (Paul de Man "Literary History and Literary Modernity")

Modernity and literary historical scholarship

Speaking of modernity is not unlike speaking of the divine—the concept adheres through a faith in its object, but nonetheless is continually contested by divergent interpretations, different narratives.[1] Thus, despite its wide acceptance and employment in different academic contexts as a reified category, modernity remains a highly problematic concept, its application often complicated by ideological considerations. Thus, modernity has retained an ambivalence captured well in the "well-qualified" comment in Jane Austen's *Persuasion* that "modern minds and manners" bring about "a state of alteration, *perhaps* of improvement" (Austen, *Persuasion*, p. 38).[2] This unease about the value of modernity is not easily discounted, despite the dominance of positivistic approaches to it; indeed most often this ambivalence flows from the very point with which I began these comments: the contested nature of modernity.

With Austen's comment comes the realization that in the "early" stages of modernity, no less than in its "late" stages, the configuration of the alterations that are encoded within this term have been viewed by many as of an uncertain value.[3] While the vulgar appellation of "the modern" often presumes a collaboration with historical positivism, and in so doing renders modernity a category apart from criticism, it is useful to recall the positions of resistance that have arisen against certain formations of modernity, in both Europe as well as in the colonized world.

Thus it is that modernity has a non-European face as well, however difficult it has been to define it.[4] Ali Gheissari, writing about the concept of modernity in Iranian intellectual history, notes, "what is defined as 'modern', however, never really became a standard or definite pattern of action, impression, or experience rooted in the society, and the experience of modernity varied" (Gheissari, *Iranian Intellectuals in the Twentieth Century*, p. 14). This reading of modernity as unevenly applied, or somehow "belated" in effect and distribution, is important to understanding the cultural history of nineteenth-century colonial societies.[5]

In thinking about the colonial context of modernity, it may be useful to revisit another foundational reference in the construction of this term, also betraying traces of uncertainty about how to value the term modernity, which comes to us from Baudelaire: "Modernity is the transient, the fleeting, the contingent; it is one half of art, the other being the eternal and immutable" (quoted in Nicholls, *Modernisms*, p. 5). This view of the modern goes much farther than Austen's somewhat cautious view, by defining the very act of change as modernity; going so far as to charge it with a central role in the conceptualization of the sublime. The Arabic poet Adonis echoes this by saying "not all modernity is creativity but creativity is eternally modern" (Adonis, *An Introduction to Arab Poetics*, p. 21). Aesthetics, when separated from its divine imperative through the project of Enlightenment, requires a new valuative basis—here Baudelaire is setting terms of aesthetic value that will come to define modernity. Baudelaire values the concept of the modern from a positivist perspective, linking the newly autonomous category of "art" to the state of modernity—indeed, in this conception neither category is redeemable without recourse to the other. Nonetheless, the autonomy presumed by Baudelaire's definition of art has an element of Euro-centrism to it. As we will discover, modernity within the colonial world is less often linked to this bifurcation of art between the aesthetic sublime and the temporal condition of the modern. However, what is useful for us in Baudelaire's definition is the acknowledgment of a bifurcation between the sublime and the temporal—it is in this space that culture gains autonomy from the clutch of religious and monarchical systems of legitimation.

For those societies that have not commonly been granted the mantle of an indigenous modernity, these concerns—about defining modernity and about valuing it—are still of fundamental importance. One affectation of the colonial project has been the claiming of modernity for colonizing societies; the experience of colonialism (in all of its forms) is thus tied closely to the genesis of the concept of modernity (Chatterjee, *The Nation and its Fragments*, pp. 237–9). This argument needs no great rehearsal here; it is carried through in much of the work of postcolonial scholarship, and has been widely discussed and debated in recent scholarship on colonial histories and cultures. Yet it has been the case that the postcolonial division of the modern as either a feature of colonial hegemony or as the defining feature of indigenous nationalisms, has limited the utility of the concept of modernity, particularly in its use in the realm of aesthetics. In colonial contexts, discussions of modernity have often been overdetermined by the political projects of colonialism and anti-colonialism. As a result, colonized societies have often found their claim to aesthetic modernities to be only validated when they have coincided with aspects of these political projects. For example, in the field of literature, the ascendance of a national-literature framework has resulted in an evaluative framework that assesses twentieth-century literary practice along lines resonating with the project of nationalism.

But to what extent is our understanding of nineteenth-century literary practice mediated by the national-literature models that we still use in approaching them today? Put differently, one may ask whether contemporary evaluations of literary texts of the nineteenth century are essentially arrived at by using the national-literature models that remain ascendant today? The answer to these questions may relate to the interplay of two terms, "nationalism," and "novelism." The latter term is defined by Clifford Siskin as "the habitual subordination of writing to the novel"—it is the prevalent tendency to approach prose writing in general using a framework of value derived from criticism on the novel (Siskin, "Rise of Novelism," p. 423). Rather than evaluating texts of this period using criteria that can be philologically ascribed to the sites of their production, we tend to a historically employ a framework of value derived from a currently ascendant form of writing. I will examine how this paradigm—what I will call the nationalist–novelist paradigm in shorthand—has limited scholarly perspectives on nineteenth-century literary practice.

The terms here employed are general ones; by speaking of nationalism, one must be careful not to dehistoricize the shifting basis of nationalist discourse even when considering even a single nation's history. Furthermore, the term *novelistic writing* must be articulated with a consideration of the manifold directions and permutations the novel form has followed. The project of the validation of texts on the basis of nationalist proclivities, which finds its parallels the centralization of novelistic writing in the evaluation of modern literature, is the central project of nationalist–novelist paradigm.[6] In a sense, each term, nationalism and novelism, presumes the other. Echoing this, Siskin argues that novelistic writing was employed by British nationalism in "domesticating" myriad practices and genres of modern writing that by the nineteenth century had come to be considered a social threat (Siskin, "Rise of Novelism," p. 424). It is widely argued that the novel is the genre of the age of nationalism. Benedict Anderson famously links national consciousness to the new temporal considerations that arise out of novelistic writing that create a conception of community central to nationalist discourse (Anderson, *Imagined Communities*, pp. 24–5). Franco Moretti goes farther in exploring the spatial and geographic homologies between the novel and the nation, relating the imaginative spaces of the novel to the material borders of the nation (Moretti, *Atlas of the European Novel*, pp. 13–73). The novel is also closely linked to colonialism—both Edward Said and Patrick Brantlinger have described the novel as the form *par excellence* of the colonial and imperial imagination, in this sense relating it to projects of nationalism, even in anti-colonial contexts.[7] As Said terms it, "the novel, as a cultural artifact of bourgeois society, and imperialism, are unthinkable without each other...imperialism and the novel fortified each other to such a degree that it is impossible, I would argue, to read one without in some way dealing with the other" (Said, *Culture and Imperialism*, pp. 70–1).

The condition of evaluating literary modernity through the rationalizing lens of nationalism, and through the criteria set by novelism, is still a prevailing method for the study of nineteenth-century literature. This paradigm has obscured the study of this period's literatures, particularly those of colonized societies: to look outside this paradigm is to consider the literary work of this period in light of the specific contingencies within various projects of modernity. Yet, the failure of these contingent modernities can not justify the historical erasure that contemporary literary historiography has enacted, by overlaying a single narrative for modernity over these divergent histories. If modernity has always been contested, writing a history of the contestations of modernity requires a consideration of its contingencies throughout its history.

The outcome of this trend has been a certain impoverishment of approaches for postcolonial scholars of the history of aesthetic modernities. Much of what has been called postcolonial scholarship on cultural modernity is marked by what Aamir Mufti has succinctly described as auratic criticism—which he describes as,

> a pervasive language and mood in the contemporary critical scene that is concerned with the inauthenticity of postcolonial culture, community, and politics, and in which authenticity comes to attach itself to the concepts of certain cultural practices as a kind of aura, as the practices themselves come to be seen as resources for the overcoming of the forms of alienation that are the result, and the subjective dimension, of the colonial encounter.
>
> (Mufti, "Aura of Authenticity," pp. 87–8)

Mufti argues that concerns with authenticity in the colonized world are part of the traumas of colonialism, and that nationalist recourse to conceptions of tradition or authenticity have stunted the comprehension and critical assessment of other forms of modernity, those he would term vernacular modernities (Mufti, "Aura of Authenticity," p. 99). For example, this is a critical problem in scholarship on modern literatures of the Islamic world, and in particular of Persian and Arabic literatures. To begin with, there has remained an unfortunate bifurcation between what may be termed local and outside scholars in both contexts, a division that any researcher of this body of literature confronts either consciously or unconsciously. By local scholars, I mean the grouping of "native" scholars who for the most part write in the language they are researching, while the latter grouping includes native-born and foreign scholars who write generally in Western European languages, most frequently English, on the literature in question—in this case, institutional bearers of the legacy of oriental studies in the West. However these groups have generally shared similar paradigms in their approach to modern literature. A generation of outside scholars of Arabic literature has focused a great portion of their attention to the development of novelistic writing, often working within the value system created by the nationalist–novelist paradigm.[8] Local scholars have also worked within a similar framework, often pioneering the canons of literary value in bibliographic scholarship that is picked up by outside scholars. For example, Egyptian critics such as Luis 'Awad and 'Abd al-Muhsin Taha Badr have had great influence in the domestic organization of evaluative methods for literary study around nationalist agendas.[9] In Lebanon 'Abd al-Majid Husayn Zaqarit; in Iraq, 'Umar Talib; and in Morocco 'Abd al-Rahim 'Allam all have provided texts focusing on a national-literary reading of Arabic literature from these countries.

Local scholars have excelled, to a great extent, in providing descriptive cultural histories of their home societies (most often defined along national lines) while outside scholars have most often engaged in analytical and conceptual approaches to these same histories, occasionally in comparative contexts. Certainly, exceptions to each of these generalizations do exist, yet this bifurcation of scholarship—marked by linguistic difference in the writing of it—has resulted in quite different agendas in the general field of the study of cultural history in these societies; one that may not be as apparent in Western European contexts, for example.

This bifurcation has complicated attempts to investigate the social history of literature within these contexts. Along with Mufti, I would argue that this is a defining problem in postcolonial criticism, which is why scholarship on certain Western European literatures to a great extent has already begun to examine the relationship of social histories to literary production. I do not point this out in order to revive the developed–underdeveloped trope that often weighs down such comparative assessments. Instead, I wish to emphasize that the development of this bifurcation between local and outside scholars is a product of the colonial and postcolonial histories of these societies, and both show traces of the traumatic search for authenticity that Mufti has identified as part of the predicament of the postcolonial world. Thus, much of the scholarship by both local and outside scholars can be characterized as auratic criticism—and so insufficient in fully assessing the critical possibilities of vernacular modernities in the colonial world.

A more significant problem in the larger field of literary scholarship concerning this period lies within the prevalent paradigms for the study of this subject. The focus of this question will necessarily center upon analytical and theoretical works, which are more abundant among "outside" scholars, and which are largely available in English. This should not be read as a marginalization of the work of "inside" scholars, which will come to provide this study with much of its detail in later chapters. In Persian, for example, the encyclopedic scope of Yahya Aryanpur's *Az Saba Ta Nima: Tarikh-i Sad u Panjah Sal-i Adab-i Farsi* (From Saba To Nima: The History of 150 Years of Persian Literature) provides unrivalled detail and depth of focus in presenting biographical and bibliographical information on the major literary figures and trends in nineteenth- and early-twentieth-century Persian literature. In Arabic, Hamdi Sakkut's multi-volume *al-Riwaya al-Arabiyya*,

Bibliyujrafiya wa Madkhal Naqdi, 1865–1995 (The Arabic Novel, Bibliography and Critical Introduction, 1865–1995), presents a similarly thorough catalogue of novelistic prose writing in the language, including significant attention paid to texts from the latter half of the nineteenth century.

On the other hand, recent outside scholarship has brought greater attention to the problem of modernity in Arabic and Persian intellectual history, and to an extent in the literary history of these languages as well.[10] Yet, even with innovating studies available, in literary historiography of Persian and Arabic overall we find a limited consideration of how to approach the changes and innovations within these literatures over the previous two centuries. Looking simply at the field of Arabic literature, the language that outside scholars have used to describe the process of innovation or change within Arabic literature is often marked by developmental metaphors and through an analysis of what is termed "influence" and "impact" of European forms and thought.[11] At times these claims have had a troubling essentialism to them—asserting, for example that

> the form of the Arabic novel is amorphous and its development reflects the belief in blind fate, divine destiny, coincidence and luck . . . The more the Arab author assimilated Western culture, the more he tended to replace fiction with truth, episodes with social criticism, the incident with the uneventful, the haphazard succession of external incidents with the determined motivation and psychological emotion of the character. He switched from black and white characters to living and real ones, from flat characters to rounded ones, from the farcical and melodramatic to the actual and trivial, from the heroic character to the victims of society, from exaggerated description of emotion to the subtle description of internal motives . . . The more westernization replaced the medieval mentality of the [Arab] writer, the more the techniques of the Arabic novel resembled those of its Western counterpart.
>
> (Moreh, "Blank Verse in Modern Arabic Literature," p. 114)

Here, the development trope often at the heart of discussions of pre-novelistic writing is tied to transformations not only in literary practice, but also to a general "assimilation" into "Western culture," as part of a "replacement" of a "medieval mentality." The reasoning is tautological—the more the Arab author releases himself from his inherent "belief in blind fate, divine destiny, coincidence and luck," the more he will be inherently Western, and a release from these traits leads him directly into novelistic writing. Undoubtedly any deviation from the path of Westernization—largely undefined by this author as it so often is—would thus be a deviation from the path of literary development, away from the "truth" that novelistic writing is concerned with. While the framework is quite familiar to students of Edward Said's *Orientalism*, and perhaps should hardly surprise us, it is worthwhile nonetheless to occasionally revisit such expressions to recall what has been (and, indeed, so often still is) at the heart of scholarship on this subject.

Such a methodology also views with greater suspicion the interrelations of Arabic texts from diverse geographic and social contexts than the relations of each of these with the legacy of colonialism and European cultural imperialism. Also, this model all but ignores the fertile connections between the national-literature canon and texts from other non-European languages. In this, the national-literature model, various texts and literary figures are absorbed into the nationalist discourse of a particular nation—some are absorbed with the conscious consent of the author, others are done so *post facto*, in a retroactive move. The canon is always contested, and the retroactive absorption of pre-nationalist texts is a tenuous game, with critics and literary historians protesting too much their claims—in a sense the very adamancy of those who do not acknowledge the multifarious nature of modernity comes to betray the weakness of their claims.

Novelism in scholarship on nineteenth-century literatures

As Michael McKeon writes of scholarship around the English novel, “the common understanding that the novel ‘rose’ around 1740 provides a *terminus ad quem* which appears to organize all that follows within the ample boundaries of the great modern form, but which also requires that what precedes this founding act will resemble chaos” (McKeon, *The Origins of the English Novel*, p. 25). Despite the fact that McKeon’s monumental text acknowledges the problem of constructing a genealogy of novelistic writing, it tends to reify the limitations imposed by traditional novelism through its singular focus and attention on the novel. This said, this work has very significantly contributed to schools of literary scholarship that have come to address more fundamentally the inherent limits of this focus. In presenting a critical reassessment of eighteenth- and nineteenth-century English prose writing Diedre Shauna Lynch presents a lucid summary of the tendencies of prevalent scholarship on the novel:

> Introducing the eighteenth-century “origins” of “the” novel, we validate the assumption that what novels are now was already immanent in what they were then. We ratify geopolitical boundaries (between, for example, England and France). We legislate for a canon of exemplary, “truly” novelistic texts and legislate against popular practices of reading and writing. These are problems endemic to efforts to ascribe a distinct, essential nature to the novel.
>
> (Lynch and Warner, *Cultural Institutions*, p. 2)

This concern with the primacy of novelistic writing, and its relationship to nationalism (the ratification of geopolitical boundaries) has resulted in two general paths for the reassessment of nineteenth-century English prose writing. The first is a trend toward scholarship on non-novelistic writing, such as memoir writing or travel writing, in the assessment of nineteenth-century “literature,” a trend which has opened new arenas for the exploration of writing and reading practices of non-dominant social groups; women, the working classes, etc.[12] The second trend is one that has not foregone the novel as a subject, but either has reassessed it within the framework of a history of material culture, as a product and commodity, or has focused on the subterranean world of counter-dominant novelistic genres, such as the Victorian proliferation of Gothic, or "sensual novels," which were objects of derision and concern for advocates of more high-minded fare such as moral tales or the adventure novel.[13] Both these approaches tend to decenter the novel from a larger view of literary practice, asking important questions about the social value of different positions of creators, vendors, and consumers of literature, as well as those at the margins of the cultural economies of Europe.

From among these trends toward a reassessment of the literary history of Victorian and nineteenth-century European literature another approach has engaged with the question how to speak of prose innovations that do not fit the criteria developed around the novel. J. Paul Hunter addresses this problem from within his genealogy of the novel, by arguing that "novels, especially early novels, often bear features that do not 'fit' later conceptions of what the novel is or ought to be" (Hunter, *Before Novels*, p. 29). Hunter argues for an expansive vision of novels (rather than "the novel") that would include works often termed "failures" in developing the realistic, individualistic criteria vaunted by scholars of the novel, for example in the classic work on the novel by Ian Watt. These new features could be identified by focusing on the needs of seventeenth- and eighteenth-century readers, rather than by relying on twentieth-century aesthetic measures (accurately termed "*arriviste* snootiness" by Hunter) (*Before Novels*, p. 29). Yet, even by setting out new criteria for defining the novel, Hunter cannot avoid the problem of having to anticipate a telos for the history of such writing, which brings its own inevitable questions raised by teleological historical narratives: How did the novel develop? Who wrote the first novel? And so forth.

Yet Hunter's work raises important questions that have helped in the reassessment of the relationship of the category "novel" to the expectations linked to the term "modern literature." These reassessments also pay homage to the achievement of Richard Altick, in his social history of reading in Britain, *The English Common Reader*, a work that in many ways anticipated some of the afore-mentioned trends in scholarship on English literature by nearly three decades, by bringing to the fore the study of social contexts for the production and consumption of literary work.[14] Altick's work dramatically challenged the dominant focus in nineteenth-century English literature—that of a narrow aesthetic measure of a small body of "high literary" texts—to make the readers of literature the object of literary history. No longer vacated by the concept of a "reading public" that so often played the role of representing the social dimension of literary production, the actual reading practices of "common" people became a subject of study. What Altick's work shows is that often the value systems of the consumers of literary work were at odds with those of the anointed critics of literature, whether in the nineteenth century or in contemporary academic scholarship. While this claim was not in and of itself surprising, it is one that has hardly been widely adopted in general scholarship on the literary history of this period. However, those scholars who have continued the work of marrying social and historical approaches to the study of literature have been instrumental to reconsidering the nationalist–novelist paradigm, in particular in the area of European literatures.

Tradition and modernity and the overpoliticization of literature

When examining the prevalent frameworks for study of literatures from the colonized world, the question of how narratives of literary modernity are constructed has often been rooted in the dialectic of traditionalism and modernism. In addition, rather than assessing the reception of literature through sociological data, postcolonial scholars have tended to emphasize questions of ideological and political orientation and influence, in evaluating modern literatures. Both of these dilemmas stem from historical considerations; the debates over tradition have strong ties to the emergence of anti-colonial nationalist movements, and the trend of reading cultural and aesthetic questions as markers of ideological formation has been widespread in particular among critics and scholars wishing to emphasize cultures of resistance, or the cooptation of cultural expressions by elites in the colonial and postcolonial world. These are quite valid areas of inquiry, but the preponderance of focus on these questions has led to an overemphasis of the centrality of these issues to the aesthetic dimension of the innovation of literary practices in the modern period, as well as to the understanding of changes to the practice and value of reading.

Ali Gheissari's history of modern intellectual thought in Iran includes a general overview of intellectual currents in the nineteenth century, focusing largely on a characterization of the period as divided between "modern" and "traditional" trends in social and political thought. He concludes that the attitudes of reformist intellectuals were formed of an "uneasy coexistence of modernity and tradition" which underlay "the contradictions that characterized individual Iranian reformists and the reform movement as a whole" (Gheissari, *Iranian Intellectuals in the Twentieth Century*, p. 15). Yet for Gheissari the modern is largely defined as a product of the material influence of the West, and consequently he sees all reactions to this influence as naturally falling into the opposing category of tradition. In addition Gheissari's chronicle of the forces for social change in the nineteenth century follows a widely employed theoretical framework concerning the idea of modernity by considering modernity as a way to term a temporal conception, while unfortunately ignoring its possible aesthetic or cultural dimensions.

Kamran Talattof's *The Politics of Writing in Iran* does consider the aesthetic dimensions of modernity, but Talattof limits his readings of nineteenth-century texts to that of a highly ideological rubric. Indeed, Talattof's endeavor is identified as "to understand the role of ideology in literature and the role of literature in social movements," so this emphasis follows from his stated goals (Talattof, *The Politics of Writing in Iran*, p. 18). In this sense, his project differs from much of what may be termed the canonical literary histories of nineteenth- and twentieth-century Persian literature.[15] But as literary modernity is not itself an ideological formation—that is modernity is not simply an ideology—it may seem insufficient to address aesthetic concerns through a specific analysis of ideological trends. Thus, Talattof tends to treat cultural modernity as flowing from the ideological.

Much of Talattof's analysis of the advent of literary modernity, while quite wide in the number of texts and literary figures it includes, centers fairly limitingly upon an analysis of the conflicts between what are termed "modernists" and "traditionalists" (Talattof, *The Politics of Writing in Iran*, pp. 23–5). In Talattof's usage, these terms are to be distinguished from their possible deployment as aesthetic categories, and relate to positions taken in a set of debates between anti-Islamic Iranian intellectuals (modernists) and others who opposed them (thus, traditionalists). In the work of both Gheissari and Talattof, the concept of an emergent modernity is largely defined by political processes and ideological formations—certainly, important perspectives on the intellectual history of Iran in this period. However, both studies leave open the question of how we may consider the genesis of literary modernity in the context of Persian literature as an aesthetic and cultural process. How, for example, do these ideological formations result in reconsiderations of how a text is written, and what form of literary imagination informs it? Do political and ideological transformations directly result in aesthetic transformations? For Talattof and Gheissari the non-ideological dimensions of literary innovation are not central to a theorization of modernity.

For example, Talattof locates the "first episode of modern Persian literature" within a current of reactionary anti-Islamic discourse among a number of late-nineteenth century Iranian writers, as if the modernity of their writing is defined by their ideological position (Talattof, *The Politics of Writing in Iran*, p. 23). He critically remarks upon the fact that their anti-Islamic position is in a more essential sense derived from a (proto-) nationalist anti-Arab ideological stance, defining Persian–Iranian national identity in opposition to that of Iran's Arab neighbors (or, indeed, Iran's Arab subjects). However, this analysis unwittingly accedes literary modernity to the quasi-racist ethno-nationalist ideological strain that would come to define Iranian official nationalism in the early twentieth century. That the emergence of this "episode" marks the advent of modernity for Talattof, further confirms that within this study modernity is largely seen as an attribute of an ideological positioning—while there are fruitful investigations to be made on the issue of the relationship of specific ideological formations to certain aesthetic considerations, this may be a rather limited way to understand a process as complex and contested as modernity.

In considering the problem of the overly ideological approach to Persian literary scholarship, Mohammad Mehdi Khorrami has argued that twentieth-century works of literary criticism have been dominated by a framework of "socio-political discourse" (Khorrami, *Modern Reflections of Classical Traditions in*

Persian Fiction, p. 128). He argues convincingly that an over-politicization of literary criticism runs the risk of relegating literary production to the ideological sphere. In these circumstances, literature as a whole becomes instrumentalized as an element representing discreet political contestations, between systems of power and among various oppositional forces. When taken to a logical conclusion, this approach has been detrimental to understanding the "literary" import of modern texts.

Another method may foreground an examination of aesthetic strategies and literary imagination, considering these alongside the social history of the sites of production, and by so doing, defining literary modernity within cultural rather than ideological terms. Tavakoli-Targhi dismisses the tendency, present in the work of both Gheissari and Talattof, to conceive of modernity as purely a European product of what has been termed "occidental rationalism"—what he terms the "conventional Enlightenment story," where "non-European societies were 'modernized' as a result of Western impact and influence" (Tavakoli-Targhi, *Refashioning Iran*, pp. 2–4). Through a reference to Foucault's conception of heterotopias as counter-sites to the conception of an Enlightened utopia (i.e. the modern occident), Tavakoli-Targhi proposes instead to view modernity as a product of "heterotopic experiences," thus reorganizing the colonial conditioning of modernity. As he argues "by recovering the significance of heterotopic experiences in the formation of the ethos of modernity, the lands beyond Europe, instead of being the reverse image of enlightenment and modernity, served as 'laboratories of modernity', as sites of the earliest sightings of 'the hallmarks of European cultural production' " (ibid., p. 3). As he correctly notes, the idea of a European production and exportation of modernity into non-European contexts most obtains within the framework of nationalist historiographies. Within this framework, the non-European nation is conceived as inhabiting a teleological position of retardation in relation to the colonial metropole; the non-European nation, as the subject of history, is following the known history of modernity paved for it by the European nation. Tavakoli-Targhi further argues that an over-reliance on this framework has allowed historians of Iran to utilize periodizations that follow the schema proposed within European historical scholarship. This phenomenon is easily observed in literary historical studies, which have often followed the widespread material success of and high social value for the novel in Europe as a measure for modern Persian writing, when the Persian novel has never enjoyed a similar popular or critical reception in Iran. While specific data are difficult to come by, it is known that the economy of book-printing in Iran is by no means comparable to that of any Western European languages, and in particular, from among the various printed commodities, novels have never been in a position of similar economic standing as they have been in Europe. By neglecting to consider the different strengths and qualities of the economies of publishing from these diverse arenas, scholars working in comparative frameworks have often made unsubstantiated claims of the social significance of the novel using the European template in non-European arguments.

Scholarship on Arabic literature, while concerned with certain different historical details, has also followed a framework of eliding a thorough discussion of modernity in its aesthetic and cultural dimensions, by also relying on the thesis of an occidental exportation of modernity. Attempts to escape this constraint have shown limited success, perhaps due to the difficulty in breaking with certain predominant frameworks. As an example, in *The Genesis of Arabic Narrative Discourse*, Sabry Hafez resituates the reading of nineteenth- and twentieth-century literary innovations in Arabic literature, using social and economic data, as well as a critical approach to the legacy of literary historiography on modern Arabic literary practice. Hafez characterizes the dilemma within prevalent scholarship on Arabic literature as represented by two general approaches—what he also terms the "traditionalist" and the "modernist" approaches to producing literary history (Hafez, *The Genesis of Arabic Narrative Discourse*, p. 16). Hafez describes traditionalism as an approach that seeks medieval antecedents to modern literary formations; thus claiming them as purely a product of classical Arabic literary heritage. The modernists have rather argued that modern Arabic literature is purely imitative, "borrowed from the West" (ibid., p. 17). The studies of the latter group rest largely on defining the influences of Western literature within Arabic literature, while the former excel at locating references to classical Arabic literature within modern work. Indeed this division is not only limited to scholars of Arabic literature, but also well characterizes scholarship on Persian–Iranian literature and it may be argued, is at least familiar to most colonized societies, particularly those that make claims of a significant classical literary heritage. At times scholars make use of both concepts in congress; Talattof, for example, makes greater recourse to the traditionalist mode of analysis of modern literary work (by highlighting possible antecedents to these texts in pre-modern literature), while at the same time, retaining a historical framework more common to modernists:

> It is true that [Persian] modernist writers used some Western models, but their works were not limited to the exigencies of Westernization or rote imitation of Western forms. Rather, in many respects, they are rooted quite purposefully in the literary traditions of Iran. Even referring to them as modernists should be done with caution, not because modernism is too broad and vague, but because, as history has proved, their movement did not lead to an overall modernity similar to that of Western modernists.
>
> (Talattof, *The Politics of Writing in Iran*, pp. 24–5)

Talattof begins in the traditionalist mode by claiming that Persian literary modernity is "rooted quite purposefully" in the "traditions of Iran"—thus exemplifying the discourse of traditionalism to which Hafez alludes. But he relies upon the modernist claim that true modernity is of Western provenance, and that presumably had the "Persian modernists" *wanted* to, they could have endeavored to reach an "overall modernity similar to that of Western modernists." Here modernity is of a local, native provenance, while at the same time the local form is doomed to fail to achieve true modernity—which is defined as Western modernity. This conflation of traditionalism and modernism closely follows trends in anti- and postcolonial nationalist discourses to present nationalism as a simultaneously traditional, inherent characteristic of a specific society, while at the same time basing the claim of its progressive aspirations on its Western roots. This duality of post-colonial nationalisms has been articulated best by Partha Chatterjee through his proposal of two domains—the "material" and the "spiritual"—within these national discourses (Chatterjee, *Nation and its Fragments*, pp. 120–1).[16]

While critical of both of the above-mentioned approaches, and presumably of their simultaneous employment as well, Hafez does not identify the common rationale that legitimizes each of them in a common discourse. Traditionalist and modernist historians of Arab culture come to different conclusions about the valuing of literary work, but do so through a similar framework; both groups tend to valorize prose narrative as high cultural writing (although they may differ in their indexing of a canon of such work), and in both groups consideration of this literary activity coalesces within the context of the nation. Put simply, neither the traditionalist nor the modernist analysis obtains legitimacy outside of the framework of nationalism.[17] For the traditionalist, the nation provides the basis for justifying the concept of tradition—following on the nationalist tropes of rebirth and resurrection, the traditionalist reads the modern work as a direct outcome of classical antecedents, and the boundaries of these antecedents are calibrated to the nation's borders. For modernists, the relation is even simpler—as much as modern literature is a reflection of the "influence" of advanced European cultural production, it is also a reflection of the positivist adoption of the nation as the modern political unit under the very same influence. In both cases, the discourse accumulates around concepts of resurrection or rebirth, although in each case the object of rebirth may differ; for traditionalists, the concept of cultural heritage gives meaning to the claims of rebirth, while modernists will tend to make the nation itself the retroactive object of the term resurrection.

As Chatterjee argues, both trends of traditionalism–nativism and modernism–liberalism share common terms of discussion, and often make reference to classical "traditions" as antecedents to the independent postcolonial nation, while casting the nation as intrinsically modern, and in a sense equivalent to (and thus imitative of) Western models. Chatterjee articulates a three-stage path through which the development of non-Western nationalisms may be narrated: the moments of departure, arrival and maneuver (Chatterjee, *Nationalist Thought and the Colonial World*, pp. 50–1). In many cases, the role of nationalist intellectuals in the development of a canon of "classical" literature is a key "moment of departure" in the articulation of a nationalist culture. While Chatterjee examines the role of cultural elites of colonized societies in the production of such a conception, he does not directly note the fact that in certain instances, the idea of a national literature is first articulated by colonial scholars, and then appropriated by nationalists. In these cases—and as the studies on *Alf layla wa layla* and *The Adventures of Hajji Baba Ispahani* in this book will show—the critical value of such a conception is different for orientalist or colonialist scholars than for nationalist ones, yet both make equal use of the conception of tradition. Another potent example of this can be found in the monumental study by E.G. Brown, *A History of Persian Literature*, which is the first articulation of a canon of Persian literature. The text is translated into Persian by 'Ali Asghar Hikmat—who, as the Iranian minister of Education under Reza Shah had a formidable role in the cultural articulation of Iranian nationalist discourse—and has played an important role in nationalist literary historiography by Iranian critics of the past century.

Hafez accurately identifies both traditionalist and modernist approaches to literary history as part of a "similar reductive methodology that attempts to explain a complex and intricate phenomenon . . . by resorting to simplifications and extrinsic reasoning" (Hafez, *The Genesis of Arabic Narrative Discourse*, p. 18). Yet, while Hafez could well have located the legitimizing function that validates both approaches within discourses that also enable nationalism, he does not do so. The lack of a clear analysis of the role of nationalism is not so much an oversight as it is a testimony to the fact that much of twentieth century literary history has been composed with the nation as a presumption fundamental to the modern field of cultural production. This may well be due to his choice of the short story as the central object for his study; Hafez's focus on the short story allows him to largely sidestep addressing the role of nationalist discourse in twentieth-century literary histories.

Indeed, these studies also share another fundamental common presence, less unconscious than that of the nation, and that is the centrality of the novel to conceptions of literary modernity. By engaging with the short story, Hafez can afford to cast his eye away from the nexus of attention in the studies of literary modernity, and thus also avoid the pitfalls that have ensnared many of his predecessors. Yet in a fundamental sense, Hafez tends to work in an analytical framework that does not greatly differ from many of the studies he implicitly critiques. For in his analysis, literary modernity is defined simply by the genesis of "narrative discourse," an object that by and large is also the focus of novelistic literary studies. While Hafez rethinks the goal of this trajectory, dislodging it from the narrow body of novelistic writing in late-nineteenth- and early-twentieth-century Arab societies, he does not reconfigure the trajectory itself. It must be said, however, that Hafez's work is useful in its mode of analysis, and attempts a rethinking of the trajectory of a development of "narrative discourse" in Arabic literature by emphasizing short story writing as a destination for literary innovations from the eighteenth to twentieth centuries. What is still left open, in an analysis such as this, is an approach that would present a fuller understanding of the generative social transformations within the unsettled period preceding the appearance of a fully developed "narrative discourse."

Another insightful critique of the trend in Arabic literary scholarship to assess the Arabic novel along Western lines comes from Roger Allen, who writes with an aim to intervene in the long-running debates concerned with producing a chronology of the Arabic novel through a comparative framework derivative of the history of the novel in Europe:

> This type of historical analysis applied to a novelistic tradition within a particular world culture leads, almost automatically, to a number of questions concerning the processes of "translation," used here in the literal sense to describe the process whereby an artifact or genre is "carried across" the divide between two literary traditions, and therefore to a (re)examination of the origins and development of the novel itself—issues of definition and development, of "the novel before the novel" and so on [. . .] Is it the fate of the Arabic novel, for example (and by extension those of other non-Western/Third World cultures) to play a continuous and eventually unsuccessful game of "catch-up" with the various subdivisions of the Western novel?
>
> ("Literary History and the Arabic Novel," p. 207)

Allen's assertion of the limitations of producing this kind of novelistic literary history for non-Western literatures calls into question much of the predominant literary scholarship on the development of literary modernity within these literatures. However in this discussion Allen also largely gives priority to the novel as the prime actor in any discussion of modern literature; the debate is how better to assess the non-Western novel, rather than to rethink its central role in these histories. His prescription is for future researchers to "change the balance" between discussions focusing on the importation of Western literary forms and those that focus largely on the "rediscovery of the cultural heritage of the past": he observes that while the former have held sway for the better part of the twentieth century, it is now time to give greater priority to the latter ("Literary History and the Arabic Novel," p. 213). Allen further argues that scholarly knowledge of the era "immediately anterior to the beginnings of a 'modern' period" is lacking, and calls for greater focus on this issue, as well as to the issue of linguistic and hence literary heterogeneity within the Arabic language itself (ibid.).

These latter assertions bring to the fore important questions about the modes of scholarship that predominate in Arabic literary studies. However, it may be necessary to go further and perhaps rethink the kinds of historical narratives that emerge from our tendency to give primacy to the novel as a literary form at all. The suggestion of giving greater priority to what Hafez may call the "traditionalist" model of literary scholarship may serve to correct some of the excesses exhibited in scholarship on modern non-Western literatures. However, this may in the end be a limited correction—as I have already argued, the debate between "traditionalist" and "modernist" perspectives largely occurs within a larger framework that continues to accommodate the imperatives of the nationalist–novelist paradigm. However, what is most prescient in Allen's argument is the identification call to engage in a deeper understanding of both the complexities and distinctions within literary productions of the Arabic language, as well as his call for greater scholarly attention to the neglected era directly preceding the "modern." Beyond these very useful proposals, one may wish to add the need to place Arabic literature within new comparative frameworks—ones that would move beyond the traditional comparisons with Western literatures—to recognize the importance of regional "translations" in the emergence of literary modernity.

Multilingualism in the study of nineteenth-century literatures

Prevalent work in the field of comparative literature is further characterized by a problem of how the question of comparison is to be framed. As a matter of course, where the study of literatures of the colonized world are concerned, comparative work has overwhelmingly taken the shape of what is often termed "East–West" or "North–South" comparisons—presumptively assessing the influence of colonial societies upon the modern cultures of the colonized world. Few studies have attempted to assess the question of innovation, and even influence, as a process that may be examined in a framework *comparing* different colonized societies. Fundamentally, this predilection follows the trends of language training both outside and inside postcolonial societies.

This condition may be termed ahistorical in that it reflects an approach to literatures that often were not common to nineteenth-century cultural figures in these societies. Speaking simply of North Africa and Western Asia, it is a fact that even until the latter period of the century, a claim to literary competency in these societies required a degree of multilingualism in regional languages, which would have included Persian, Turkish, Arabic, and often other "minor" languages and dialects. Thus it is no surprise that Hajj Sayyah Mahalati, the late nineteenth-century author of travelogues and historical commentaries was fluent not only in Persian, but also claimed various levels of fluency in Turkish, Armenian, and Arabic as well as a number of European languages. It was also a matter of course that Muhammad 'Abduh, the Egyptian cultural and religious reformer, should translate the Persian writings of Jamal al-Din al-Afghani into Arabic, who was himself literate in Persian, Arabic, and Turkish as well conversant in French and English. Zayn al-'Abidin al-Maraghihi, the author of *Siyahatnamih-yi Ibrahim Bayg* was apparently fluent in Turkish, Russian, Persian, and Arabic. These citations are not of exceptional cases, but reflect the average aspirations of linguistic ability for cultural figures in these societies in this period. Yet, general literary histories of Arabic and Persian literature, at least, rarely if ever account for this multilingualism except as a marginal issue. Even among contemporary Iranian literary figures, few indeed are those individuals such as Muhammad Reza Shafi'i

Kadkani, an eminent poet and literary scholar, who have had the training and active inclination to engage with modern Arabic literature (in conversation with Persian literature), as an object of study or literary inspiration. Figures such as Shafi'i Kadkani are largely products of a generation who emerged into the secular arena of literary production through the traditional educational systems that have continued to require a thorough training in and estimation of Arabic language and literatures, as part of a traditional religious training. With the exception of Shafi'i Kadkani, most scholars who have shown such an interest (and fewer still are those with the training to make a claim to such multilingualism) tend to operate on the margins of the mainstream of Iranian literary scholarship.[18] Also the modern secular education systems in the Arab world, as in Iran, devalue the learning of regional languages beyond perhaps the most elementary level.[19]

Where comparative approaches have excelled, they have encompassed frameworks such as Arabic and English literatures, or Persian and French, etc., to the neglect of regional interlinguistic themes. The cause of this is perhaps clear enough, and relates to the cultural capital accorded to working with metropolitan languages, or to simplistic nationalist proclivities (perhaps more intense in the case of Persian than of Arabic), as well as to institutional prestige and standing within the academy in both local and outside contexts. The outcome of this is that no major literary study of Arabic or Persian nineteenth-century literatures has employed a comparative framework across the two languages, or indeed of any other regional language. What has been lost is the consideration that relations between these two and other regional languages could account for any major part of the genesis of literary modernity in these languages—indeed, instead it has legitimized the parallel opposition outlined by Hafez between traditional and modernist approaches to literary study of this period. Traditionalists, on the whole, have emphasized a simply monolinguistic approach, fundamentally discounting comparative frameworks. Modernists have most often been comparatists who have worked to locate evidence of "influence" from Western literary contexts into that of either Arabic or Persian.

Yet the limitations of this narrow kind of comparative approach have led to the marginalization of the study of regional and sub-national comparative literatures. For example, J. Strauss has presented this critique of the predominant trends in literary historiography of nineteenth- and early twentieth-century Ottoman literatures: "Modern historians have tended to create a separate literary identity for each [linguistic and ethnic group in the Ottoman Empire] according to the Western European concept of 'national' literature" (Strauss, "Who Read What in the Ottoman Empire," p. 39). While Strauss is interested in recovering the literary work of various communities in late-Ottoman society within a single coherent category of "Ottoman literature," his critique has implications outside of the Ottoman context.

> Literature is restricted to the production of one "nation" in one single language; the established canon consists, of course, of original works, emphasizing specimens of the different genres which had developed in

> the West (novel, drama) [. . .] In particular, literatures which do not fit the nationalist paradigm, such as that of the Turkish speaking Greek-Orthodox (Karamanli) or the Turcophone Armenians, fall between two stools. Generally, they are not regarded either by Turkish or Greek and Armenian scholars as part of their literary heritage, and have been studied only by specialists.
>
> (Strauss, "Who Read What in the Ottoman Empire," p. 39)

Indeed, Strauss' concerns go farther beyond the range of this study, and present a cogent reminder of the limitations of the framework here proposed—his call is for the studying of a greater range of "minority" or marginal languages within the rubric of the Middle East than a narrow focus on Arabic, Persian, and Turkish may afford. He is justified in pointing out that even comparative studies across the range of these languages tends to replicate the nationalist paradigms of the twentieth century—his interest is in an expansion of the study of multilingualism, in particular within religious minority communities such as Sephardic Jewry, Bulgarians, Greeks, and Armenians within the Ottoman polity. Clearly, the present study can only be one contribution to a puzzle still missing many of its key pieces.[20]

The promise of engaging in comparative literary study across Persian and Arabic frameworks (as well as those of other regional languages) is that such scholarship may serve to more fully return the study of these bodies of work to the historically situated conditions of their production. If multilingualism was *pro forma* for cultural figures of these societies, then the study of the social conditions of cultural production may be enhanced by greater sensitivity to interlinguistic, intertextual threads that exist between them. Furthermore, such a sensitivity may open new vistas for understanding the processes of innovation and change that are so often the subjects of study in these languages, while re-evaluating the relations between these literatures and those of the colonial West. As Elleke Boehmer argues, studies of colonialism have almost universally disregarded "anti-imperial, cross border strategies" such as those that linked Irish and Indian nationalist sympathies during the colonial era (Boehmer, *Empire the National and the Postcolonial*, p. 5). Through such a framework, she further argues, we may be able to trace hitherto disregarded features of a "globalized and constellated modernism" decentered from the predominant narrative of Western modernity's influence on colonized societies (ibid., p. 175).[21]

Here it must be said that the intention of this reordering is not to discount or erase the fact of interlinguistic relations between Western languages and Persian or Arabic. Rather, it more fully accounts for the complexity of exchange between these literary arenas. It does so by considering the possibility for exchange of literary material not only in a dialogic relation between monolithically termed Western and Eastern social arenas, but also of the re-echoing or mutation of such material through three or more linguistic stages. Indeed the breaking of the prevalent dialogic mould for literary study of these languages also introduces a question concerning the "flow" of literary material. This prevalent approach has tracked, to the extent possible, "influences" along lines of colonial hegemony and domination—which explains the underlying rationale for what Hafez terms the modernist approach. Although this methodology does certainly offer insight to certain processes of literary exchange, the overall picture remains limited.

Textual transactions and the autonomous field of literary production

The call to consider nineteenth-century literary histories anew requires a theoretical framework able to account for the fluid cultural dynamics in this period. In the societies discussed in this study, the nineteenth century is a time of unprecedented social transformations, a period of political revolutions, reconfigured identities, and the upturning of traditional economic and social systems. The outcome of these transformations in the cultural field was to present a relatively unstable and fast-changing order of social values, where the estimation and role of cultural productions, and the work that produced them, came into a new organization.

What Pierre Bourdieu terms the *field of cultural production* presents a useful framework from which to trace these cultural transformations and innovations. Bourdieu uses the field of cultural production to describe the system of social values and beliefs that, working in a complex network of relations, make legible and accede material and immaterial value to the work of the artist or cultural producer. The structure of the field is defined by the possible positions made up by the "structure of the distribution of the capital of specific properties which governs success in the field and the winning of the external or specific profits (such as literary prestige) which are at stake in the field" (Bourdieu, *Field of Cultural Production*, p. 30). Bourdieu's emphasis is that these positions are neither static nor immutable, but rather characterized by contestation within the field. The field may be termed a field of forces, just as it is a "*field of struggles*, tending to transform or conserve this field of forces" (ibid., p. 31). In this framework, any work of literature (or any cultural production) is marked indelibly with the social conditions that make possible its production, from its value (material or otherwise) and the cultural capital that it accords to its producer(s), to the modes of its reproduction and consumption. Thus any comprehensive literary study, if considerate of the fields of cultural production within which it was generated, must also be to some extent a study of social values, and if the study is historical in nature, may be termed social–historical as well as literary.

This foregrounding of social history in the study of literary texts thus highlights the social contestations that are present in the history of the production of all texts, requiring the literary scholar to make recourse to certain secondary materials—archival materials, autobiographical writing, commentary of contemporaries—to achieve a view of the context of the production of the text that is as thorough as may be possible. This focus illuminates the struggles that are at the centre of the field of literary productions. Bourdieu notes "the impetus for change in cultural works—language, art, literature, science, etc.—resides in the struggles that take place in the corresponding fields of production" (Bourdieu, p. 183). Thus this model of literary study not only highlights the struggles in the field that define the value of the text, but more essentially highlights transformations in the field through its sensitivity to the impetus for change that is part of the field. The constant change that characterizes the field is at odds with its self-image, which presents its dominant values at any time as permanent and timeless. Thus to be a part of the field of cultural production is to subscribe to its values and to have faith in it, much as economic markets are said to rise and fall on faith in their integrity and promise.

As Bourdieu argues, "the artistic field is a universe of belief" (Bourdieu, p. 164). This relation of the field to ideas of the sacred is more than simply a poetic gesture. In the context of conflicts between the secular and religious domains, it is important to note that the distinction between divine ordination and other manners for the evaluation of cultural texts is not as great as post-Enlightenment thought would posit. Each system works within a world of signs that Adorno terms "enchantment" despite the claim of the Enlightenment to enact the opposite, a disenchantment of the world through the secularization of aesthetics. Within the field of cultural production, the values of secular aesthetic systems—for example, European bourgeois aesthetics—must be analyzed no differently than those of sacred systems. In the context of literary study, this posits a significant challenge to frameworks that presume "high" aesthetic judgment for novelistic writing, while discounting other writing. Indeed, this framework begs the critic or scholar to attempt to see the valuative order that has engendered distinctions between high and low aesthetic forms, not simply to replicate it. This, again, requires the study of the sociology of literary production alongside historical and more literary methodologies.

Yet, Bourdieu does make an important distinction between a sociology of the field of cultural production, and a "sociological approach" to literature, which has often meant a determinist or causal framework for the study of literature. This follows on certain, often Marxist, schools of theory that have attempted to study literature purely as manifestations of material and social conditions, with little sensitivity to the specificity of the conditions of possibility that create value for a specific text in a specific historical context. Instead a sociology of the literary field would consider the relation of the individual to the social within a historically informed framework; thus neither "macrohistorical" (or culturalist) nor "microhistorical" (textual or personality-driven) in its methodology (Bourdieu, p. 165).

If Bourdieu shows favor for a certain selection of literary texts, it is less derived from "new" high-aesthetic parameters—Adorno's famous disdain for jazz is a kind of example of this—but rather, it is for those texts that are at once a product of certain constellation of social forces, while simultaneously representing or critiquing the same system of values that gave rise to it (thus his adoration of Flaubert's *Sentimental Education*). While this does direct the literary scholar to certain trends in post-Romantic European literatures, it is not as narrow a measure as it may seem. We may read beyond Bourdieu's personal predilection for self-reflexivity and locate the germ of auto-criticism far beyond the confines of a turn to aesthetic modernism—in this sense, the valorization of modernism as the (sometimes perverse) fulfillment of the telos of aesthetic modernity itself needs careful examination. Central to an understanding of the logic of the field of cultural production is the concept of cultural capital, and its development.

The appearance of a field of cultural production regulated by competition for cultural capital in a market of symbolic goods is in a profound sense a defining characteristic of modernity. Where pre-modern cultural life was marked by aristocratic as well as ecclesiastical tutelage and legitimization, a defining element of modernity is the development of an autonomous artistic field. This autonomization brought with it measures of cultural capital, which gains through complex relations between various sites of power. An important and new element in consecration of legitimacy is the conception of mass consumption, and a public audience. Any study of the genesis of cultural modernity needs to account for the shift away from pre-modern sources of legitimation of cultural productions, to that of the autonomous cultural field. In the modern context, this brought with it the professionalization of cultural work, and a turn toward sponsorship for artistic work outside of traditional venues, toward new classes of cultural consumers emerging out of a transformed social estimation for the acts of reading, writing, and for participation in and consumption of literary productions—what Siskin calls the "the work of writing" (Siskin, *Work of Writing*, p. 16). If the definition of modernity has been contested, the development of the field of cultural production is one manner in which cultural modernities may be identified. This study will use the framework of the theory of the autonomous cultural field by way of tracing the appearance of what will be termed literary modernities. This does not mean that an analysis of the early stages of cultural modernity need follow a narrow trajectory toward a singular ideal of modernity—quite the opposite. What may be most useful to this study is how Bourdieu's theory of the field of cultural production opens a door to the integration of competing trajectories of modernity within the field, just as the sites of power in the field, and the mechanisms of legitimization, are in constant struggle. Thus, the use of a singular narrative of modernity—such as that embraced by the nationalist–novelist paradigm—can be eschewed; instead various narratives can be considered in a common accounting. Through this perspective we may also begin to see this paradigm as simply one of the various mechanisms of legitimation in the field.

Any multilingual approach to nineteenth-century literatures, when focusing on an examination of the literary fields and the works that make them up, presents a profound challenge to the nationalist–novelist paradigm. Yet Bourdieu's work presents certain limitations to such an ideal that must be contended with—specifically, a kind of Eurocentrism where the fundamental values of the field of cultural production are identified, as well as a lack of consideration for interlinguistic and inter-societal literary relations. By using the European bourgeois system of values as the central paradigm for his theorization of the field of cultural productions, Bourdieu forecloses on the applicability of some of his nuanced explications of the systems of relations within the field to arenas outside of a Western European context, despite the global reach of the latter. More difficult, even for a comparatist is to understand how the theory of the field can accommodate the study of a text that transcends a specific social order (or literary field) and moves into another social setting with very different historical and political exigencies for the value acceded to the same text. The point of exchange across these different social settings may be identified and articulated with recourse to the same methods that present a sociology of the literary fields involved, yet the concepts that are at the heart of Bourdieu's work are somewhat inflexible for such work.

These concerns are not significant enough to discount the use of the theory of the field of cultural production outside the confines that Bourdieu himself used it for. As a productive framework, it may be extended to accommodate different cultural settings, and multiple cultural settings, through a following of its own fundamental claims—in particular, that logic of the cultural field is an economic logic. In a Western European context, the collaboration between capitalist economic theories and bourgeois aesthetics generated the cultural field within which Bourdieu situates his analysis (again, with a focus on post-Romantic French literature and arts). Within the context of nineteenth century Arab or Iranian societies, we may find a more complex network of interests, both economic and ideological, that can identify the nature of the field. These fields of cultural production would necessarily raise questions about colonial and regional economic systems that were set to compete with vested and deeply rooted pre-modern economic systems. In terms of the ideological, arraying the various struggles between elite and colonial powers and religious- and secular-reformist movements would require careful attention, in addition to coalitional social movements such as those that produced the Iranian Constitutional Revolution of 1906, or the Egyptian 'Urabi revolt of 1881. The collaboration of these various economic and ideological forces can be conceived as the basis for the cultural fields in these societies, in this period.

A consideration of the circulation of texts across these discrete literary fields will require the complication of Bourdieu's theory. As cultural capital accrues from the logic of a specific field, and from the struggle between forces within each field, it will be necessary to conceive of how such cultural capital is affected in its transfer between different social settings. This study will work with this problem by suggesting the term *transaction* as the way to narrate and analyze the movement of texts across different fields of cultural production.[22] By terming these exchanges transactional, an emphasis is placed on not only the transmission of the text, but also the possible costs or gains of such a transmission. While it is well within the boundaries of a study such as this to account for the material exchanges that often accompany the transaction of a text from one social context to another (one may think of the price Galland paid for the manuscript of *Alf layla wa layla* he translated into *Mille Nuits et Nuit*), in a more fundamental sense the concept of transaction within the study of cultural capital centers more on the shifts in cultural value, legitimacy, and utility that may be associated with such textual circulation. To return to the example of *Alf layla wa layla* (which will be discussed at greater length in Part 2 of this study), to discuss the text as transactional, we will need to also consider the shift in the value of the text within an urban Arab context, from the pre-European translations of it—when it was generally considered a work of profane, urban, light entertainment—to the nineteenth-century reemergence of the text as an example of a popular classical Arabic heritage.

By considering the points of contact between cultural fields, I aim to show the central role played by textual transactions in the development of literary modernities in Arabic, English and Persian literatures. An examination of textual transactions in these languages during the nineteenth century, and particularly the mid- to late-nineteenth century, presents a picture of highly dynamic cultural fields across these diverse cultural settings. Also, this approach allows us to consider alongside one another texts of different genre and forms, evaluating them not on the basis of a well-qualified measure of "literariness" but rather on the basis of criteria arising from their possible functionality within specific social arenas. Catalyzed by internal reformist movements, colonial geopolitics and the transformation of the regional and global economies of which these societies were a part, social values around literary production and consumption were to be fundamentally reconfigured. Once denuded of the laurels of Enlightenment's aesthetic sublime, literary production is approached appropriately as a social activity within a socio-cultural arena, the field of cultural production, and is endowed with the aura of autonomy. The need to understand the value that literature is given within cultural and social arenas relates to material and political contestations that define both the production and consumption of such work. Modernity is a key concept to this understanding. As Marshall Berman has suggested:

> It may turn out, then, that going back can be a way to go forward: That remembering the modernisms of the nineteenth century can give us the vision and courage to create the modernisms of the twenty-first. This act of remembering can help us bring modernism back to its roots, so that it can nourish and renew itself, to confront the adventures and dangers that lie ahead. To appropriate the modernities of yesterday can be at once a critique of the modernities of today and an act of faith in the modernities—and in the modern men and women—of tomorrow and the day after tomorrow.
>
> (Berman, *All That Is Solid Melts into Air*, p. 36)

This is not to argue for simple materialistic analyses of writing and reading activities, but rather to look more closely at the social values that enable certain kinds of creative acts within specific historical circumstances. Methodologically, a philological approach to these contested texts, rooted in a critical historical framework, will revalue that which is innovative, transgressive or deconstructive in them—bringing to the fore a reconsideration of the temporal contingencies of modernity in the nineteenth century.

Part 2

NINETEENTH-CENTURY *ARABIAN NIGHTS'* BIOGRAPHIES

With the seeds of desire tunnelling deep in their entrails, artists in the West embarked on their desperate attempts. They filled the pages of their sketchbooks in a defiant response to the reflection of the light rippling along the nap, trying to corral its richness. Sulayman the Magnificent entered from the most beautiful gate ever opened in a wall. And he stayed there in the blazing imagination, in the pages of the earliest translations of *The Thousand and One Nights*.

(Huda Barakat, *Tiller of the Waters*)

2

BIOGRAPHIES OF THE *ARABIAN NIGHTS*, AN ENGLISH CHAPTER

There is perhaps no better example of textual transaction than the interlinguistic exchanges that enabled the modern incarnations of *Alf layla wa layla*, known most widely in English as the *Arabian Nights*. As a text—or, rather, a series of texts—of uncertain origin, translated numerous times and produced as a book in edition after edition over the course of the eighteenth, nineteenth and twentieth centuries, tracing the variegated uses of the text in different social and historical contexts can be a bewildering task. To follow the thread of the modern *Nights*, even limiting oneself to its use as a printed book, takes one from the libraries of royal courts, to educational and cultural institutions, the offices of newspapers and periodicals and down alleyways to back-street printing houses publishing pamphlets and cheap books for expanding markets of readers.[1] The transformation of this group of tales into a coherent text, organized, printed, and consumed in an expanding market for books, is rather remarkable. This is especially so considering that these narratives represent what in the pre-modern and early modern Arabic context would be considered a rather minor, popular, literary arena, despite evidence of its longevity in the region.[2]

Scholars of the *Nights* have filled bookshelves with critiques, analyses, and commentaries upon the various editions, translations, and histories of the text. Disputes remain to be settled over the authenticity of certain manuscripts, and assessments rise and fall over the quality of the countless available translations into dozens of languages. But few scholarly works have focused on the social value accorded the modern *Nights* in its different incarnations and permutations, the measure of which has been fluid and in contestation in each site of the appearance of the book. This is despite the fact that from the time of the text's construction as a book onward, there has been a recurring fascination with its history, or as Sir Richard Burton terms it, the "Biography of the Book." In the case of Burton (whose *Nights* appeared in 1885–1888), this biography was internalized within a supplement to the published translation, as well as through his footnotes and appendices. These appendices had already become a recognized feature of printed book editions, as E.W. Lane (1838–1841) and John Payne (1882–1884) had already arranged critical apparati for their translations; later translators would continue to do the same. Yet these biographies of the *Nights* have been largely directed at uncovering certain essential or generic qualities that may explain their supposedly timeless virtues as a text. It would seem the universalist drive to appropriate the *Nights* to the project Goethe termed *Weltliteratur* would leave Western readers with a text the values of which should be little in dispute. The actuality is quite the opposite. To speak simply of the English *Nights*, the appearance of the different major editions of the text served only to kindle repeated controversies in public fora over its value. Perhaps the most notorious of these was the charge of pornography adduced to Burton's edition; however earlier editions also sparked degrees of scorn, fear, and anger on the part of different institutions and individuals—emotions that followed the text over the course of the nineteenth century.

It is possible to see the disputations around the value of the *Nights* as a measure of the transactional qualities of the text. The *Nights* was uniquely situated, both in time and place, to galvanize public interest and imagination for different ideals. The measure of the text's undoubtedly singular qualities may best be affirmed by the way in which the text was to come to represent different ideals for different readerships over the course of the nineteenth century. One need only look at any number of other texts translated or written at different points of the nineteenth century, promoted or upheld by critics as "timeless" or "universal," which were to all but shortly disappear from notice after the evaporation of public or critical interest. The history of the *Arabian Nights'* appearance into Europe, and the development of the various collections, editions and translations over the course of the eighteenth and nineteenth centuries—in particular in English, French, and German language contexts—has been the subject of several studies.[3] A number of scholars—perhaps foremost among them Muhsin al-Musawi and Muhsin Mahdi—have shone light over questions concerning the seam between the nineteenth-century Arabic and English editions. Others have begun to do similar work on the genealogies of the Persian translation—here, the work of Ulrich Marzolph bears direct mention, although a generation before him Muhammad Ja'far Mahjub provided important scholarship on the same subject. While some questions concerning historical details pertaining to various manuscripts and extant recensions of the text remain unanswered, the same historical rigor has not been applied to understanding the social dimensions of the production and consumption of the *Nights* at this time, either in Europe or in the Arab world. Few if any studies have devoted significant attention to the question of the translation of the *Nights* into other non-European languages, despite the explosion of interest in the text in recent years, and despite increasing interest in scholarship on the expansion of non-European readerships in the nineteenth century.

In the case of that chapter of the *Nights'* historical odyssey that is set in Western Europe, the richness of the text's biography is rarely exhausted in reiterations. This chapter begins in 1701, when the French numismatist Antoine Galland purchased a manuscript entitled *Alf layla wa layla*, beginning the European chapter of the odyssey of the circulation of the body of texts best known in English as *The Arabian Nights*.[4] Within the subsequent two centuries, many authoritative editions and countless others would appear in print not only in French and English, but also in other languages, including Arabic and Persian. A text with roots in scattered pre-modern narratives extant only in a small group of apparently incomplete manuscripts of different length and content, in the eighteenth and nineteenth centuries, this body would come to be seen as unified and consumed as a singular work. The Galland translation begins the European chapter, and it is his edition that defined his own century—unchallenged by other editions, all European translations prepared in the eighteenth century are in one way or another derived from Galland. So dominating was Galland's work that no alternate complete translation would be prepared in French until the early twentieth century, and even then the first effort at a new translation directly from the Arabic, that of Joseph Charles Madrus, would shortly be shown to be an act of forgery and plagiarism (Irwin, *Arabian Nights*, p. 36). Yet the nineteenth century would be defined by the English translations, despite continuing disputes between devotees of Lane, Burton, and others, about which edition, translation, and organization was most "faithful." Despite these academic trifles, over the course of the eighteenth and nineteenth century, the various manifestations of the *Nights*, both in English and French, would come to be regarded as being among the most successful commodities in the new economy of book publishing in Europe.

A genealogy of the value of the English *Nights*

An important marker of late eighteenth-century considerations of the value of the *Nights* for an English readership is Richard Hole's *Remarks on the Arabian Nights Entertainments* (1797). This monograph, originally prepared as a lecture for the Literary Society in Exeter, bears witness to the emergence of a conflicted framework for English evaluation of the *Nights*. In the instance of Hole's lecture, the details of the original setting for the lecture is not known—how many of his audience were readers of the *Nights*? What social classes were represented? For now, these and other questions must be left to conjecture. Yet, in preparing these comments for print, Hole's thesis would be transformed from the learned musings of a lecturer to an important critical text with implications for subsequent studies and criticism for decades to come. While proposing that the *Nights* preserves elements from classical texts and traditions long forgotten to Europe, Hole develops a thesis that the work's merits lie in its representation of contemporary oriental manners and customs. Yet the latter view forms a very small part of his dissertation as a whole, and the weight of his analysis is given to researching of traces of antiquity within the *Nights*, through a close reading of the Sindbad tale.

Hole begins with the proposition that the tales of the *Nights* may be derived from ancient Greek (and to a lesser extent, Indian) myths and fables. As Musawi notes, this thesis is "one of many zealous attempts to vindicate the supernatural element in the *Nights* on classical premises and, ultimately, to rescue the tales from belittling criticism" (Ali, *Scheherazade in England*, pp. 24–5). This attempt followed a trend already mapped by orientalist scholars, articulating Arab Islamic cultural achievements as the product of a synthesis or appropriation of elements of Greek (and again, to a lesser extent, Indo-Persian) antiquities. By locating the origins of the *Nights* within a Hellenic setting, Hole anticipated solving a confounding problem, namely, why it was that adult European contemporaries were only "occasionally amused by [the *Nights'*] wild and diversified incidents," (being "seldom relished but by children") while it had been recorded in travel accounts such as those of one Colonel Capper, that the *Nights* were "universally read throughout Asia by all ranks of men both old and young" (Hole, *Remarks on the Arabian Nights Entertainments*, p. 8). Beyond the likelihood that Capper overstated the significance of the oriental audience for the *Nights*, the idea of the text as co-equivalent to the orient—a slippage between the text and the society it was said to represent—was important to eighteenth- and nineteenth-century European travelers, who were themselves seeking the living settings of the *Nights* on their travels, as well as to critics such as Hole.

Hole is not predisposed to dismiss the value of the tales, as he is "convinced that these tales possess merit of some kind or other, however it may have eluded our notice" (ibid., pp. 8–9). Neither does he carry the prejudice of "consider[ing] the Arabians, notwithstanding what we have heard of them, as children in intellect, and ourselves arrived at the maturity of knowledge" (ibid., p. 9). So how to resolve this apparent discrepancy between the estimation of the value of the *Nights* for its "Arabian" and "European" audiences? For Hole and his audience, a palpable anxiety frames their relation to the *Nights*. Between the sanctification of the text as the highest achievement of the secular imagination of Arabian civilization, and its ability to stimulate a child's delight for "wild and diversified incidents," we may understand Hole's, or more generally any discerning European gentleman's, predicament. How is he to resolve his objective judgment that the tales do "possess merit," without infantilizing the Arab genius which bears responsibility for the text as it has been translated?[5]

The focus on pre-Arab and pre-Islamic sources, in particular the likelihood of some shared source with Hellenic myths and tales, gives Hole a space from which to argue the miscomprehension of the text by some of his fellow European readers. The appropriation of these Greek elements within the *Nights* accounts for the natural affinity French and English readers should feel for the text (of course by this period the theory that Western Europe was civilizationally a product of ancient Greece and Rome had few opponents). By discovering these elemental appropriations, Hole wishes to Europeanize the text, and to loosen the knot of anxiety the text generated in many European readers. To no small extent, this anxiety resulted from the pleasure readers sensed from experiencing an unfamiliar social and literary repertoire, in some cases using social and sexual mores deemed corrupting or dangerous to some segments of English society. Hole is writing in reaction to European critics who found the *Nights* tales extravagant exaggerations, and thus wished to dismiss them as fantastic inventions without social merit, or even as dangerous for the common reader, particularly for children and women. By disclosing the classical sources for these tales, Hole cautions these critics from "indulg[ing] a too hasty contempt for things apparently trivial and insignificant; which may in fact exceed our apprehension... [and which] may at last yield some valuable and unexpected discovery" (Hole, p. 250). While Musawi argues that Hole's "main appeal is to the classical preferences of the literati" (Ali, *Scheherazade in England*, p. 24), Hole also clearly viewed the text as going far beyond the appeal of its representation of classical civilizations: by outlining the text as possibly "yield[ing] some valuable and unexpected discovery," he shows an affinity with themes of adventure, exploration and exploitation that would serve as the underpinning of colonial discourse. Also, by cautioning against "too hasty contempt for things trivial and insignificant," Hole presages the admonitions of later colonial officials and scholars against those who would see the orient as a simple subject, thus evading the opportunities inherent in the colonial project.

Hole's thesis had a long-standing influence on evaluations of the *Nights* for decades to come. As far away as the United States, a lengthy (20-pages long) 1829 review article of Jonathan Scott's 1811 edition of the *Nights* attempted to place the *Nights* within a larger history of oriental and Arabic literature. Hole's thesis, termed a "lively and erudite volume" is quoted at length, concluding similarly but less categorically that at least some of the value of the *Nights* is derived from its use of Hellenic materials, or "how far the author of that fiction [Sinbad the Sailor] has drawn his materials from the Greek writers" (*The Arabian Nights Entertainments*, 1829, p. 295).[6] While less deliberate than Hole in claiming the *Nights'* general origin to be from Greek sources, the anonymous American reviewer still concludes that Arabic literature is highly defined by Greek influences—a point that would hardly be controversial today. The section on Hole concludes, "all this shows the influence the Greek writers had on Arabic literature, and how well the Arabian Nights have represented the general national belief" (ibid., p. 297). What is novel in this review is its reliance on a discourse of "national" characteristics to determine the value of the *Nights*, a very different framework than that employed by Hole's original piece. The article concludes by arguing that "we consider [the *Nights*] as powerful delineations of national character, seen through a veil of delicately wrought fiction" (ibid., p. 302). In this view, the appropriation of an ancient nation's literary legacy by other later nations is organic to the development of national character, which as a matter of course would legitimate the appropriation of the Hellenic legacy in American as well as European centers. By structuring the value of the *Nights* around a discussion of national characteristics, this review would attempt to draw a continuity between the Greek sources and the contemporary consumption of the *Nights*, showing that the text was useful for American and European readers as a repository of a heritage no less essentially deemed their own. Hole was not the first to promote this view—as Musawi notes, in *Progress of Romance* (1787), Clara Reeve promotes a similar thesis (Ali, *Scheherazadein England*, p. 22). However, Hole's work is more substantive and sustaining than Reeve, and devotes more attention to the question of the *Nights'* value for English readers.

Despite the efforts—exemplified by Hole's thesis—to bolster the social value of the *Nights*, anxieties over the perceived perils of the text remained high over the course of the century. Concerns for the dangers the *Nights* posed to young readers and women were most often spelled out in moral and religious terms. One enterprising effort to find accord between these anxieties and the wide popularity of the various editions of the *Nights* attempts to reinfuse a religious and moral ethic into the familiar tales of the text. In *The Oriental Moralist, or the Beauties of the Arabian Nights Entertainments*, the Rev. Mr. Cooper, attempts to do this through "hav[ing] selected a few of the most interesting tales, hav[ing] given them a new dress in point of language, and hav[ing] carefully expunged everything that could give the least offence to the most delicate reader" (*Oriental Moralist, a*). The Rev. Cooper's work is the outcome of a simple concern for the virtue of a significant part of the public readership. Speaking more freely later in his introduction, he states that this new and reworked edition has been crafted so as to "promote the love of virtue, to fortify the youthful heart against the impressions of vice…" (*Oriental Moralist, b*). With these rather lofty goals, he seeks to transform what seems "a wild and weeded spot" back into the "rich and luxuriant garden" it once had been (ibid.). Through a discourse of religious virtues, Cooper aims to rework the text within an operative field of religious and moral legitimation—to do so, he must carry out a radical surgery of the work (or extending his own metaphor, a thorough weeding) so as to render the text accessible and appropriate to the younger and more sensitive reader.

It is in the face of such anxiety that Richard Hole articulates the transactional possibilities of the *Nights.* He does so through an indexing of the work within a framework that argues against the essential unfamiliarity of the text, by reconciling it with its perceived European cultural roots. Yet at the same time the alienating aspects of the unfamiliar text are resurrected, within limits, as the case for the text's merit. Hole argues that

> in exhibiting the merits of this work, I ought not to omit that it is generally allowed to delineate justly the manners of the Eastern nations: and even its *miraculous circumstances*, as was before remarked, are not always to be condemned as absurd and ridiculous because bold and fanciful. They are frequently to be traced to a classic origin, or to other sources, which on a cursory view would be little suspected. The author is not always *erring in his extravagance.*
>
> (Hole, *Remarks on the Arabian Nights Entertainments*, p. 17)

Here Hole sets forward a hint of what will, in later generations, become the primary motivating criteria for high valuations of the oriental tale—the merits of the genre for "delineating justly the manners" of contemporary oriental societies, despite the element of the fantastic within much of the genre. Yet, the primary value of these tales is their "preservation of those valuable remains of antiquity" (Hole, p. 2). Rather than considered "ridiculous," such efforts should be considered "bold," and the extravagance is often well justified.

We now know that Hole's entire thesis suffers from a rather fundamental flaw, which he had no means to ascertain in his own time. Despite engaging in a close reading of the Sindbad episode—the text he references was Galland's *Nuits* or a translation of it—Hole had no way to corroborate the translation against an Arabic manuscript, as he was not fluent in Arabic. It has recently been shown that Sindbad was inserted by Galland in the *Nights* surreptitiously, and that its later acceptance as part of the claim was largely due to his false claim that it had been a part of the manuscript of the *Nights* he possessed. The problem had puzzled scholars for years, in that Galland's original Arabic manuscript is extant, yet lacks the Sindbad sequence—many presumed Galland had a second manuscript that has been since lost. Yet it has been conclusively shown that the Sindbad sequence originated from an entirely separate manuscript, not of the *Nights* tales, and was inserted into the *Nights* sequence, as part of the third volume of Galland's translation.[7] Thus, Hole's thesis is not wholly inaccurate to the extent that it draws conclusions about Arabic literature, however, it cannot have a direct bearing on the origins of the *Nights* as such.

The critics of the *Nights* that Hole intended to address—the Rev. Cooper in some ways articulates their position, albeit in a move toward reconciliation—were, as has been mentioned, seemingly motivated by an anxiety for the dangers the text's excesses were thought to give rise to. Most troubling for them was what they viewed as the text's oblique or often non-existent moral or ethical structure, the shocking absence of admonitions or examples. Devoid of the merits of delivering a moral education, the text would need to find value through another mode of legitimacy. This transformation of the text must be looked at through the perspective of contestations between forms of religious legitimization, and those of an emerging, more autonomous mode. Hole's reading of the *Nights* strips it of the religiously ordained anxieties articulated by readers such as the Rev. Mr. Cooper, transforming the value of the text through its reading within an autonomous framework of cultural value, one that derives its legitimacy through the institutions of the educational establishment, in collaboration with a market of cultural goods for a society educated in their consumption.

By the early nineteenth century, the oriental tale had coalesced into being a recognized market category within the expanding English print-book economy. Yet the development of this sector of the market was by no means a cause for comfort for British elites.[8] By this time the diversity and wide range of texts appealing to the "reading public" presented concerns for some critics. Coinciding with the expansion of British colonial ambitions in India, competition between British and French interests in the Near East, and the threat of Russian imperialism in the Central Asian "Great Game," the dizzying range of these books may well have caused anxieties for intellectual and political elites who wished for common cause between the literary market and the political policies of the Empire.

The most significant effort to organize and evaluate the body of available texts is carried out by Henry Weber in his 1812 compendium *Tales of the East: Comprising the Most Popular Romances of Oriental Origin: And the Best Imitations by European Authors*. This canonizing collection, made up of excerpts from texts already published as well as new translations and selections, presents a valuative scheme by which the merit and value of the field may be assessed.

Weber outlines his evaluative schema through an introductory essay, which recognizes the economic basis of the legitimacy of the oriental tale when he says that its history shows "how eager European story-tellers were to profit by the fictions of the eastern imagination whenever they could obtain access to them" (Weber, *Tales of the East*, p. xii). Writing just 16 years after Hole, Weber does largely replicate Hole's thesis on the value of the *Nights* as a repository of classical knowledge (including quoting from Hole's dissertation at great length in his introduction), yet he tends to emphasize more strongly the reading of the *Nights* as a representation of the "manners and customs" of the orient.

> As conveying in general a true and striking picture of the manners and customs prevalent amongst some of the most interesting nations of the earth, the value of these tales has not been disputed, particularly since the authenticity and *vraisemblance* of the portraits they convey has been established by the authority of some of the most faithful and best informed travelers in the East. By the perusal of the Arabian Nights' Entertainments, and other collections of a similar nature, we obtain, in a manner the most impressive on the memory, and the most pleasing to the mind, a perfect insight into the private habits, the domestic comforts and deprivations of the orientals; we are led to participate in their favorite amusements, and acquire a knowledge of their religious sentiments and superstitions.
>
> (Ibid., p. ii)

A generation of scholars have reflected on issues such as why the "domestic comforts and deprivations" of the people of the East would be a matter of much concern for an English readership. However, beyond the particular and very important question of (mis-) representation raised by much of the post-*Orientalism* scholarship, it remains unclear what *function and value* is such knowledge to serve for the estimated public readership? Reading Weber, a fundamental question emerges at the heart of much public discourse on the dangers of mass literacy and readership—specifically, who is the intended audience of the romance, the gothic novel, or the oriental tale? In the midst of critical concerns for the effect of such literature on various social groups—women, the working classes, the young—Weber attempts to recover the oriental tale as endowed with a common, if nonetheless limited, educational value. He makes this explicit by imagining that "a boy, who has been indulged in the perusal of these ingenious fictions, is made well acquainted with the peculiarities of oriental manners, and the tenets of the Mahommedan faith, during the time of relaxation, as he is, during his school hours, with the customs and mythology of the Greeks and Romans" (ibid., pp. ii–iii). Neither a fanciful act befitting leisure, nor the stuff of academic enrichment, the oriental tale has value as a window upon the manners of an unfamiliar setting not addressed in his formal education. By emphasizing the educational possibilities of the *Nights*, Weber rescues it from accusations of its powers of corruption, while admitting its proper setting—the "time of relaxation"—as an supplementary activity within an educational setting.

This new social valuation of the *Nights* articulates its particularly social function as a literary utility in the quest for authentic knowledge of the orient. The claim of its authentic, even mimetic, powers of representation are carried out in numerous reviews and articles through the course of the next decades of the nineteenth century. For example, a *Times'* reviewer of an 1826 edition of the *Nights* rehearses much of Weber's language.[9] This edition is vaulted by the reviewer precisely for the improvements it makes over earlier editions, addressing it within an ethnographic valuative framework. The reviewer addresses the specifically social function of the *Nights* in stating "the chief merit of the new tales is, that they give singular and authentic pictures of the domestic manners of the Arabs, and convey, without the formality of descriptions, some very satisfactory information on subjects which are not commonly treated by travelers or historians" ("New Arabian Nights Entertainments," *The Times*, 4 May 1826, p. 3). Here the language reflects a transformation in the *Nights* from a text of conflicted values in the sacral or moral sphere, particularly as the education of youth were concerned, to a text of clear and simple utility as an ethnographic portrait of contemporary foreign peoples. That this knowledge was tied to Great Britain's colonial ambitions was a point needing no rehearsal. However, it would have to be later in the century before the colonial position was most fully articulated by another commentator, as will be shortly discussed.

This shift marks a subtle but important re-evaluation in the transactional value of the text. Its status as an authentic work of the orient, and its apparent timelessness (unencumbered as any European reading of the text was with assessing the historical contingencies of the production of the text in Arabic), made this set of narratives excellently suited for the role they were to play. Given the high degree of artifice involved in the production of their "authenticity," it may not be entirely speculative to say the text was made to fill this role for European, and in particular English, audiences. Indeed, the text was largely a referent to what was from a literary standpoint, a minor, populist strain in certain parts of the Islamic world, yet attempts continued to endow it with a centrality and significance for Arab and Muslim societies that it certainly did not enjoy.[10] The *Times* review of Van Hammer's translation claims that the *Nights* "are universally popular in Arabia," with no consideration of historical or social specificity ("New Arabian Nights Entertainments," p. 3). Furthermore, the significance of the text within Arab domains is measured economically, as its recitation is said to "furnish employment to a large body of the community" (ibid.). Outside of the fanciful claims of a few travelers claiming to have seen performances of the *Nights* by storytellers in cafes and public spaces, stating this also makes material the purported value of the *Nights* to Arab societies. In a way that perhaps matched the expanding economic value of the text within European literary marketplaces, the *Nights* also was deemed to command a position of economic significance in the Arab world.

E.W. Lane and the science of the *Nights*

We have seen how, for the most part, early nineteenth-century reviewers and scholars found much of this value deriving from the use of the *Nights* in the development of a universalist perspective on mankind. Yet, from Hole's thesis on the *Nights* onward, evaluations of the text almost invariably included references to its high premium as a catalogue of the true East, an index of the timeless characteristics of oriental, or Arabian, life. While this would not mean that the *Nights* betrayed truths much relevant to modern European societies—and hence fears of its "amorality" were quite understandable—the truths of the East were deemed valuable to an understanding of the past of and sources of European civilizations. Some, like the *American Quarterly Review* writer, would set the terms in definable "national" categories. While a religious perspective struggled to accommodate itself to the popularity (and marketability) of the *Nights*, either through condemning their spread or by reconsidering their use to religious concepts and goals, the utilitarian perspective also struggled to legitimize public consumption of the *Nights* through its own value systems.

A new and significant development in the late 1830s would again redefine the terms of these debates: Edward William Lane's translation of the 1835 Bulaq edition of the *Nights*, published between 1838 and 1841. Lane's edition, and critical responses to it, would set the measure of the value of the *Nights* and much more narrowly to its use as an ethnographic window upon the Arab world. Discussion of the *Nights'* Hellenic origins would die out, as would arguments of its use to modern European readers as a universal repository of the contributions of oriental thought to European civilizations, such as Weber's notion that the *Nights* complimented the schoolboy's study of the classics. Emboldened by Lane's critical introduction and notes to his translation, critics began to discuss the *Nights* as very specifically with exacting verisimilitude representing the timeless realities of Arab society. While containing a historical dimension, this representation had more importantly a trans-historical validity, presenting actual facts about Arab customs, institutions, relations, and aspirations that were true for all time.

As a young man, Lane had spent three years in Egypt, and had produced a ground-breaking text, *Manners and Customs of the Modern Egyptians* (1836), which would be considered an important proto-anthropological text on modern Egypt for decades to come. *Manners and Customs* brought to the fore the ability of the European to represent in text and image (Lane had been trained as a lithographer) the truths of a foreign society.[11] Encyclopedic in ambition, the book intended to complement the value of *Description de L'Egypte*, which was produced as a result of the French invasion of Egypt in 1798. Yet, rather than employing the dizzyingly panoptic methodology of *Description*, Lane aimed for concise and penetrating observations to create a field manual for understanding modern Egypt—a methodology emerging from the development of Ethnology as a field apart from Philology. Lane masterfully worked between the lines of the two fields, and through his interdisciplinary methods, produced a popularly accessible approach to the study of distant cultures.

These works were never meant to be scholarly in a proper sense—both *Manners and Customs* and *The Arabian Nights* were published by the Society for the Diffusion of Useful Knowledge, an important publishing institution in Victorian England. Founded in 1826, the Society's aims were to serve as a "vendor of wholesome reading matter" for the "skilled workingman and their families" (Altick, *English Common Reader*, p. 269). This goal was advanced by series of cheaply printed texts offering "useful" reading to a social class earlier largely targeted by a market of cheap diversionary books. The Society published Lane's *Manners and Customs* as part of its Library of Entertaining Knowledge—a selection of the offerings of this "entertaining" series, which would include other works such as *The Elgin Marbles*, *Secret Societies of the Middle Ages* and a three volume collection entitled *Vegetable Substances*, gives an indication of the kinds of texts considered wholesome and useful by the Society (ibid., p. 270). Marketed to the lower-middle and working classes, these texts were part of a larger movement to extend considerations of who was included within the British reading public. By offering "serious" works to these classes, the members of the Society were determined to disprove the widespread view that literature was as dangerous as it was beneficial, and that the working classes should *ipso facto* be considered among the sectors of the public for whom reading could be harmful or dangerous.

The election of Lane's *Nights* by this institution for its catalogue is a fact quite telling of the important role the text was to play again in defining the terms for debates on how to evaluate literature. With Lane, a sacralization of the *Nights* for the orient would enhance the empirical charge of the text for the English reader. Over the course of the nineteenth century, the English imagination of the social function of the *Nights* among Eastern societies highly exaggerated the significance of the text so as to fit it well within the function it had come to serve within English society. Given the fact that this was likely the *only* text from an Arab–Islamic context that the average English reader would encounter, it assumed a representative status for these readers, a burden that was clearly quite significant—the text was made to serve social, historical, and religious claims about, varyingly, Arabs, Islam, or the orient. This was driven not only by the continuing competition between sacred and secular institutions for cultural legitimacy (and the role of assessing cultural legitimacy), but also by the incremental deepening of Imperial concerns for the orient as part of a comprehensive vision of the colonial world.

As English readers consumed, and English authors produced, new editions of the *Nights*, the text came to occupy a singular location within the English literary imagination, this is well reflected in the critical responses to the *Nights* during this period. The *Times* reviewer, Weber, the Rev. Cooper and Hole all mark positions on a range of evaluative formulations—intimately related, if articulated in manners which show the slight and major differences in rationale between them—for assessing the merits of the *Nights* for an English audience. Certain ambivalences mark the statements of each: Hole is unable to reconcile the value of the *Nights* as a possible repository for antiquity with the disdain of English readers for its fantastic exaggerations, inappropriate for educated adults; Rev. Cooper is moved to excise the text of its excesses and rework its amoral structure, yet defends the use of the text as a gateway to educate youth; Weber places the text precariously on a pedestal between leisure and education, while emphasizing its use as a reference-book or window upon contemporary oriental societies. This determination is emphasized in the *Times* review, which gives the ethnographic reading of the *Nights* a context for a larger reading public in the new translation by von Hammer. Lane made the *Nights* part of a new and popularly accessible science, a hybrid of ethnology and philology that well suited the perspective of a burgeoning colonial interest in the Arab world. By reading the *Nights* as an encyclopedic repertoire of Arabian social life, the value of Lane's edition would be found to be in its highlighting of the social element, both in the text and in his copious notes that accompanied and explained it. Its publication by the Society for the Diffusion of Useful Knowledge placed the text squarely in an economy of publishing devoted to popularizing and expanding the audience of literature of value to society as a whole. Through his expurgations, and with his footnotes, Lane wrested the *Nights* from the clutches of the moralists who found it a text of no value—as the need to know the orient gained a higher premium, the *Nights* as presented by Lane, were to come to serve a function central to meeting this need.

Burton's labors: imbuing the *nights* with a "new vitality"

> And here we were confronted by a serious question, What number of copies would suffice my public? A distinguished Professor who had published some 160,000 texts with prices ranging from 6d. to 50 guineas, wrote to me in all kindness advising an issue of 150 to 250: an eminent printer–publisher would have ventured upon some 500: others rose to 750 with a warning-note anent "wreckage," great risk and ruinous expenditure, while only one friend—and he not in business—urged an edition of 2,000 to 3,000 with encouraging words as to its probable reception. After long forethought I chose 1,000 as a just middle.
>
> (Burton, *Supplemental Nights*, Vol. VII, p. 460)

The initial response to Richard Burton's edition of the *Nights* was notoriously mixed, in particular due to the controversy over his inclusion of relatively sexually graphic passages and tales that had earlier been subject to editorial abridgement. These and other concerns (such as Burton's application of a quasi-archaic style of English for his rendering, which he mixed with sometimes jarring elements of colloquial dialects) led to clear divisions among literary critics. But the tide worked in the favor of his supporters, a fact that is confirmed not only by the material success of the 1885 edition, but also by the supplements and stream of reissues that were to come in the following years. Indeed, Sir Richard Burton's concerns about the risks involved in the self-publication of his translation of the *Thousand Nights and One Night*, proved to be unfounded. In fact, the subscription series, published in a limited edition of 1,000 copies, which sold out within weeks of their release, may be thought of as a coup of late nineteenth-century literary marketing. No other book, purporting to be for limited academic use, had gained as great a public notoriety as this. Indeed, masquerading as a "limited edition" for academic subscribers, Burton's *Nights* acted much as the canonizing triple-decker novels did. The typical triple-decker, the favored form for "high" literary novels aimed at middle-class readers, was published in editions of 500–1,000 copies, and the relative speed with which this initial offering was bought up often set the measure for the book's long-term prospects in terms of cheaper reissues in yellowback or other forms (Eliot, "The Business of Victorian Publishing," p. 55). Once Burton's initial offering was sold out, he too moved to provide for this market in different ways, through publishing extra supplementary volumes of *Nights* tales, and eventually publishing an expurgated edition for general consumption under the supervision of his wife, Isabella Burton, a prolific author in her own right.

As numerous periodicals noted, the initial demand for the edition far outpaced the available copies, and the rising market resell value of the edition was frequently noted in reviews and articles in the press. Initial reviews of the 1885 edition were already attentive to its rising value, even listing resale prices. An early review, coming only weeks after the edition's publication, noted "the copies published a month ago at a guinea have gone up in value to ten... a few of the volumes were to be had in Holywell-street, but these have all been bought up at big prices" (quoted in *Supplemental Nights*, Vol. VII, p. 494).[12] Others set the price by less material measures, noting that within three weeks of distribution, "it is not longer to be had for love or money" (quoted in ibid., p. 462). By 1886, the price had risen even higher, "Sir Richard Burton's version... is now unobtainable. The edition sold off immediately, and the price has already reached twenty-six guineas" (ibid., p. 467). It should be noted that even the one pound price placed the text far out of reach of most "leisurely" readers, much less the price of 26 pounds, which would have been more than the monthly income of an average middle-class family (Eliot, "The Business of Victorian Publishing," p. 38). As noted by one 1888 review of the *Supplementary Nights*, a seven-volume appendix Burton assembled of disparate material in response to the interest generated by his original *Nights*, the material value of this edition of the *Nights* did not quickly wane. "The fixed price is pretty high, but so overmastering is the purely literary curiosity in the matter that not only was the original edition sold to the last copy, but the book is now at very considerable premium on the market" (quoted in *Supplemental Nights*, Vol. VII, p. 494). The economic calculus was a point of pride for Burton, as he placed these and many other reviews and included them in an appendix to the final volume of the *Supplementary Nights*, integrating the discussion of the edition's rising material value into the physical book—perhaps one of the first attempts at making the critical response of a text a part of the text itself.

The rising material value of Burton's edition of the *Nights* is one part of a wider picture of the transactionary role the text played in late nineteenth-century Britain. The market interest in this edition coincided with changes in the nature of the reading public, and follows the increasing autonomy of the literary field from the previous determinants of literary value. The masterful oversight of the production of this edition—from the subterfuge of imprinting the text with a fictitious publishing concern ("The Kama Shastra Society of London and Benares," as improbable as it seems) to the limitation of its acquisition to subscribers (in order to avoid obscenity charges), to the choice of cover, design and paper, all worked as factors in the high status the edition was to gain with the majority of critics and cultural institutions in Britain. Ironically, his detractors largely served to do the same.

The ripostes targeting Burton's *Nights* came fast and furious immediately upon its publication. One of the most vehement of the initial attacks came from the *Edinburgh Review* whose author offered a crib summary of the major editions. "Galland for the nursery, Lane for the library, Payne for the study, and Burton for the sewer" (quoted in Irwin, *Arabian Nights*, p. 36). The domestic metaphor highlighted the nature of the threat to the family, with a rational division of the editions between family members and roles disrupted by the appearance of the Burton edition. *Pall Mall Gazette* also joined the fray, with two articles terming the collection "pornography."[13] The conflict that played out in reviews of Burton's *Nights* was more than an academic dispute. Rather, it may be thought to present a marker of the "crumbling of a Victorian consensus," at the end of the century (Kennedy, "Captain Burton's Oriental Muck Heap," p. 318). This process was accompanied by a reorganization of priorities in cultural value discourse; Burton read the shifting grounds shrewdly, and targeted his work to take advantage of what he saw as an open opportunity in the cultural reconfigurations of late Victorian Britain. That Burton expected his planned publication to be notably successful is apparent in a dedication of Vol. III, addressed to the writer Henry Irving, encouraging the latter to create theatrical works based on the new rendition: "The *Nights* still offers many a virgin mine to the Playwright [. . .] In the hope that you will find means of exploiting the hidden wealth which awaits you" (Burton, *Thousand Nights* (1897) Vol. III, dedication). The use of materialist metaphors, in an imaginative return to the colonial adventure, quite clearly shows a regard of the *Nights* as a kind of reservoir of natural resources for cultural production. The careful "exploitation" of these resources will confer a "hidden wealth" to the writer. Burton's enthusiasm is somewhat vulgar, perhaps, but no less so than the reviewers of the *Nights* who endlessly focused on calculating the "hidden wealth" possible for readers and the translator of the *Nights* alike.

Over the following years Burton's edition eventually came to be considered the popular standard-bearer, even if sometimes remaining out of favor with connoisseurs and specialists. By 1923, T.E. Lawrence held all the major English translators in disfavor, oddly echoing the *Edinburgh Review* in opining, "Payne crabbed. Burton unreadable. Lane pompous" (Irwin, *Arabian Nights*, p. 39). He rather tellingly preferred the French 1899–1904 Joseph Charles Mardrus edition, which has since been shown to have been constructed of both newly fabricated stories and fancifully reconfigured material from previous available editions—so much for Lawrence's conceits as an amateur Arabist on the order of Richard Burton.

But beyond the discussion of the book's material value, which factored centrally in its initial reviews, there are other signs of the translator/publisher's larger personal, social and cultural interests in publishing this edition. Some of these are evident from Burton's own comments that appear in the introductory, supplementary and critical additions to the translation of the *Nights*. Burton introduces his translation with a series of intimate and delicate images. In poetic and intimate terms, Burton leads the reader through a set of visual associations the tales bring forth in his own mind; they take him from his " 'respectable' surroundings" to "the land of my predilection, Arabia" (Burton, *Arabian Nights*, p. xxiiii).[14] There, undifferentiated images of "diaphanous skies" and "the evening star, hanging like a solitaire from the pure front of the western firmament" materialize into the setting of a Bedouin encampment, where further images testify to the simple lives of its inhabitants, as night begins to fall (ibid., p. xxiv). This is the theatre of Burton's mind, with himself as director, made clear by his announcement of "a change of scene." The curtain rises on a tribal gathering around the campfire, Burton himself among those gathered, now as an actor upon the stage of his imagination. These images, triggered by his reading of the *Nights*, feed back upon themselves, for sitting confidently among the Bedouin, it is *Burton* who is reciting the tales of the *Nights* to his hosts, as "a reward [for] their hospitality" (ibid.). What better image exists of the transactional role of the *Nights*, than in his description of the Bedouin women and children who "seem to drink in the words with eyes and mouths as well as ears" (ibid.).

Burton's "reward" to his nomadic hosts is to tell them tales from a book that is their own; the transaction of the text takes an almost literal reversal. But for Burton's narrative, the merit of the text is not only in its exchange-value, but also in its use as a representational archive from which to draw a specific way of reading the Arabian locale. From the sensuous experience of the evening air, to the sighting of the evening star, Burton makes clear that the *Nights* played a central role in making this space legible, and the societies found there, during the course of a lifetime of colonial service. It is in this context that he explains that the *Nights* did him "noble service" not only as a payment for the kindness of Arabs he stayed with, but also for shaping an understanding of the lands he traversed in a way that could be shared by both himself and his company. "In Somali-land," he notes, "no one was deaf to the charm [of the *Nights*] and the two women-cooks of my caravan, on its way to Harar, were incontinently dubbed by my men 'Shahrazad' and 'Dinazad'" (Burton, *Arabian Nights*, pp. xxiv–xxv). Burton reads this episode as a moment where his retelling of the *Nights* to his Eastern employees, results in their appropriation of the tales for their own description of their world. Hence the local guides assisting Burton came to read the world around them—including the women hired as cooks for his caravan—in terms he had introduced through his telling of these tales.

Burton's introduction had a greater purpose than to simply recall his days in Arabia—this *mis en-scene* intended to place Burton at the centre of the text, to identify himself with it integrally, and to furthermore beckon to the reader to take Burton's place at the fireside. This image sparked the imagination of one contemporary reviewer, who noted "clearly an Englishman who can thus hold an Arab encampment spellbound by reciting to them their own tales has at least one indisputable qualification for translating the famous collection of these stories embodied in *Alf layla wa layla*" (quoted in *Supplemental Nights*, Vol. VII, p. 484). The value of Burton's text measured not only as a compensation for the hospitality of his previous Arabian hosts, but also as a qualification for the reproduction and marketing of these tales within England.

Burton was to legitimize his addition of a new translation of the *Nights* to the large stack of preceding efforts by arguing that his predecessors "one and all degrade a chef-d'oevre of the highest anthropological and ethnographical interest and importance to a mere fairy-book, a nice present for little boys" (Burton, *Arabian Nights*, p. xxvi). This, despite the fact that John Payne had presented a very similar translation of the same *Nights* only one year before Burton—indeed, large portions of Burton's work are deemed by some as plagiarizations of Payne's edition (Irwin, *Arabian Nights*, p. 30). Yet equally does Burton bemoan the moralist's strain in the English approach to the *Nights*, followed from Rev. Cooper's minor edition through to Lane's stately 1839 edition, which avoided the "objectionable" to be found in the Arabic—a rather remarkable point, as his text was largely based upon the Egyptian Bulaq edition, which had already expurgated many of the more saucy elements of most extant manuscripts (Burton, *Arabian Nights*, p. xxvi). Burton has no patience for such temerity—for he sees the value of the *Nights* not in the conflicted terms set by some of his predecessors. Unaffected by claims of their use as either leisure-reading, or as moral tales (if only just touched up), Burton sets an agenda for valuing the *Nights* in very stark, absolute terms. Burton sees his contribution to the legacy of the *Nights* as reflecting on its value within the logic of the colonial project.

> This book is indeed a legacy which I bequeath to my fellow-countrymen in their hour of need. [. . .] Apparently England is ever forgetting that she is at present the greatest Mohammedan empire in the world. [. . .] He who would deal with them successfully must be, firstly, honest and truthful and, secondly, familiar with and favorably inclined to their manners and customs if not to their law and religion. We may, perhaps

> find it hard to restore to England those pristine virtues, that tone and temper, which made her what she is; but at any rate we (myself and a host of others) can offer her the means of dispelling her ignorance concerning the Eastern races with whom she is continually in contact.
>
> (Ibid., p. xxxvi)

Burton's articulation of the value of the text explicitly links colonialism with the merit of the *Nights* for an English readership. In comparison to Weber, Burton makes little effort to elaborate upon the supposedly canonical nature of the *Nights* within oriental societies—in fact, such a concern seems entirely irrelevant to him. In Burton's narration, the *Nights* is a text *re*-introduced to Arabia from Europe; the matter of its origins is of lesser importance to him than *use* of the text by Europeans in their relationship with the orient. Burton calls for a rigorous engagement with the text, through which the English colonial officer could become equipped to unveil the text for his Arab audience, and in so doing, make legible their own world for themselves. The terms of the *Nights* were not only useful for the English reader to better fulfill his role in the empire, but also could assist in bringing the native oriental to better understand his or her own world as well.[15]

Some of the critical responses to Burton's work also recognized the value of the text for social and political concerns, while others tied their estimation to a more universalist discourse, itself no less implicated in the colonial project. The metaphors reviewers used are illustrative of a linking of material and cultural values. One early commentator noted that this edition "enriches the world of Oriental investigation." Another remarked that with Burton's edition, it is ever more clear that the *Nights* "marks the continuity of Oriental political ideas" (*Supplemental Nights*, Vol. VII, p. 486). Other reviewers see Burton's work not simply as a work of literary genius, but emphasize the value of his labors as "a service" to England, "priceless to anyone who concerns himself with such subjects" (ibid., p. 457). Of special mention in this regard are the notes prepared by Burton, which one reviewer argued "have a value which is simply unique." Another also found the greatest value of the edition to lie within these notes, because "Captain Burton's minute acquaintance with Eastern life makes his comments invaluable" (ibid., p. 458). However, Burton's final flourish, linking his labors on the *Nights* directly to the exigencies of the colonial project, may also serve as an obfuscation of certain facts. Despite the common reference in reviews to Burton's "service" for having translated the *Nights*, it is clear that after a run of minor and widely ignored translations (many of them as if not more erotic than his *Nights*), Burton was quite attentive to the financial and more ephemerally "cultural" value a translation of the *Nights* would be able confer upon him. As a sort of literary entrepreneur, Burton showed an uncommon knack for mining his formative experiences in the Arab world for capital that would sustain his final years, and not only financially. Famously disgruntled for the professional disappointments he endured as a faithful diplomatic officer, Burton was quite intent to find just compensation by accumulating cultural capital for his talents as an author, able Arabist, ethnologist, and entrepreneur. Indeed, the return on this investment was not insignificant "The *Nights* were not only a critical but also a financial success. Burton spent 6,000 guineas on printing sixteen volumes, and gained a profit of 10,000 guineas"—after the success of his *Nights*, Burton was to conclude that, "now that I know the taste of England, we need never be without money" (Brodie, *Devil Drives*, p. 309).

Through this accumulation of both cultural and material capital, Burton was further able to enter into an ongoing public clash on British Victorian mores and attitudes, and to have an impact on the course of this debate. In Burton's time these concerns were in fact yet another variation on earlier contentions over the utility and interpretation of the practice and economies of both writing and reading. The key dispute remained the struggle between moralist–religious interpretations and those of utilitarian mode. What remained at stake was the nature and mode of legitimation of "literature" as an autonomous cultural arena. As a text generated by a series of transactions between European and oriental literary fields, over the course of the late eighteenth and nineteenth centuries, the varying editions based on the Arabic tales of *Alf layla wa layla* played a consistent if ever-shifting role in the shaping of debates over the purpose and value of literature in society. By the late nineteenth century, the terms of this clash had changed somewhat—few articulated the moralist position through the use of purely religious discourse, although traces of it certainly remained. The utilitarian approach had largely overtaken the centre ground, framing the rhetorics and terms of the debate. Yet, there remained a significant disquiet, especially among the elites and the middle-classes, for the possibilities of recognizing literature as a truly self-legitimating social arena.

3

MODERN ARABIC AND PERSIAN BIOGRAPHIES OF THE *ARABIAN NIGHTS*

The European value of *Alf layla wa layla* was initially defined by the popularity and commercial success of the *Arabian Nights* franchise—a fact that raises questions about the essential appeal of the text that remain difficult to answer. Just as the category of modern literature was coalescing into a discrete subject, and just as the ascendant genre of the novel was gaining in popularity, a text of distant temporal and geographic sources came to occupy a prominent place in discussions on literature's value in modern society. The debates around the use of the *Nights* for moral, utilitarian, romantic, or other ends show how widely the range of possible merits of the text extended, and the extent to which the text was made to speak for social anxieties and aspirations that were tied generally to the emergence of the categories of modern literature and mass readerships. As the previous chapter has argued, the text's flexibilities were part of its appeal, and very much arose from its transactability.

Shorn of a clear historical, cultural, or even geographic center, the *Nights* were able to be read in such a way as to be representative of a wide range of social expectations and desires. As translated texts for which an authentic *ur*text was absent, the fabric and sensibility of these various translations were able to very freely accommodate different audiences and therefore different social imaginaries. Other translations of major pre-modern texts were often produced on the basis of a better-defined master text—yet, because of their fastidious commitment to the source text, the resulting books published from these translations often alienated almost all readers but enthusiasts, scholars, and those for whom the text had a religious significance. In addition, the very structure of the *Nights* also allowed for it to act as a transactionary text. As various tales or strands of the *Nights* were to appear in periodicals, journals and abridgements, the fame, and relative popularity of certain stories would often set the terms of discussion for the work as a whole—in fact, it is likely that a significant proportion of European readers were familiar only with selected stories of the collection, and that relatively few readers were reading the unabridged collections of the *Nights*.

It is perhaps ironic that given that the roots of the *Nights* are most likely Indo-Persian and their longevity owes a great deal to the Arabic enhancements and rearticulations of the original tradition, the modern resurrection of the *Nights* in Persian and Arabic owe a significant debt to the European fascination with them. The emergence of modern editions of the *Nights* in Arabic and Persian circumstances may be dated to the early nineteenth century—one measure of this milestone is the first appearance of print editions of the text, 1814 in the Arabic case, in the 1840s in the Persian. In the Arabic context, the first printings of *Alf layla wa layla* were directly tied to colonial British institutions, and the eventual reappropriation of the text by Arab publishers was deeply affected by the European debates of the merits of the text. It has been observed that "the *Nights'* popularity in the 'West' in turn created within Arabic culture an interest in this corpus of stories, which has until recently been marginal to the Arabic literary and cultural tradition" (Ouyang, "Genres, Ideologies," p. 127). The Persian *Hizar u yik shab* was in one sense a later ripple emanating from the same colonial project, yet carried out in a very different cultural and political environment, marked by the anxieties found in Qajar Iran concerning reforms to the country's elite. Yet shortly after its translation, the text was to first be appropriated by the Shah Nasir al-Din as part of his diversions from the responsibilities of rulership, and later, with the rise of nationalism, the text would be recovered for the emergence of an Iranian national readership.

Arabic print editions of the *Nights* appeared first in the early nineteenth century, and between 1814 and 1842 four were issued; named by scholars as the Calcutta (I), the Breslau, the Calcutta (II) and the Bulaq editions. None of the first three was based upon a single manuscript—both Calcutta editions are thought to be compendia from different sources and the claim of the authenticity of the Breslau edition has been shown to be suspect (Mahdi, *The Thousand and One Nights*, p. 96).[1] The remaining Bulaq edition is likely derived largely or exclusively from a single manuscript, which has not been located. The major English translations of this period are based upon these four Arabic editions—in particular the latter two. Lane worked from the Bulaq press edition, while Burton relied largely on the Calcutta (II) for his translation. An important issue, which cannot be sufficiently attended to here, is the possible effect of the eighteenth-century European editions (which largely derive from Galland's text) upon the contents or organization of the Arabic print editions. By what can only be a pure historical coincidence, or a fact more telling than many scholars have allowed, Galland's manuscript has been shown to be the oldest, and most complete, extant manuscript of the *Nights*.

The first Calcutta edition of the *Nights* (printed in two volumes, 1814–1818) was a direct product of British colonial policy and its educational institutions in India, which, simply put, "exercised a decisive influence on the textual history of the *Arabian Nights*" (Marzolph, "The Persian Nights," p. 282). The editor of this work, Shaykh Ahmad Shirwani al-Yamani taught at the East India Company's Fort William College, and so had intimate knowledge of the English translations of the *Nights*. Mahdi states that the first Calcutta edition was produced by the college "as a textbook for teaching Arabic to Company officers" as part of colonial administrative duties "for the study and administration of Islamic (Mohammadan) law" (Mahdi, *The Thousand and One Nights*, p. 89). Shirwani used an eighteenth-century Syrian manuscript (or, more likely, a copy of it made in 1811) for his edition. Yet, in consideration of the purpose of the text—to instruct English colonial officers in Arabic—he "took the liberty of extensively editing the manuscript from which he was preparing the edition [. . .] with the overall intention of preparing a useful manual for teaching Arabic at the College and elsewhere" (ibid., p. 91). The organization of the tales, and the inclusion of certain stories from the Galland edition (such as the Sindbad sequence) also show that Shirwani was directly influenced by the European editions, despite having access to an original Arabic manuscript.

The 1835 Bulaq edition, which follows Shirwani's by some eighteen years, would appear to represent a more autonomous work, given that it was issued by an Egyptian government printing press with little direct interaction with European interests. Yet, as Mahdi has argued, "the widespread interest in the *Nights* in France and Great Britain did concern not the text of the first Bulaq, but rather the production and composition of its exemplar" (ibid., p. 97). The Bulaq edition came at a time when European travelers were making Cairo one of the most popular destinations for travel outside of Europe; one mid-century commentator would be able to remark that "there is no country in Europe where one could live in such perfect luxury as during six months in Egypt" (quoted in Gregory, "Scripting Egypt," p. 127). Among these travelers, not a small number of book antiquarians and collectors were arriving in the manuscript and book market with requests for manuscripts of *Alf layla wa layla*, which likely impacted upon the manuscript trade of late-eighteenth century Cairo (Mahdi, *The Thousand and One Nights*, p. 98). The recension of the *Nights* that is considered to have been the basis for the Bulaq press edition was from a line of a relatively recent vintage, dating no earlier than to the 1770s, or perhaps later. In addition, the continuity of content between various recensions of the Nights were notoriously uneven—as Heinz Grotzfeld has noted:

> In Egypt, complete sets of the recension directly preceding the one known as Zotenberg's Egyptian Recension (henceforth ZER) must have been extremely scarce in the last quarter of the eighteenth century. In consequence, there was a need to compose a new recension—ZER. This new recension, of which complete copies could be easily purchased in Cairo at the beginning of the nineteenth century, became scarce in the late 1820s (Lane, Manners 420), hereby again prompting a new recension—the Reinhardt manuscript in Strasbourg. In the course of some forty to fifty years, a new recension disintegrated and was replaced by a new composition prepared both from parts of the preceding recensions and additional materials that were not included previously in a recension of the Nights. In this manner, the development of manuscript tradition prevented the formation of a canonical repertoire of *Alf layla*.
>
> (Grotzfeld, "Creativity, Random Selection, and pia fraus," p. 219)

Grotzfeld comments on the transformation of the repertoire of *Alf layla* within different recensions, but does not offer a view upon the reasons for these changes. Eva Sallis has argued that the transformations of nineteenth-century Arabic recensions were due to what was seen as a need to "improve the story art" of the *Nights* in comparison to earlier manuscripts (Sallis, *Sheherazade Looking through the Looking Glass*, p. 37). This assessment, necessarily subjective, follows on a valuative framework for what David Pinault terms "creativity"—this may well reflect the desires of late eighteenth-century European manuscript buyers in the Cairo markets (Pinault, "Bulaq, Macnaughten and the New Leiden Edition Compared," p. 127). Among nineteenth-century scholars of the *Nights*, finding evidence of the text's true origin came to be the holy grail of the field. Not a few leading lights of this period's scholars of the orient devoted significant portions of their lives to the search for the Rosetta stone of the *Nights*—a manuscript or fragment that would unlock the hidden history of the text, and explain its true origin. Some scholars were even driven to ignore contradicting evidence in making claims of having found significant texts relevant to this search, others opportunistically forged what they needed to make claims of having located such texts (Irwin, *Arabian Nights*, pp. 37–8). As they were largely philologists, these scholars focused their efforts on locating textual evidence of an originating point for what was largely presumed to have been, at one time, a complete book. It is perhaps not surprising that among these scholars the status of the tales within oral literature was largely neglected, even if their presence within various oral cultures was occasionally noted. For many scholars of this period, the value of the *Nights* was tied to the idea of an original, authored, text. Mahdi cautiously advances a hint of what effect this search may have had on the Arabic *Nights* by arguing,

> It is therefore possible to suggest that the common exemplar of the late Egyptian recension was complied in 1775 to meet the demand created for a "complete" *Nights* copy. But it may also have been commissioned by European travelers, or by dragomans or other functionaries in the consulates and embassies of the European powers in the Arab parts of the Ottoman Empire, acquainted with Galland's *Nights* and wishing to acquire a more complete manuscript of the original.
>
> (Mahdi, *The Thousand and One Nights*, p. 103)

The Bulaq edition not only appears to meet the demands of this market of European enthusiasts and book dealers in Arabic literature, but also must be thought to address the interests and values of a small but engaged market of Egyptian consumers, particularly those who were emerging from the new educational institutions in Egypt, supported by the same governmental reform plans that had supported the publication of the Bulaq *Nights*.[2] Al-Musawi further elaborates on this issue, centering the role of European values in an articulation of the Arabic cultural revival of the mid-nineteenth century. "Even the publication of the Bulaq edition in 1835 should be seen in contexts of expediency and acquiescence to the prevailing European enthusiasm for the tales . . . the publication of the collection could be seen as catering to the European interest in the tales, while simultaneously appropriating them to the growing revivalist tendency" (Al-Musawi, *The Postcolonial Arabic Novel*, p. 71). We will look more carefully at the appropriation of the *Nights* by late-nineteenth century figures of the Arab *nahda* in more detail shortly; yet it is necessary to understand this new interest in the text as relating to and perhaps arising from the creation of a manuscript economy for new versions of the *Nights* as a result of European interest in it.

It is remarkable that given the claims of English commentators (e.g. Hole and Weber) of the absolutely canonical nature of the *Nights* to "oriental" or at least "Arabian" literature, very little critical commentary on the text was produced by Arab literary figures over the course of the nineteenth century. The two or three generations of *nahda* intellectuals, who worked diligently to comment on much of what was thought to be the classical Arabic literary heritage, devoted remarkably little attention to the *Nights*, just at a time when English commentators were claiming that Arabs were steeped in this single text more than any other. Gerhardt reports that "for centuries, cultured Oriental readers did not count [the *Nights*] as literature at all, the European enthusiasm about it seemed a slightly painful and comic misunderstanding" (Gerhardt, *The Art of Story-Telling*, pp. 2–3).

Thus, it is justifiable to say that European claims to the popularity of the text within an Arabic context were largely overstated, if not a pure fabrication. While four Arabic editions were prepared for printing during the course of the century, only one has a nominal claim to responding to a domestic Arabic readership, that of the Bulaq Press. Yet, as Mahdi and al-Musawi both indicate, the exemplar for this edition was likely prepared in response to European demand for Arabic manuscripts of the *Nights*. Despite the production of the Calcutta versions (both of direct colonial heritage) and the Bulaq edition, (which as has been discussed, likely emanated from a manuscript market which was significantly affected by European demands) the *Nights* appear to have made little impression on the literary debates of the early *nahda* period—this matter will be discussed later and at greater length. In the late nineteenth century, as the European fascination with the *Nights* began to be registered within the Arab literary classes, an educational endeavor was introduced, attempting to inform Arab readerships of the value of the *Nights*.

Educating Arab readers in the value of the *Nights*

The educational imperative provides the context for the following question in the October 1, 1894 issue of *al-Hilal* magazine, sent by the Aleppo-based Hikmat Bey Sharif to the Cairene offices of one of the most influential Arabic cultural and scientific publications of the late-nineteenth century: "I request that you enhance [our knowledge of] the merits of the famous book *Alf Lalya wa Layla*: Who wrote it, and at what time? Because it is not an exaggeration to say that, given who did write it, this book shows that the Arabs have talents in the art of story and narrative" (al-Hilal, "Alf layla wa layla," 1894, p. 107). The editors of the journal, which was published by a luminary of the *nahda* movement, Jurji Zaydan, responded at length.

Their answer outlines different theories on the origins of the *Nights*, the anonymity of its author or authors, and presents a brief categorization of the kinds of tales found within the text. This response makes clear the presumption that the readership of *al-Hilal*, while on the whole being literate, educated, and well-attuned to issues of literary and cultural import, had little real knowledge of *Alf layla* beyond a possible familiarity with its title. *Al-Hilal's* typology implies a valuative framework for assessing the text, one that may seem familiar: "The contents of the book are of two sorts: The first are the superstitions and fantasies (*khaz'ablat*) such as demons and genies and similar beings, and the second are manners (*'awa'id*) of the Arabs in the height of Islam and their morals and their traditions and the description of the court of the caliphs and their feasts and related issues" (al-Hilal, "Alf layla wa layla," 1894, p. 107). The division of the text into the fantastical and the historical follows the general outlines of some of the English critics already discussed, in contending with "superstitions" in the text, while elaborating the use of the text as a window onto the "manners," "morals," and "traditions" of the "height of Islam"—in essence imagining the text as a document of the achievements of classical Islamic thought. While the framework is familiar, the content is different. Where Hole and Weber speak of the book as a repository of knowledge about antiquity, or of the ancient East—in particular Persian and Indian civilizations—*al-Hilal*'s commentator finds the book a testament to an entirely different historical and social context, that of 'Abbasid Islam, and in particular the Arab identity of that caliphate. Unable to reconcile the Persian elements of the frame story to the view of the text as primarily of an Arab nature, the *al-Hilal* author proposes to accept the hypothesis that the book may be a composition by Persians intending to present a description of the Arab caliphate. Yet the question of its original authorship is a minor issue, as the question of ethnic particularism is not central to the discussion of the *al-Hilal* commentator.

However, the question opens the doors to further discussion for *al-Hilal* and its readership. Hikmat Bey, who had addressed his initial question to the publication, writes again several months later, offering his own short analytical essay on the origins and influences of *Alf layla* (Sharif, "Alf layla wa layla," p. 852). Several issues later, another brief article appears in response to Hikmat Bey's research on the origins of *Alf layla*, but argues for the consideration of another influence as well. A reader writes in support of the theory that the text is indeed of Persian origin, and not of Hellenic sources, "as some Europeans believe" (al-Hilal, "Alf layla wa layla," December 1895, p. 253). The author makes reference to classical Arabic works on literature—in particular *al-Fihrist* of ibn Nadim—in defense of this assertion. From this discussion it would seem that European neo-classical discourse on the *Nights*—represented for example, by Hole's thesis on the Sindbad narrative—was a topic now familiar to Arab critics. The reference to European attitudes concerning the text in this discussion of "Alf layla" in *al-Hilal* indicates that these attitudes were at least generally familiar to these Arab intellectuals, and shows that their effect upon them was not negligible.

Al-Hilal supplies further evidence of the social reception of *Alf layla* for a *nahda* Arab audience during this period. In a section of the periodical devoted to announcements of new publications, the May 1, 1901 issue announces and reviews a new edition of *Alf layla*:

> *Alf layla wa layla* is an Eastern fictional narrative (*riwaya sharqiyya*), representing the customs of people and their morals and traditions (*adab*) in the Islamic middle ages in Iraq, Syria and Egypt. [. . .] It represents the traditions of people in their gatherings and their stories as well as their economic and legal and family transactions. It explains the conditions of women in those days in a faithful manner. And *Alf layla wa layla* has been published numerous times, and has been translated into most European languages. Each Arabic edition has strengths differing from the others, and the most complete is from Egypt. However, in it there are terms and words that would make the polite man embarrassed, much less the modest woman (*al-'adhra'*). And we are now in an age where both sexes are reading literary books, and this narrative (*riwaya*), despite its faults, is one of the most beautiful books of customs and traditions. And able scholars in Beirut have addressed this problem and have abridged it and have published it twice. [. . .] It has undergone a thorough abridgement so that no modest woman could be embarrassed by reading it.
>
> (al-Hilal, "Alf layla wa layla," May 1901, p. 446)

This announcement presents several points central to conceiving of the merits of the text for the editors of *al-Hilal*. First, is its articulation of the merits of the text on its representation of "customs" and "moral traditions" in the Islamic middle ages—closely related to European claims about the text, if differentiated for its historical perspective. The book's value is furthermore attested to not only by its several printings in Arabic, but also by its translation into European languages. Finally, this edition foregrounds concerns for the text's transgressive elements, and promises a careful abridgement, suitable for "the modest woman"—a matter of new concern for the new definition of reading as an activity for both sexes.

The *al-Hilal* article indicates how, with the transformation of *Alf layla* into a popularly accessible text, new segments of Arab society may benefit from its merits—despite the dangers it also poses them. The terms, while in some sense tailored to an Arab audience (despite the conflation involved in deploying the concept of "an Eastern novel" to a text that may solely concern "Iraq, Syria, and Egypt") share an articulation of a valuative scheme no longer hinged to the categories of classical *adab* traditions, nor to religious legitimacy, but bespeaking the development of an autonomous field of literature. One sign of this is the use, by *al-Hilal*, of the term of "riwaya" to describe *Alf layla*. While the term generically denotes a narrative, it is to be distinguished from other established genres, such as the *maqama*. It was not until the 1940s that the word began to be more widely accepted as conveying the same meaning as the English word "novel," although it was utilized by some commentators as such much earlier on.[3] "Riwaya" does not retain the innovative implications the English word inherently carries, but its use as a marker of a literary genre begins to coincide with conceptions of literary modernity.

Al-Hilal's announcement was for a reprinting of an edition prepared in Beirut in 1881. This edition also corresponds to the *al-Hilal* announcement in its combination of according value to *Alf layla* for its transmission of elements of a classical heritage. Yet these merits are to be considered alongside what dangers it may also present.

> The book *Alf layla wa layla*, which was compiled more than three hundred years ago, and intended for light heartedness and moral correction, was one of the best books to address these subjects. Woven within it are customs and proverbs, and commands and warnings, and poetry of exquisite rhyme by the highest and best composers of poetry. However, even with what it has of literary merit, it is not devoid of concerns that contradict refined taste or terms unacceptable for good conduct. It is likely that its publication, even in an abridged form, will not remove concerns arising from [the consequences of] its entrance into homes of good taste and standing. And young ladies cannot be deprived of reading it; for the arena of knowledge in this new age (*al-'asr al-jadid*) has been opened more than ever, and the race to compete in rhetoric and literature includes both sexes. The woman claims the same rights as the man, to wade into the seas of glorious sciences and reading useful desirable information (*al-akhbar al-mufida al-sha'iqa*). For this reason, we have cleansed this book and edited it where possible in such a way as to not detract from the benefits from reading it, and not to excise its humor and beauty for its student.
>
> (*Alf layla wa layla*, 1888–1890, p. i)[4]

The valuative framework for the Beirut editor of the *Nights* here follows, in a manner, the significant moralist backlash to the work found in England. Although the moral contexts were no doubt different, as with Hole, or the Rev. Cooper, the Beirut editor is attempting to recover the text from what seems to be present and unresolved anxieties over its presumed unsuitability for certain readerships. This passage perhaps most clearly relates to the question of the dangers of the text for a readership that now includes women. The issue of how a public readership is imagined within Arab societies in the nineteenth century requires a greater and more materially grounded study than can be afforded here, but the hints presented by this introduction are those of a complex and changing conception of who may read, who does read literature in this new/modern period (*al-'asr al-jadid*), and what use can be made of reading the *Nights*.

The question of women's consumption of literature was quite pertinent to contemporary debates among the Arab literati. The Beirut edition of the Nights precedes the emergence of a "women's press" in Egypt by only a few years. *Al-Fatat* magazine ("The Young Woman"), which was the first publication to address a readership of women, was begun in 1892, and "heralded the founding by women of many periodicals by women in Egypt" (Booth, *Woman in Islam*, p. 171). The almost entirely male-dominated *nahda* press (what Booth terms "the malestream press") devoted significant attention to the issue of women's new public social roles as consumers of literature and the press, and by the early twentieth century, a number of publications were also begun by men with the aim of addressing women readers. The subsumption of writing by women and that for women (by both men and women) into one category has resulted in an unfortunate watering-down of the vitality of the actions of a small but energetic grouping of Arab women in setting the terms of discourse around women's access to the written word in this period. In any case, the attention paid by both press and book editors to perceived social concerns involved in the acknowledgment of women as consumers of literature is an indication of the shifting value accorded to literature, which was by now no longer the sole provenance of men. Transformations in texts of some significance—such as the editing of *Alf layla*'s provocative passages—was clearly to be deemed a necessary process in the expansion of the readership of Arabic texts.

But the claims of women were not the sole concerns of the *al-nahda* literati—transforming *Alf layla* was generally deemed necessary for more general reasons. Ibrahim al-Yaziji, one of the most influential Arab literary figures of his generation, devoted a page of *al-Dhiya'*, his "scientific, Literary, Medical and Economic Magazine" to a review of the 1901 edition of *Alf layla* published by the *al-Hilal* Press, which would appear also as intending to address the problems perceived with "deficiencies" making the text inappropriate for an expanding readership.

> *Alf layla wa layla*—There is no need to describe this book since the fame it has accumulated in both East and West when it was translated into the majority of the languages of Europe [. . .] Despite what is of value in it, including stories and beautiful storytelling and literary and historical value, it is not empty of subjects that distort the face of life and provoke hatred on the part of the guardians [of social and religious morality], and others. Because of this, certain literary figures of our time were charged with reducing these defects within it, desiring to make its reading popular, while defending of the traditions of reading, so that the book has become generally consumable [*sa'igh al-masharib*], accessible to either solitary [*khalawat*] or group [*majalis*] readings, appropriate for both the old [*al-'atiq*] and the young [*al-ghulam*].
>
> (al-Dhiya, "Athar Adabiyya," p. 564)

While *al-Dhiya'* does not appear as concerned as *al-Hilal* about the dangers of a specifically female readership, this review does shed further light on other anxieties for the Arab cultural elite over the expansion of a public readership. The review juxtaposes modes of reading (solitary vs. group) and generational divisions (old vs. young) hinting that while previously texts with undesirable qualities were not off limits for solitary reading by mature readers, the expansion of reading to include group (or perhaps public—the Arabic *majalis* intimates a social gathering) readings, as well as the reading of such texts by the young required a text that would be "generally consumable" or literally, "permissible for consumption." The reference to group readings is in fact quite important, as it confirms what is known of the widespread practice of public readings of published works at this time. Given the relatively small proportion of the public who are known to have been literate, it has been a point of frequent debate as to whether the late-nineteenth-century Arabic press and publications were socially consequential. This passage by *al-Dhiya'* confirms that through the multiplication of categories of readerships, as well as the expansion of settings for it, a new problem of how to make literature permissible for general consumption has now emerged. The role of *Alf layla* in this debate seems quite unique, and the transactional nature of the text—acknowledged in the repeated refrain of its having been translated into European languages—is key to this role.

These debates in *al-Hilal* and *al-Dhiya'* raise a series of important questions concerning the value of *Alf layla* for Arab readerships over the course of the nineteenth century. Late-nineteenth-century *nahda* intellectuals were as yet engaging in a rudimentary discourse about the text, as the 1894–1895 articles in *al-Hilal* show, confirming that the text did not figure centrally in previous conceptions of canonical Arabic literature. Despite *al-Hilal*'s mission to increase awareness of the merits of *Alf layla* for Arab readerships, evidence remains that the effects of this program were limited. Occasionally editors seemed exasperated with the level of detail readers requested about this text. In the May 1901 issue of another influential Egyptian journal, *al-Muqtataf*, a letter was sent by a reader requesting some basic information on *Alf layla*. Here, a letter appears from one Iskandar Bey asking simply, "who composed the book *Alf layla wa layla*, and into what language was it first translated? Who transmitted it to French and so on to English, German and Russian?" (al-Muqtataf, *Alf layla wa layla*, p. 474).[5] The response to the question is curiously impatient, even brusque: "Indians composed it, and the Persians first translated it, as has been noted in its own introduction and preface. And we do not know what you or anyone else would gain in knowing the names of the translators—does it serve any purpose to toil in the research and investigation of their names?" (ibid., p. 475). One may still ask such questions. Yet again it would seem that even by the turn of the twentieth century, the innovation of the text for an Arab context lies in its double legitimacy; arising both from its association with a classical heritage, as well as its translation and popularity in European contexts. Public interest accumulated around this still-unfamiliar text—word circulated from various sources of the regard for the *Nights* in European societies, and, now living largely under one form or another of colonial hegemony, Arab readers could not ignore this fact.

But important details were still not commonly known—such as whom the various translators of the text had been. The exasperated reaction of the *al-Muqtataf* editor is perhaps understandable—as cultural arbiters, such journals were expected to know all-important details pertaining to important literary texts. The *Nights* were now perceived as being such a text, yet the facts around it were still difficult to come by.

By being both a reflection of classical literary heritage, and of a contemporary European adoption, *Alf layla wa layla* was uniquely situated to play an enabling role in the transformation of categories of legitimacy into ones that affirmed the autonomy of the literary field. Figures such as *al-Hilal*'s Jurji Zaydan and Ibrahim al-Yaziji of *al-Dhiya'* are precisely those that were invested in such a move, by their fastidious observation of the power and significance of a classical heritage (coded, most often, as Islamic, even by Christians such as Zaydan) as well as their own participation in institutions that promoted the autonomy of literature from its previous legitimizing elements.

Reviving the Persian *Nights*

In a February 1929 meeting of the Iranian Literary Society (*Anjuman-i Adabi*), the Iranian minister of Education and Religious Charities, 'Ali Asghar Hikmat offered a lecture on the history of *Alf layla wa layla*, or *Hizar u yik shab*, as it is known in Persian. In order to better sense the atmosphere of this talk, one may visualize a photo of Reza Shah Pahlavi, now in the fifth year of his reign, hanging prominently somewhere in the hall where the society was gathering. What did this portrait look like? In the early years of his rule, the official images of the shah show him in full profile, with a formidable military headdress. It was not until the mid-1930s that the official pictures took on a stern half-profile, evoking to some extent, a mustachioed Mussolini. The name Pahlavi was a recent addition to the identity of the former Iranian Cossack Brigade commander, in whose administration Hikmat was serving. As the usurper of the 150-year-old Qajar dynasty, Reza Shah was understandably sensitive about his relatively modest and decidedly non-aristocratic background, and determined to style himself a modern ruler in the line of ancient Persian rulers—hence the new nomenclature, Pahlavi, a reference to the pre-Islamic language of the Persian Empire. In this period, copious and self-conscious references to ancient Iran were part of the nationalist discourse of the Iranian government. This conception was reflected throughout public discourse by the elite and intelligentsia, who largely collaborated with and advanced the new regime's nationalist ideals. In this setting, on a wintry February evening, Hikmat began his talk:

> The book that has come to known in the East and West as *Alf layla wa layla* is one of only a few books that speaks of the conditions of antiquity, and is the finest remaining reminder of the customs of the ancient nations of the Eastern Lands (*mashriq-zamin*). Articulating the

> importance of this book, both from a historical perspective and a literary one, is a greater task than one may be able to correctly express in the short period of time that I have a claim to. And I fear that even if dawn should break, the matter will only be half-said.
>
> (*Hizar u yik shab*, 1938, p. i)

After reassuring his audience of the anticipated brevity of his presentation, Hikmat continued by remarking on various historical and literary lessons retained by the text, as well as the many moral (*akhlaqi*) ones. In terms of its history, he estimates the stories to date back two millennia, having benefited from the "finer customs of the ancient races of the East," such as "India and Iran and the Arabs and the Turks," and suggests that these stories circulated among the civilizations of "the Sassanians, and Islam, and the Abbasid and Fatimid caliphs" (*Hizar u yik shab*, p. ii). The typology employed by Hikmat in estimating the origins of the text is not original, but attention may be drawn to the mode of his description of the nations that make up the East (*mashriq-zamin*). Although categorically uneven, his conception of the text as the compilation of a shared "Eastern" heritage across the common etho-linguistic groupings of Western and Southern Asia is rather generous. He finds the tales to deliver codes of moral or honorable behavior that are the unifying characteristics of these diverse social groupings. He comments on the nineteenth century translation of the text into Persian, carried out by ‘Abd al-Latif Tasuji (with poems composed by Mirza Surush), and notes its "innovating" effect on Persian prose writing (*Hizar u yik shab*, p. vi).[6] Yet, the latter fact is outlined without touching on one important question: What circumstances led to the translation of the text into Persian only as late as the 1830s, if the text had been known from antiquity for its rich and authentic heritage, particularly in relation to Iran?

Despite Hikmat's foregrounding of classical Persian elements in the work, his evaluative schema does not vary greatly from that which we find utilized in *al-Hilal*. While he notes the fact that Tasuji's 1830's translation of *Alf layla* is the earliest extant Persian manifestation of the text, he does not view this as worthy of particular concern or further consideration (p. x). He comfortably implies a direct link between the Tasuji text, and those references to it in classical Arabic catalogues, such as *al-Fihrist*. The claim of Tasuji's primacy—perhaps understandable given the context of its production—seems to be an exaggeration. Four unexamined manuscripts containing early nineteenth-century Persian translations (presumably predating Tasuji's) of the *Nights* have been recorded in catalogues worldwide. Yet, there are no other known translations dating from before the nineteenth century (Marzolph, "The Persian Nights," p. 282).

Thus, Hikmat's is a largely ahistorical perspective on the text, and despite his references to and consideration of ‘Abd al-Latif Tasuji's work as a prose innovator, Hikmat does not contextualize the social and cultural dynamics, only a century before him, which led to the translation and publication of *Hizar u yik shab*. These circumstances raise questions about the supposed centrality of

Alf layla to Persian–Iranian literature, and emanates from a colonial framework as much as it points to the continuing connections between Arabic and Persian cultural spheres during this period—all points willfully overlooked by Hikmat. Sadly, what is known of Tasuji presents an incomplete picture of the context of the text's translation. However, the details that are known are quite salient to this discussion. Muhammad Ja'far Mahjub, an Iranian scholar of popular and folk literature active in 1950s and 1960s, undertook to seek out the progeny of Tasuji and relates, from his grandson, much more information than has been preserved in writing: his findings are well worth summarizing here (Mahjub, "Tarjumih-yi Farsi-yi Alf layla wa layla," pp. 34–53). Mahjub reports that Tasuji lived in Tabriz, in north-eastern Iran, and was trained as a cleric at a young age. In this, he followed in his father's footsteps, and had achieved a position in Tabriz as an Imam. His family was steeped in the institutions of traditional religious education, and his father, as a *mujtahid*, was considered a high religious authority in his lifetime (ibid., p. 50). Tasuji thus became a religious authority in a provincial city that had come to be the seat of the royal crown prince during the course of the Qajar dynasty. This allowed him to come into regular contact with high members of the royal court while carrying out his duties as cleric.

These contacts led to his gaining an appointment as a tutor of the children of Bahman Mirza, the brother of Muhammad Shah, and a governor with clear aspirations to the throne. Yet, when the shah's son Nasir al-Din was named crown prince, these aspirations were dashed. Despite this, Bahman Mirza accepted his new role as the regent to the prince, and appointed his confidant Tasuji to tutor the young Nasir al-Din.[7] The governorship of Bahman Mirza was marked by a continuation of the policies of his predecessor, 'Abbas Mirza, who had initiated wide-ranging reform programs (such as the sponsorship of students sent for study in England and France), and who became a faithful patron of the literary arts. During the course of 'Abbas Mirza's governorship, Tabriz became a major cultural center, a role also enabled by the city's geographic location at a crossroads of Ottoman, Central Asian, Iranian, and Russian cultural influences.[8] His policies, and their continuation under Bahman Mirza, would develop Tabriz into the most culturally progressive of Iran's cities. For his work as a royal tutor, Tasuji gained the title of *Mulla Bashi* and a position within the court.[9] His commission to undertake a translation of *Alf layla wa layla* into Persian was made by Bahman Mirza sometime around this same time.

Tasuji most likely began his translation during the reign of Muhammad Shah Qajar, as the first volume manuscript bears a dedication to the latter ruler, and it is presumed that he completed it during the first years of Nasir al-Din's rule, as the second volume bears his name as its patron. Yet it must have been completed very shortly after the death of the father, as after accompanying the new shah to the capitol, Tasuji requested orders to leave his previous post so as to travel to Najaf for pilgrimage. He was granted this wish, and his family was entrusted to the court's care. Tasuji left, apparently never to return to Iran. It is reported that he spent his last years among the shrines of Najaf, in study and prayer. The exact date of his death is not known.

While this ending to the narrative of Tasuji's biography emphasizes the piety and dedication he espoused in his religious duties, there is evidence that he may have left the shah's entourage for other, more worldly, concerns: the changeover of administrations in the Qajar period were often contentious affairs, and Tasuji may well have left for reasons such as duress or a concerns for his life. But we have little information to justify further speculation in this matter. Whatever the political standing he may have gained or lost at court, his translation of *Alf layla wa layla*—the only example of his literary talents known to have survived—shows evidence of a mature, confident, and innovative writer, with impressive fluency in Arabic and in both literary and colloquial Persian idioms.

Mahjub's efforts to seek out Tasuji's family also yielded details not often found in the conventional biographies of notables of the Qajar era—important among them is the assertion that Tasuji's wife, known as Kulsum Khanum, being highly literate and educated, "participated with her husband on the translation of *Alf layla wa layla*, and from what is said among Hajj Mulla Bashi's family, she played a major role in this work" (Mahjub, "Tarjumih-yi Farsi-yi Alf layla wa layla," p. 37).[10] The daughters of Kulsum Khanum apparently followed in her footsteps, as one of them, Nusrat Khanum, was known at court for her wit and skills as a poet. The fame she enjoyed from her talents reportedly led to her marriage with Zill al-Sultan, one of the Qajar princes, and the governor of Isfahan (ibid.).[11] These biographical details shed light on Tasuji's specific social position as a transitional figure between religious, monarchical, and more autonomous systems of legitimization. Tasuji, "a cleric of mildly unorthodox leanings" was an exemplary product of the traditional educational system, one that served him well in its focus on training in Arabic rhetoric and grammar (Amanat, *Pivot of the Universe*, p. 66). Yet he seems to have displayed interests or talents that were less common among those who used their educations to pursue a conventional clerical position, as he had. Furthermore, he appears to have won favor with Bahman Mirza who, as has been noted, pursued reformist policies and was a patron of the arts as the governor of Tabriz. In addition, he is reported to have collaborated with his wife on this project—indeed, the report from his family leaves open the question of whether she was not in fact the more significant partner in this effort. It is also noteworthy that one of his sons, Muhsin, initially followed in the family tradition of pursuing a clerical education and work, going so far as to wear the clothing of a cleric. Yet later in his life, he changed dress to the modern style, and entered the court service (given the title Muzaffar al-Mulk) during the course of the reign of Nasir al-Din Shah. Tasuji's grandson, who also was granted the title Muzaffar al-Mulk, was a bureaucrat in the late Qajar and early Pahlavi ministries of the interior (Mahjub, "Tarjumih-yi Farsi-yi Alf layla wa layla," p. 36).

In addition to considering Tasuji's social standing within the Tabriz court, there are hints that the court may have had specific knowledge of the European translations of the *Nights*. Once again, this point requires a degree of conjecture—the following paragraph may be no more than a fictive digression: It is known that other than Tasuji, another tutor of Nasir al-Din, and a familiar figure within the Tabriz elite, was one Madame Gulsaz, the French wife of an Iranian court artisan. A convert to Islam and fluent in Persian, she came to Iran in the 1830s, and quickly gained a position as a tutor and advisor to the young crown prince, as well as teaching decorative arts to the wives of the court elite (Gulsaz means "flower-maker," a reference to her husband's vocation as a flower arranger at court) (Amanat, *Pivot of the Universe*, pp. 59–60). Madame Gulsaz, who as an educated woman with an obvious interest in the orient, was almost certainly familiar with Galland's *Nights*, which were in relatively wide circulation in France during her childhood. Could she have been one conduit of the tales—á la Burton, to an audience of rapt Iranian listeners—did she kindle an interest in their translation, leading to the commission by Bahman Mirza? Clearly, further investigation is needed to fill out the details of this hypothesis.

While Tasuji's translation was prepared for court use as a lavish manuscript accompanied by numerous illustrations, it was also fairly quickly prepared for lithographic printing and issued in book form—the earliest suggested printing of the book is 1843, although the exact date remains in some dispute (ibid., p. 48).[12] The speed with which it entered the print market indicates that Tasuji and his royal patrons likely had the production of a printed book in mind all along. It is widely accepted that Tasuji worked from the Bulaq press editions, and not from a manuscript, in his translation—this would certainly have affected his own vision of the social function of this work (Aryanpur, *Az Saba ta Nima*, Vol. 1, p. 183).[13] As a point of comparison, it is instructive to learn that the *Nights* was similarly modernized in the Turkish context, albeit with new tensions and dilemmas surrounding its perceived value in late-Ottoman society. The first print editions of the *Nights* in Turkish appear between 1842 and 1851, meaning they are almost simultaneous with the publication of Tasuji's editions (Birkalan, *The Thousand and One Nights*, p. 225). By the late nineteenth century, perhaps due to the ascendancy of anti-Arab tendencies among Westernized Ottoman elites, new Turkish editions would only be prepared from the French translations rather than from Arabic editions (ibid., p. 226).

The early history of the printed book in Iran coincides closely with the life of Tasuji, as the first printing presses were introduced in 1816–1817, in Tabriz (Ringer, *Education, Religion and the Discourse of Cultural Reform*, p. 11). He was quite likely among the earliest Iranians to come in contact with this new technology. The social context for the production of *Hizar u yik shab* is linked closely to developments in the conception of "literature" in Iran. It has been suggested that

> the traditional understanding of "literature" in the Persian context would primarily denote works of the classical poets that in written format were solely available as manuscripts. The introduction of printing to Iran in the early nineteenth century resulted in new modes of text production, transmission, and distribution. The wider—though still limited—accessibility

> of written matter possessed the potential to distribute to a large number of people, and thus to literally "popularize" all kinds of literature that previously had mostly been available by way of recitation or oral performance from a manuscript source.
>
> (Marzolph, "Persian Popular Literature," p. 218)

While to term the small run of lithographed texts that may have been issued by a single printing "popular" is to perhaps over-extend a definition of popular culture, it is worthwhile to note that Tasuji's translation enjoyed many reprintings, from different lithographic set-ups, in the decades that followed its completion. It has been said "the impact of the text on the Persian reading public can be gauged by the numerous editions produced in the nineteenth century" (Amanat, *Pivot of the Universe*, p. 461). Here, the constitution of this "reading public" is not elaborated upon, but Tasuji's work is certainly one of the first in Persian which may be associated with the nascent concept of a reading public. Technological limitations on lithographic printing at this time limited the copies of each run to a number between 300 and 400 copies, and some runs were smaller (Marzolph, "Persian Popular Literature," p. 215). Even in relatively small print runs, the text was published in new editions several times over the following decades, apparently enjoying a consistent demand in the literary market. Mahjub reports a cataloguing of three runs of the text, reportedly published in Tabriz, between the years 1843 and 1845, but finds this claim suspect, given the date of Nasir al-Din's ascension to the throne, and the dedications found in the royal manuscript (Mahjub, "Tarjumih-yi Farsi-yi Alf layla wa layla," p. 42). Yet, after the first two editions (1843–1845 and 1855), seven further lithographic editions would be issued between 1872 and 1938. It is also noteworthy that the 1855 edition, and all further lithographed editions, were complemented by illustrations to the text—this edition would be the first non-European edition of the *Nights* to appear with illustration (Marzolph, "Persian Nights," p. 285).

Tasuji's translation served not only to provide the text for one of the earliest printed books in Iran, but also was utilized for the production of what would be "the last outstanding specimen of the traditional art of the book in Qajar Iran" (Marzolph, "Persian Nights," p. 284). For a young Nasir al-Din Shah, very shortly after taking the throne, lavished a great fortune on the production of a hand-illustrated copy of the text for court use. The first lithographic printing of the book had been available to him as a boy, and he was already an avid reader of this edition (Amanat, *Pivot of the Universe*, p. 66). The resulting calligraphically-enscribed and hand-illustrated book, taking up some 570 text and 570 illustrated folios of 2279 pages, took seven years and a team of forty artisans to complete. So the *Nights* not only marked the transition to print production, they served as a last testament to what had been considered the highest mode of book production in pre-modern and early-modern Iran—the exquisite work done on the production of this edition indicates that it was not for lack of inspiration, but much more likely for economic reasons, that no further traditional books were to be commissioned by Iran's rulers (Marzolph, "Persian Nights," pp. 283–5).

Insufficient as these details may be in leading us to definite conclusions about Tasuji's motivations, or to the evaluation of the text by his peers, we must see him as a transitional figure in the movement away from a religiously codified system of knowledge, by way of royal patronage, into another developing, yet already more autonomous, cultural arena. This sense of transition is also confirmed by the transformation of his family from one of a traditional clerical and jurisprudential identity, to that of a modern bureaucratic character, within two generations. While the specific reasons of his election to carry out the translation of *Alf layla* into Persian remain obscure, his tendency toward "unorthodox" views indicates an interest in the dual nature that the text held, as both exemplary of a classical heritage, and yet innovative in its most recent form—the Bulaq edition, which he used for his translation. Comparing this work to other early products of the Tabriz printing presses, it is further noteworthy that it is one of the first of an entirely secular nature (Ringer, *Education, Religion and the Discourse of Cultural Reform*, p. 34). His exceptional literary achievement, which may owe a great deal to the talents of Kulsum Khanum, stands as a monumental if somewhat unconventional testament to the complexity of the literary and cultural imaginations of this period of Iranian history—a period beset by the traumas of multiple defeats at the hand of imperial Russia, as well as unprecedented anxieties of English and to some extent French colonial encroachments into regional and domestic affairs. At the same time, the speed with which the Tabriz court appears to have gained access to a copy of the Bulaq press edition of *Alf layla* is evidence of exchange and contact on literary and cultural levels, with Egypt and other parts of the Arab world. For the literary circles of Tabriz, enervated by the relative liberalism of 'Abbas Mirza and Bahman Mirza, the Bulaq edition of *Alf layla* represented an innovative text, if one that bore legitimizing references to the idea of a classical heritage, yet modern in terms of its articulation and production.

***

Returning again to Burton's potent image—of the European colonialist–adventurer sitting in the centre of a primitive Bedouin encampment, reciting tales of the *Arabian Nights* to his hosts as a repayment for their hospitality—clearly, locating a starting point for the narrative of the *Nights* is a quest largely in vain. Just as the text itself is constituted by complex historical conjectures and coincidences, assessing the value of the text for the various societies that it has been canonized within is similarly an inexact science.

In the Arab and Iranian contexts, the *Nights* are also constituted for a local audience through a transactional process, translated under circumstances that were enabled not only by the circulation of textual materials from Arab Ottoman contexts, through a multilinguistic network of readers, to the Tabriz court, but also by European circulations of implicit (through their effects upon the Bulaq edition) and more explicit natures. While the heritage of the *Nights* cannot be denied a claim to Persian, Arabic, Greek, and Indian classical origins, the particular material circumstances that led to its appearance cannot be detached from the conditions of modernity, in European, Ottoman, Arab, Indian colonial, and Qajar Iranian domains. If not for the nearly coincidental "discovery" of a manuscript by Galland—reworked through and overlaid by the very specific local market pressures he faced—it remains very uncertain that Arabic and Persian-reading audiences would have come to even know the text, much less to evaluate it as canonical to their literary heritage. Instead of resting upon the classical evocations of the text, the editing, and translation of the *Nights* for nineteenth-century Arabic and Persian readerships resulted in texts marked by their "innovation" in style, and autonomy from traditional forms of legitimization. Thus, the values accorded to *Alf layla wa layla* and *Hizar u yik shab* are distinctly tied to the condition of modernity, as contingent as their modernities may have been.

By 1929, this collection came to be termed by an Iranian minister of education as representing the moral traditions not only of ancient Persia (and hence, a testament to prior glories of Iran) but also of "the East" as a whole. From the time of Galland's first translations through to Hikmat's speech, *The Arabian Nights* had thoroughly been revalued and had come to impact upon the frameworks of literary value of both "East" and "West." The magnitude of this impact, perhaps, is the finest testament to the singularity of the *Nights*—but it may well be that the social circumstances surrounding the transaction of this text between Arabic, French, English, and Persian sources may be more significant than its approximation as a work of sublime promise. At the same time, this text, in its various permutations, has suffered from constant contestation over how it has been valued. Since its (re-)emergence through transactions between European, Arab, and Iranian social contexts, the text's perceived merits have been offset by the tenuous threat of its ethical, moral, and religious shortcomings. In the British context, as a consequence of disputes between religious moralist arguments and those by utilitarian secularists about the social role of literary practice, the *Nights* remained stained by its disreputable effect on the reading public. Ironically, what saved the text from the onslaught of such readings has been the ascendant capitalist valuation of it—its popularity and place in the publishing economy became the foundation for its defense, even by readers as divergent as Hole and Burton. Traces of these ambivalences are visible in later criticism on these texts, in particular their irreconcilability to nationalist preconceptions. As evinced by Hikmat's ambivalences in characterizing the text's merits within the context of Reza Shah's nationalist project, or earlier in its assessment by *al-Hilal*'s writers, Iranian and Arab critics were at pains to read the text with the agenda of canonizing it into a national literature—these moves required an elision or erasure of the transactional moment, when the text was recreated for nineteenth-century readerships in Western Europe, Iran, and the Arab world. Yet, even in these and later evaluations, the text has continued to show a tenacity to resist a simple cooptation into such discourse, just as its place in genealogies of novelistic writing has remained controversial.

Other questions remain—in particular, it remains to be seen what an analysis of the transacted texts themselves will tell us about the process of translation, and how the social and critical environments here discussed affected the individual decisions and choices available to translators, and how these limitations or opportunities manifested themselves upon the written page. More importantly, the material and language used, and the evolution of different manuscripts show that the *Nights* belonged to a much vaster middle literature (neither popular or oral) that uses literary material as well as folklore, and includes hundreds of other similar manuscripts. It may well be that the *Nights* was so often reproduced through textual transactions not only because of the structure and "translatability" of the text—existing as it does outside of religious and monarchical systems of legitimacy—but also because ideologically, it partakes of a system of values that largely esteems "right" transactions rather than "righteous" ones. Although at times the *Nights* seems to be the object of too great a deal of scholarly interest, the persistence of these and other questions continue to legitimize further examination of this most extraordinary text and its variegated uses. It has been often suggested that certain inherent structural and logical coherences within the text had an important role to play in the rapid diffusion of the text in a particular set of cultural contexts and into modes of literary representation associated with literary modernity. For example, in attempting to account for the text's success within different social settings, Aboubakr Chraibi has briefly sketched out the successive transformations of the *Nights*, from the presumed Persian origins through to its modern incarnations, as

> starting from the Persian book *Hezar afsane* (Thousand Tales), one composed another book, giving it a new title (The Thousand and One Nights), new contents (khurafa) and a "commercial" ideological orientation. This currently dominant ideological orientation, similar to the Judeo-Christian or the Muslim model, is based on a final exchange (good deeds are exchanged for paradise; good stories are exchanged for life).
>
> (Chraibi, "Texts of the Arabian Nights," p. 156)

This sketch highlights the inner transactions that characterize the narratives of this textual body—by linking the *Nights'* narrative logic to the "dominant ideological orientation" central to the Abrahamic traditions, Chraibi suggests that the transactionary ideals of the text (what he terms the "commercial" ideological orientation) appeal equally to Jewish, Christian, and Islamic traditions. While on one hand perhaps too general to be accepted as a full accounting for the remarkable trans-literary history of this text, this thesis offers a point of departure for further studies of the value of the *Nights* for the many very different readerships that have read—indeed, consumed—the innumerable versions of this text produced for over a millennium.

Part 3

WRITING TRAVELS AND OTHER TRANSACTIONS

. . . strange cities are then never completely strange.
(Mourid Barghouti, *I Saw Ramallah*)

4

THE INNER SUBJECTS OF ARABIC AND PERSIAN TRAVEL TEXTS ON EUROPE

> THERE: The time-machine stares at us, leaving far behind the sea's whiteness. We're carried by the voyage, away from the race's stubbornness.
>
> (Etel Adnan, *There*)

The following three chapters will propose an approach to the question of literary modernity through focusing upon the literary consequences of travel. The intersection of temporal disjunctures in the experience of travel is evoked by Etel Adnan's definition of THERE as a place arrived through time-travel, "leaving far behind the sea's whiteness"—the temporal disjuncture in this travel experience is constitutive to a conception of modernity, of a disjuncture that marks present time as distinct from that which came before it. Where in the previous discussion of *Alf layla wa laya*, the act of translation itself has been shown to be implicated in a process of cultural re-evaluation of the category of literature, here I would now like to look at a similar process traceable in changes in the conventions of writing travel texts in the nineteenth century. The following chapters will present readings on travelogues and faux/fictive travelogues, pursuing the sometimes elusive narrators of these texts as their subjects. Where the previous discussions of *Alf layla wa layla* and its European incarnations looked purely at the category of literature and the manner by which this category was filled with new criteria of value, the following readings will instead look to the question of subjectivity and character in the authorial/narrating voice of the travel account. Through the discussion of real and fictional travel accounts I intend to construct a genealogy of self-representation as it begins to emerge in literary productions of the nineteenth century. As I will also discuss, this genealogy is a key element to the conception of literary modernity, and sets in motion a trajectory for modernity that exposes the ambivalence for these texts as they have been valued by scholars and readers working within the nationalist–novelist paradigm.

Travel writing and genealogies of the novel

Cultural modernity may be defined twice: once in material terms and once in representational terms. I have argued that modernity may be defined as the attainment of a level of autonomy in the cultural field, and is measurable through the shifting of terms of legitimation within the field itself. So, one definition of cultural modernity centers on the development of autonomy in cultural value and legitimation. In representational terms, modernity is defined as a historical narrative, asserting its own unique disjunction with past narratives. The representational terms of modernity have been often traced back to the Cartesian elaboration of subject–object relations. The narrative of the "Cartesian cogito," as Jameson terms it, is central to narratives of modernity as that of "the coming to consciousness" of man (Jameson, A *Singular Modernity*, p. 35). Yet, such a conception of modernity often directs investigations of this concept into the realms of representation—the conflation of *becoming* with *representing* becomes a mark of self-consciousness, a common trope of modern literature. Jameson argues that this is a misapplication of Descartes' famous postulation; for the naming of man is not the same as the representation of him.

This conception of modernity has direct bearing on the valuation of novelistic writing—indeed, the innovation of highly subjective narrative structures makes an analysis of the novel as a kind of literary manifestation of Cartesian logic quite a fertile ground for investigation. Thus as Jameson argues, the conflation of being with representing becomes one of the fundamental problematics of theorization on modernity. We may well consider Jameson's caveat when considering Georg Lukács' influential work on the novel, and his theorization of the form and its role within conceptions of literary modernity. Lukács celebrates the "inner form" of the novel as a crucial distinguishing mark of the form: "the novel, in contrast to other genres whose existence resides within the finished form, appears as something in process of becoming" (Lukács, *Theory of the Novel*, pp. 72–3). The " 'appearance' of the novel to be 'something in process of becoming' " speaks to the double representational role of the novel—while relating the representational role to the Cartesian formula, what we may also call a coming to consciousness, the fulfillment of subjectivity.

While Lukács is here distinguishing the novel from epic narrative, there is no reason for his attention to a "process of becoming" to be limited to the particular genre of the novel. Indeed, Lukács' argument does not explicitly attempt to evaluate the novel as a manifestation of modernity (however implicit such a concept may be to his work). In the absence of such an explicit assertion, what may be derived from this argument is specifically a relation between the Cartesian cogito and the representational production of narrative spaces where a process of becoming is the work of the text which can be considered as symphonous (Lukács, *Theory of the Novel*, p. 73). Lukács identifies the novel in opposition to the epic by focusing upon the narrative priority of the development of subjectivity found in the novel, which he identifies as achieved through its alienation of the modern subject. In this way, the framework offered by Lukács has furthered the novelistic valuation of the novel as *the* manifestation of literary modernity. Lukács' characterization of the novel as displaying "a virile maturity" certainly matches with the sometimes triumphalist view theoreticians of the novel have adopted, however nuanced their reading of this virility has been (ibid., p. 71).[1]

In rethinking the appearance of this "virile" form, and its perceived opposition or synonymy with other forms, we will find it necessary to engage with a form of prose writing often given the role of being a precursor to the novel within novelistic literary histories. As a prose literary form, travel writing has often been considered as an important germinating genre for early novelistic writing. Thus, much of the consideration of nineteenth-century travel writing, in particular Arabic and Persian examples of this form, has been limited to tracing the degree to which certain travelogues can be said to have presupposed the narrative imperatives of novelistic writing.

Subjective transactions in writing on travels to Europe

By the nineteenth century, within Arabic and Persian literary imaginations the travelogue came to bear traces of no less deliberate a turn to a "process of becoming." As a "genre" marked by a very wide range of textual and aesthetic strategies, when creating categorizations of the travelogue we must consider this range and diversity while speaking of the legitimacy of this "genre." And yet, travelogues are on the whole a neglected area in discussions of literary modernity, in particular in scholarship of Arabic and Persian literary production. While attention to this body of literary work is not negligible, most often Arabic and Persian travelogues have served as sources for intellectual or political histories, and less often accorded consideration as *literary* texts.[2] Part of this problem may well reflect the bias of some literary scholarship in failing to distinguish between the presumed empirical purposes of travel writing and the undeniably imaginative aesthetic strategies that enframe the genre.

In the early nineteenth century, travelogues in both Persian and Arabic began to diverge from the classical genres of travel writing, the *safarnamih* (in Persian) or the *rihla* (in Arabic), both of which related primarily either to the sacred experience of religious pilgrimage, including the *hajj*, or notes recording services rendered to a sovereign during diplomatic or trade-related duties. It would be incorrect to view the small number of early-nineteenth-century Arabic and Persian travelogues describing travel to European societies as entirely without precedent. Indeed, in Arabic a body of such works can be traced back to the seventeenth century, relating the travels of Arab diplomats and emissaries, largely from North Africa, to Western Europe.[3]

In this period, the travelogue, both as a literary "genre" and as a mode of narrative construction (with consideration of the already-fictional nature of the travelogue, in the distances that inevitably pass between the experience and its writing) may be divided into two general types. The first, following from certain institutional and utilitarian exigencies, is the reportage mode of travel writing. The second, reflecting the increasing consolidation of a literary field in degrees autonomous from the preceding systems of value, is characterized by an interiorization of the narrative, thus centralizing a "process of becoming" absent in work of the reportage mode of travel writing. The period in question may be best thought of as a time of synchretic experimentation in nineteenth-century travel writing, as both tendencies are present, even within the same text.

What is innovative about these travelogues is the degree of autonomy they come to assume as texts with a social value beyond either religious or royal systems of patronage. These texts are transactional; unmoored from traditional poles of literary legitimation, finding value in and through new systems and institutions. These texts are transactional not only by representing the experience of travel textually, but more importantly by doing so in a context that is more and more legislated by a need to narrate this experience subjectively. The development of a subjective voice occurs simultaneously to the development of a new mode of social relation, one that is represented through the act of writing. This is a mode of material relations at odds with the selfless and immaterial narration of a pilgrim's progress, or the clerical service of a loyal servant of the court. In this period, travel writing begins to uncover the material links that bind the home societies of their authors to the colonial metropoles they are traveling to. Through travel, these authors are compelled to face a changing set of material relations that are manifest even at an individual level, and to choose how to act within them. This crisis, and its textual representation, creates a text that is fundamentally transactional. In travel writing nothing exemplifies this more clearly than the narration of material relations within these texts. The subjective turn in travel writing is most often centered around a narration of the subject's emergence into a world defined by a new economy of social relations defined by intercultural transactions.

Historians of Iran have devoted significant attention to the travelogue of Mirza Salih Shirazi, titled simply *Guzarish-i Safar-i Mirza Salih Shirazi* (A Chronicle of the Travels of Mirza Salih Shirazi), which relates his travel experiences journeying from Iran to St. Petersburg and London in 1815. Although noteworthy as being among the first examples of a Persian-language travelogue concerning Europe, Shirazi's work was still very specifically a result of the duties conferred upon him in his official, court-appointed position, as one of the first Iranian students sent to England for training in modern sciences.[4] In generic terms, Shirazi's *Safarnamih* can be related to the influential Arabic travelogue, *Takhlis al-ibriz fi talkhis baris* by Rifa'a Rafi' al-Tahtawi (1801–1873), which relates the chronicle of his stay in Paris between 1826 and 1831, as part of his service to the Egyptian ruler Muhammad 'Ali to study translation and to act as a religious counselor to the first group of Egyptian students dispatched to Europe.[5]

Both of these travelogues were highly influential in setting a discursive field for imagining Europe for their readerships, and follow very closely a template of travelogue as intelligence-gathering and ethnographic reportage with a focus on concerns of perceived importance for diplomatic, military and governing policy—that is, they use a framework established by the reportage genre of official or diplomatic travel-writing already discussed. In both cases Shirazi and al-Tahtawi make use of their position and the opportunity afforded by their role as travelogue writers to advocate specific reforms of the ruling system or of social and government institutions. In both texts, a subjective narrative thread runs through the work—specifically in episodes concerning the difficult journey to Western Europe from Iran and Egypt respectively, and both generally follow the significant personal developments experienced by each author during their respective stays in Britain and France. Yet the subjective content is not to any great extent part of a narrative of personal development (much less transformation), and serves largely to simply account for particular decisions made during the journey. These are still travelogues as professional reports, and so often highlight issues such as the difficulties resulting from a lack of funds, or the diligence of each author in protecting the honor of their homeland, religion, or ruler, in the face of criticism from Europeans they met. For example, they might narrate a meeting with a skeptical European who, out of ignorance, attempts to prove the tenets of Islam false—such an episode invariably would end with the author besting his intellectual adversary through recourse to such sources as the biblical traditions or through logical reasoning. Beyond these digressions into the personal, in the case of both al-Tahtawi and Shirazi, the larger part of the work of each text is made up of highly descriptive passages outlining the institutions and customs of the societies observed, interwoven with historical narratives and translations of religious, political, or legal documents.

The transactional nature of these texts arises in part from their willful appropriation of textual materials from other social contexts, often through direct or approximate translation. The travelogues of Shirazi and al-Tahtawi both reproduce translated materials from a variety of European sources, often uncited, within their accounts. For example, Shirazi appropriates historical material for a long digression in the text to provide a history of England from the fifth through the eighth centuries (Shirazi, *Guzarish-i Safar-i Mirza Salih Shirazi*, pp. 205–77).[6] In al-Tahtawi's *Takhlis al-ibriz*, his translation of historical and legal materials served as an introduction to what was to be a prolific career as an official translator, among the many other positions he was to hold in Egyptian public life.[7] Thus al-Tahtawi translates much of the French *Charte Constitutionnelle* of 1814 in *Takhlis al-ibriz*.[8] An examination of these early nineteenth-century travelogues, particularly with a focus on the presence of textual material reproduced in them, may open the door to a consideration of transactional textual circulation between, for example, Arabic and French, or Persian and English texts within the genre.

A common assessment of al-Tahtawi is reflected in the comment that he was "the great revivalist of the nineteenth century" linking the nineteenth-century Arab *nahda* movement to his works, central among them his travel writing (Brugman, *An Introduction to the History of Modern Arabic Literature*, p. 24). It is worth noting that evidence has been presented giving greater credit for his achievements as a revivalist to the efforts of his teacher Hasan al-'Attar (1766–1835) (to whom *Takhlis al-ibriz* is dedicated). Al-'Attar likely had a more formidable role in initiating the innovations that often have been attributed to his student al-Tahtawi—al-'Attar in fact authorized the travels al-Tahtawi and the other Egyptians of his delegation were to make (al-Tahtawi, *An Imam in Paris*, pp. 37–8).[9] The significance of this fact would be to date the inception of the "revival" movement to at least one generation earlier than has generally been presumed by literary historians, a fact which further weakens the claims of nationalist scholars that the *nahda* was in essence a proto-nationalist intellectual trend, and places its origins more firmly within strands of local innovations within the Ottoman imperial polity.

Nevertheless, al-Tahtawi's social impact would be formidable and enduring, particular in his appointment to oversee the reform of national educational institutions, where he was a leading contributor to policy decisions for the innovation and expansion of state education institutions in Egypt. Yet within the corpus of his work, *Takhlis al-ibriz* was to remain the most influential and widely read text of his authorship. Beyond its popularity in the Ottoman domains during his lifetime (it was translated into Ottoman Turkish and was said to have been widely read by Ottoman administrators), this text is often cited as one of the initiating works of the *nahda* movement itself (al-Tahtawi, *An Imam in Paris*, p. 44).[10] Given these qualifications, some modern readers have been disappointed to read *Takhlis al-ibriz*, only to find that a good deal of its text is made up of excerpts and abridgements of other texts, mostly of French origin, concerning the history, society, and political institutions of France. Nonetheless, its innovating effect from a lexical standpoint has been significant.[11]

As has been already argued, from a formal standpoint it would be an error to assess these works as exemplifying significantly innovative literary strategies, although they do transform the content of travel writing to include materials that had never been part of the genre in earlier periods. Neither al-Tahtawi nor Shirazi envisioned their projects as falling outside of preceding formal conventions for travel reportage, although given their attention to a new subject matter, and the introduction of textual materials from European sources, their work embodies what can be termed modern discursive or literary elements. Their formal conservatism is largely due to the fact that the travelogues of al-Tahtawi and Shirazi reflect the imperative placed upon the authors to address their texts to their patrons' presumed needs. In so doing, the texts were authorized through their inherent presumption of a literary field legitimized by the values of their sovereigns, being initially prepared and presented within the court scribal and curatorial systems, and preserved in court libraries. Furthermore, the texts served primarily as compensation to the court for the support of the latter for their travels. Indeed, in the years after al-Tahtawi's return to Egypt, Muhammad 'Ali has been reported to have required each student or official whose studies and travels to Europe were supported by the court to present a text—most often a translation from a European language—for inclusion in the Khedival Library.[12] Thus the act of writing and preparing a travelogue was legitimized within an economy that derived its logic and value directly from the court and its needs. Working within this context, al-Tahtawi's work strove to address matters with a direct policy application to Egyptian rulership, especially in the field of education. As Mitchell has observed, the modern Arabic term for education, *tarbiya*, was a new coinage in al-Tahtawi's travelogue (Mitchell, *Colonising Egypt*, p. 88). These innovations were intended solely to influence the Egyptian administrators and served no role to either elucidate al-Tahtawi's own subjective experience of travel, or to report on the quotidian details of his time in Europe.

Indeed in the Western European context a similar economy—the economy of "official" patronage and legitimation—led to the production of several notable travelogues of the early nineteenth century; although the wider development of a market-based literary economy also accorded value to some of these same texts. But one should not overestimate the strength of this economy; even in the early nineteenth century in Britain a successful print run of a text "for the public" would rarely exceed several thousand copies, and few were the authors who could expect to derive a significant portion of their income from such publishing. An excellent example is James Morier's *A Journey Through Persia, Armenia, and Asia Minor, to Constantinople.*[13] Inasmuch as his work was defined by his duties as a secretary charged with recording diplomatic exchanges and with organizing intelligence gathering and reportage concerning Iranian society and the court, Morier's initiation into the writing of travelogues about the region reflected closely his work as a colonial administrator. The differentiation between the economy of travel writing and the emerging autonomous literary field in early-nineteenth-century England is captured well in the distinction between the number of copies his travel writings would sell, and the many fictionalized oriental tales he would later pen.

Given his later entrance into the economy of fiction narrative writing, Morier's origins as a travel writer and government bureaucrat are important origins to consider. Al-Tahtawi also made forays into more specifically literary kinds of writing after the success of *Takhlis al-ibriz*. His initial positions in Egypt, after returning from Paris, were first as a translator in a new government school, and later as director of the School of Languages, an early Egyptian institution of higher education (Hourani, *Arabic Thought in the Liberal Age*, p. 71). In these posts, al-Tahtawi focused much of his efforts on the translation of textbooks for students in the natural and military sciences, but also found time to pursue translations of philosophical and literary works of both classical and a post-Enlightenment texts in French (ibid., p. 72). After the death of Muhammad 'Ali, al-Tahtawi's star waned, and he was soon sent into exile in the Sudan. Despite contending with material deprivation and the relative isolation of the Sudan (in comparison to the cosmopolitanism of Cairo) al-Tahtawi made use of this period to take on his largest single "literary" translation, that of Fénélon's *Télémaque* in 1867 (Mitchell, *Colonising Egypt*, p. 75).[14] It is no surprise that the major themes of this text—the suffering of Telemachus in exile, and his eventual triumphal return—were salient for al-Tahtawi at a point of great despair in his life, as well as the text's construction as a instructive text in the genre of "Mirrors for Princes" (al-Tahtawi, *An Imam in Paris*, p. 53). Once again, as with *Takhlis al-ibriz*, al-Tahtawi directed his work to the legitimizing framework of court consumption, rather than directing his prodigious talents toward the construction of a subjective narrative.

It may be dangerous to make simple assertions concerning a temporal marker for the "emergence" of a subject-centered body of travel texts in Arabic or in Persian—indeed examples of a certain kind of subject-centered text, articulated through a travel narrative, can be found in some genres of medieval Persian and Arabic travel writing, in particular those of Sufis or other religious mendicants and pilgrims. Yet, in the dialectics conceived by Lukács—between epic and novel—a body of nineteenth-century Persian and Arabic travelogues offer a view of a narrative imagination that, while adhering to certain structural features that may be termed as modern (and which Lukács relates to the novel), cannot be accommodated by the identity of the novel. Indeed, considering those who have offered critiques of the novel as an Enlightenment corollary of myth, we may categorize these travelogues within a framework that does not conflate modernity with the novel, but which avails the term modernity of other narrative and non-narrative trajectories.

Hajj Sayyah: narrative travel and a process of becoming

It would seem that Muhammad 'Ali Mahalati (1836–1924) better known as "Hajj Sayyah" (his *laqab* or informal title meaning "The Traveling Haji") had such precendents—that is, Sufi or pilgrimage travel accounts—in mind as he composed his expansive *safarnamih.* This work published as *Safarnamih-i Hajj Sayyah bi farang* (The Travelogue of Hajj Sayyah to Europe), encompassing his travels over the course of several years, is an early example of a subject-centered, interiorized travel narrative tracing personal transformations in a progressive arc over the course of the text. This travelogue is one of the first such texts in Persian; while numerous travel texts from the nineteenth century relate variegated experiences of travel—be they local, regional, or much farther afield—the travelogue of Hajj Sayyah presents a subtle but important innovation on the author-centered perspective within a travel narrative.

Sayyah spent many years of his life traveling—indeed many details of these travels are present within his *safarnamih*, which chronicles his life from 1859, ending at some undisclosed point before his return to Iran in 1877. Schematically, the text presents itself as a rather characteristic nineteenth-century reportage travelogue; being divided under headings of various cities and regions visited by Sayyah, outlining his travels from Iran through Armenia and Ottoman Turkey across Eastern Europe, to France and England. Yet the text is incomplete—published editions of the travelogue are based on a manuscript in the Mashhad University library which ends quite abruptly, in mid-sentence. No other manuscripts are known to exist, but a later book by Sayyah, *Khatirat-i Hajj Sayyah, ya dorih-yi khauf u vahshat* ("The Memoir of Hajj Sayyah, or: The Period of Fear and Terror") makes references to his having undertaken further travels in the Americas. It has been ascertained that Sayyah crossed the Atlantic, traveled across the American continent and returned to Asia via the Pacific. Further evidence of such travels is shown by the fact that after returning to Iran, when once threatened with arrest, Sayyah found refuge in the US embassy in Tehran on the basis of having attained American citizenship during his travels.[15] While much of the text is comprised of the presentation of details concerning the natural settings of the locations visited, estimations of population, cultural and social peculiarities, and regional economic data, and the like, there are several episodes that break from the objective, reportage-style of travelogue writing, evincing the emergence of a progressive internalized narrative style, a narrative centering on the author's "process of becoming" a worldly, critical advocate of reformism and cultural modernity for Iran.

In comparison to the reportage mode of travel writing, exemplified by the travelogues of Shirazi and al-Tahtawi, Sayyah's travels initiate from very personal considerations—a factor which frames the interiorized narrative that emerges through the work. Indeed, within Sayyah's travelogue, the subjective narrative themes of this work are laid out from the very first page, and give a meaning and legitimacy to the work that is carried out through the entire text. Sayyah begins his text by explaining how preordained family obligations that would have forced him into an unwanted marriage with his cousin compelled him to flee with no particular destination in mind. From the beginning, Sayyah styles himself an ascetic "seeker of knowledge" as he wanders the roads between the provincial towns and cities of Iran. This initial episode contains the seeds of what will be the larger themes of the work. Sayyah begins by explaining that as a young man he was sent to live with his uncle, ostensibly to learn a trade. After arriving in Moharejan, at his uncle's house, he learns of another motive: the arranged marriage with his cousin. The winter being a poor time for the marriage, he is sent to carry out religious studies in a nearby town until the spring. He recalls: "I was called to return to Moharejan, and on Monday the 21st of *Shavval*, I was gripped with fear that whenever this command [to marry my cousin] was to become a deed, I would have to spend the rest of my life here. I would learn nothing of any place or any thing. Little by little my imagination (*khiyal*) gained strength that it would be better I should leave with no one's knowledge, and so I set upon my travels" (*Safarnamih*, p. 25). His travels are then explained as motivated by a desire to "learn of other places and other things," and it is through the strength of his imagination (*ghuvvat-i khiyal*) that the determination to change the course of his destiny manifests itself. The language of this passage contains the rhetorical themes that are revisited throughout the travelogue—a fear of ignorance, the strength of his imagination, his desire for knowledge.

In subsequent episodes, another recurring theme within the narrative is established—the tension Sayyah experiences between his own ethical attraction to asceticism and increasing social exigencies that demand his entrance into material relations with individuals in the communities through which he is traveling. His antipathy toward the traditional role presented him—to marry his cousin and to settle as a petty merchant in his uncle's town—is the initiating factor of his rejection of such social responsibilities. The narrative follows his attempts to adhere to an ascetic ideal and to the inevitable difficulties these attempts lead to; his solutions of these problems as they occur chart a slow transformation of Sayyah from the role of an anti-materialist dervish to a fundamentally different social subjectivity.

Circumstances lead him to travel to Armenia, where a particularly difficult period is narrated. In this episode, Sayyah passes through a nearly deadly gauntlet, skirting starvation as a consequence of his stubborn commitment to a vow to refuse charity. This episode, set early in the travelogue, focuses on the transformative power of this experience. Upon arriving in the city of Tiflis (Tbilisi), Sayyah decides to learn Armenian and finds a student with whom he begins a language-exchange. Yet, given his poverty, hunger encroaches on his obsessive program of language study—he describes sitting in his small room, wasting away while continuing his studies of Armenian for hours at a stretch. As he is informed by a ideal of spiritual asceticism and of material mendicancy (earlier he is attacked at a religious school for espousing views that are termed those of an "irreligious sufi") he finds himself in a paradoxical situation—he cannot accept charity, and yet fails at earning his keep through work as a scribe, and eventually finds himself without either income or food (*Safarnamih*, p. 28). He obsesses over what he views as the likelihood of his demise.[16]

The experience gives him cause for two general conclusions that inform his further travels. The first is that his primary life's goal will be the seeking of "education" (*tahsil kardan*). He reports that when in the throes of hunger he is asked by a prominent local Armenian what he is suffering from, he replies "ignorance" (*nadani*). Even in the most dire of physical circumstances, he reports himself to be fixated on the goal of education. The second conclusion, no less profound but less explicit, is an acceptance of the need to enter into the world of material social transactions.

This transformation is addressed in the hunger episode, when through the intervention of local notables, he is compelled to end his fast, and comes to enter the social and cultural economy of Tiblis. Impressed by his studying of languages, he is employed in a local school to teach Persian, and becomes an apprentice at a local printing press where he is taught the craft of typesetting. Now a well-fed and respectable member of Tiblisi society, he reflects upon these recent personal transformations. "Every evening I would take walks in the streets and the gardens [of the city]. There was a garden maintained by a local Muslim authority, and I would often go to wander in that place. By and by my clothes became cleaner and better. One day I thought to myself (*bi khud khiyal kardam*) that a few months ago you knew neither languages nor a craft (*san'at*). Now typesetting is an art (*honar*) that I know, and also I have learned some languages. I became very happy and grateful, that in that city I had gained fame and honor" (*Safarnamih*, p. 59). He affirms to himself that none of this would have been possible without the generosity and care shown him by the local notables who have made these appointments possible, and notes his debt to them.

While on one hand this affiliation affirms the development of what may be termed a materialist view of his social and in particular his inter-communal relations—a theme in his later engagements with various individuals across Europe—on the other, it plays a specific narrative role, as a large portion of his travels through Western Europe are made as the companion and translator for an Armenian merchant, with whom he becomes very close. It represents a subjective transformation from an isolated, ascetic ideal to one of a certain cosmopolitanism, no less one more accepting of the material relations such a transformation engenders. Thus, the improvement of his clothes precedes an appreciation for his gaining of skills in new arts and languages. Undoubtedly, for Sayyah this narrative progression may also serve as a metaphor for his homeland—isolated and ascetic—entering "the world" by recasting itself as cosmopolitan, embracing transactionary social and material relations outside its ephemeral borders. As Sayyah travels westward across Europe, this narrative develops in a variety of registers, tracing out transformations and improvements to his person and his thinking. He learns new languages, enters into higher and higher social circles and his attention is drawn more and more to material relations. Where, in the beginning of the text, Sayyah portrays himself as a seeker of knowledge of "other places and other things," he ends with a collection of personal memorabilia representing the many places he has traveled to, and makes use of the fame he gains from his formidable collection of coins from across the world, which are often used as a pretext for his gaining audiences before notables and leaders in the different areas he visits.

The improvements charted in Sayyah's narrative follow a trajectory toward the transformation of certain social value systems, thus critically reflecting upon them. Sayyah's early idealization of a traditional asceticism—an ideal invested with high value within the classical Iranian literary and cultural imagination—is negated by the material relations that arise from engaging with the social systems he enters. Turning from a fetishization of the mendicant's denial of the world, Sayyah turns to the worldly concerns of *knowledge*—not of esoteric arts, but applied skills relating to languages, trades, and institutions. Through this turn, we may trace the emergence of Sayyah as the *subject* of his text. As a travel text, the narrative follows this transformation as if it were a cartographic feature of Sayyah's road-map from Iran across Europe.

In this sense, the thread of narrative that relates Sayyah's emergence into the material world as a subject is fundamentally transactional. His transformation is informed by his own circulation within multiple social settings, and reflects kinds of transactions demanded by the specific exigencies of traversing these new, unfamiliar settings. These changes are undertaken at a cost, however, as Sayyah's episode of near-starvation informs us; resolving the conflicts of different systems of social value often requires a degree of accommodation—material, or otherwise. Hajj Sayyah's text is exemplary of the way in which textual transactions innovate the travelogue. Given the tropes that are most often availed of within this genre, travel writing can very easily serve as an index of the transactions engendered by literary modernities.

For Sayyah as an author, these transactions involve a reconfiguration of the value-systems that his character "Sayyah" aspires to embody. These values then return to embody the text's own self-legitimation. As Sayyah begins to enter the materialist relations his travels have introduced him to, so does the text become comprehensible through these relations. In fact, for Sayyah material relations and literary work begin to overlap, their boundaries blurring—this, one may argue, is largely an attribute of the text's estimation of an autonomous field of literature, and its self-consciousness of its own role within this field. The blurring of the boundaries between the material and the literary is rather clear at several points in the work—in particular in episodes where Sayyah encounters individuals who offer him services or goods, whose requested compensation is merely to be mentioned in the book he tells them he will write of his experiences.

The transactional dimension of this text is also a function of the way in which the question of individual transformations to the character of Sayyah are shown to be a function of the discrete relations he establishes with the communities he visits during his travels. His experiences in Armenian areas, being that they are the first experience of his alienation from the social setting of "home" (given the linguistic and religious differences between himself and the local Armenian community), are represented as the breaking point for Sayyah's transformation. As "factual" as the *Safarnamih* may be, by presenting an intersecting set of interests within a thread of narrative illuminated by subjective transformation, Sayyah anticipates the appearance of more consciously fictional "travel texts" that would utilize the framework of the travelogue toward differing ends. Rather than using the conceit of subjective transformations through an interiorized narrative these fictive travelogues employ a framework that is not subjectively driven, but which rather idealize a different subject for its narrative logic, that of *society*. The emergence of this narrative subject was to no small extent a product of the loosening bonds of the previous systems of cultural legitimization, and a reconfiguration of the social values for writing, enabling new social classes, and actors to participate in the work of literature.

The social turn in fictional travelogues—*Ibrahim Bayg* and *'Isa ibn Hisham*

Speaking generally, by the final years of the nineteenth century, the literary transactions between colonial societies and those of colonized peoples had entered a new register. Exploration, both geographical and literary, had become more refined, empirical and fell into ever more proscribed conventions. Indeed, for most of the non-European world, intercultural relations had fundamentally changed—the last decade of the nineteenth century made this a more "universal" experience than it had been at any previous period. In these years, Arab and Iranian cultural figures were caught up as never before in the tumultuous effects of social and political upheavals within their societies. European colonialism, although dating a full century back to the French expedition to Egypt and the encroachment of the British and Russian Empires onto Iranian domains and interests, was by the end of the century an unavoidable and dominating political factor across much of the non-European world. Ottoman hegemony of the Arab world was slowly unraveling—North Africa was by this point almost entirely outside of the Porte's authority, and even in the Levant, the Ottoman systems of authority were greatly mitigated by the influence of British and French colonial interests. Iran was heavily influenced by the ongoing competition between Russian and English imperial aspirations, and a weak central government ceded much of its authority to more and more intrusive colonial intrusions.

The effects of these worldly affairs upon the literary production of the late nineteenth century are inestimable. Authors from North African and West Asian societies were now confronted not only with the material subjugation of their societies but also with the cultural conditions of the later stages of colonialism, which flowed from this new arrangement of material relations. What this meant for literary production in these areas is that less and less did authors have the ability to creatively or innovatively interact with "regional" or "local" interlocutors, and rarely if ever was such a relationship with Western European productions in the realm of possibilities. While hopes for the achievement of an indigenous articulation of modernity were perceived to be slowly slipping away, authors proposed innovations full of ambivalence for their uses within the highly charged social arenas that were now defined by terms such as "colonialism," "reform," "constitutionalism," and "independence."

Muhammad al-Muwaylihi's *Hadith 'Isa ibn Hisham*, and Zayn al-'Abedin Maraghihi's *Siyahatnamih-yi Ibrahim Bayg* are exemplary of the ambivalences of late-nineteenth-century literary innovations in Arabic and Persian. Both offer an insight into how literary resistance to colonialism, when it found its articulation through colonial terms, was to come to be allied with nationalist discourses and political configurations. Although both texts have long been termed novelistic, their modes of address and categorical imaginations are difficult to characterize as fitting the novel's framework. Nevertheless, these works have been appropriated into the nationalist–novelist narrative of literary modernity—indeed, they have in some cases been cited as foundational to this framework of literary history.

Zayn al-'Abedin Maraghihi (1839–1909), lived as an expatriate from Iran for much of his adult life, moving between various cities in the Caucasus—largely Tblisi and Yalta—and the Ottoman capital, as an active trader and businessman, occasional civil servant, and erstwhile literary provocateur.[17] His achievements in the latter regard begin and end with the three volumes published as *Siyahatnamih-yi Ibrahim Bayg*.[18] This trilogy, or collection—termed by one scholar as "the first critical Persian novel"—was written and published over the course of some fourteen or so years, and is best characterized as a mélange of disparate textual material (Aryanpur, *Az Saba ta Nima*, Vol. 1, p. 305). Over the course of the century or so since its publication, most critical regard for the text has focused upon the first volume, which is largely made up of one distinct fictional narrative. The second and third volumes are less easy to define, and are made up of autobiographical, poetic, and political excursa, tied together by a passionate advocacy of the imperative for social and political reform in Iran.

The first volume of *Siyahatnamih* most likely dates to 1895/6; its second volume appeared about a decade later, in 1905/6; and the final volume was published in 1909 (Mirabedini, *Sad sal-i dastan nivisi-i Iran*, p. 23). This first volume contains a *faux*-travelogue of Ibrahim Bayg's journey to Iran from Egypt, as well as the details of his circulation throughout Iran. A brief introduction gives us the reason for his journey—the son of an Iranian expatriate who has lived in Egypt for his entire life, Ibrahim follows his father's nationalist proclivities despite having no experience of his homeland. Iranian travelers bring him news of the poor state of the nation.

> [They bring news of] the lack of organization in Iran, of barefooted soldiers, of the selling off of the country for any paltry bribe offered to a ruler, of the imprisonment or fining of people (*khalq*) by the ruler, the governor, the mayor, the feudal lord, each one for any pretext they wish, and of the existence in each city of fifteen institutions for imprisonment with chains . . . of the filth in the streets, of the chaotic mosques which are closed for eleven of twelve months, and of how in the fall, uncouth people fill the mosques with watermelons and honeydew, of the disgusting condition of the *hammams* and their fetid water.
>
> (Maraghihi, *Siyahatnamih-yi Ibrahim Bayg*, 2006, p. 29)

These and other details drive Ibrahim to distraction, and result in his repeatedly coming to blows with the bearers of this manner of report, such is his sense of honor concerning his national origin.[19] We learn about Ibrahim Bayg's disposition from the book's frame-story, told by an Istanbul-residing merchant, who obtains the travelogue upon being visited by his friend Ibrahim Bayg, while the latter returns from Iran to Egypt. It is obvious to the narrator that Ibrahim's earlier well known idealism has dissipated, a sense that is corroborated by the text of the travelogue, which he begins to read. Undertaking this reading, the narrator learns that during the course of his travels in Iran, Ibrahim Bayg finds his expectations dashed at every turn. As he stumbles from disappointment to disillusionment, from humiliation to anger, he finds himself growing increasingly confrontational toward the elites and rulers who he concludes are primarily responsible for the corruption, decay, and despair he finds everywhere. The book ends with a call for radical reforms of Iranian political institutions, essentially endorsing the platform of ideals that were to gain definition through the course of the Constitutional Revolution of 1906.

Ibrahim Bayg's narrative makes copious use of the conventions of travelogue writing. For example, in the final episodes of volume one, Ibrahim apologizes for not fulfilling the readers' expectations to be supplied certain empirical data, such as accountings of the populations of the various cities he has traveled to—a convention of the reportage style of travelogue writing. However, he asserts, the lack of any reliable census data or scientific institutions in Iran prevents anything but hollow conjecture about such matters (*Siyahatnamih*, pp. 222–3). In this, he ascribes the failings of his writing to follow the prescriptions of travelogues to the backwardness and corruption of the Iranian government. His use of the travelogue structure is one indication of the perceived success of the genre as a modern literary form, with application for social and political as well as literary achievements. By this time Maraghihi may well have read or at least been aware of the works of Mirza Salih, Hajj Sayyah, or any of the other early or mid nineteenth-century Persian travelogues, and likely was impressed by the manner in the genre intersected social and literary arenas.

References within *Siyahatnamih* do also point to other sources of inspiration, in particular the exilic Persian press. From Calcutta to Istanbul to Cairo to London, by the last decade of the nineteenth century a wide network of periodicals formed an informal association of critical voices for the reform of political and social institutions in Iran, while advocating new concepts of communal relations, as well as advancing critical literary and aesthetic debates on a number of subjects. Ibrahim Bayg makes direct references, for example, to *Habl al-Matin*, the Calcutta-based Persian newspaper and printing house that acted as a disseminator of revolutionary, and culturally critical thought. In Istanbul, *Akhtar* also pursued a similar agenda, often engaging in direct debate with the authors of *Habl al-Matin*. These and several other publications such as *Hikmat* and *Chehrih-Nama* were of critical importance to the sizeable Iranian community in Cairo (and likely would have served as reading material for Ibrahim Bayg were he a living character). These journals were largely published by small and devoted communities of exilic Iranians, with little financial motivation, and most depended on a close association between local diaspora merchants and traders, political activists, and literary figures.[20] Given the significant expense of printing and distribution of these newspapers and pamphlets, local merchants were often required to offset set-up expenses for these publications. For example, the publisher of *Chehrih-Nama* in Cairo used his early anniversary issues to explain to his readers the great debts this publication was incurring, and the improbability of its survival outside of the generosity of established figures in the Iranian expatriate community.[21] Given their institutional association outside of the historical benefactory centers—the government or the religious foundations and charities—these publications show further evidence of the emergence of an autonomous field of literary production, a field that would have to develop new measures of self-authorization and legitimacy. Given their diasporic settings, these publications were also well-situated to establish networks and relationships with local institutions and groups in their host societies. *Chehrih-Nama* would often report on local political issues and translated articles from Arabic periodicals (in particular Jurji Zaydan's *al-Hilal*).

Maraghihi was an exemplary audience member for these journals—a literate and educated member of the mercantile class, he had the skills, the means, and an interest in consuming these publications. That, later in his life, he was inspired to take pen in hand with a literary aim, may to some extent be credited to the legacy of these publications. Maraghihi's writing makes use not only of the framework of the travelogue but also bears traces of conventions developed in these publications' journalistic prose. Maraghihi may be thought of as a member of a generation of literary-activists who entered into the literary field—with some success—from a professional or vocational background neither of religious training nor of rigorous literary study. 'Abd al-Rahim Talibof (1834–1911), the author of another widely read and cited late-nineteenth century text, the semi-fictional semi-narrative work *Kitab-i Ahmad*, shared with Maraghihi a class-identity rooted in the traditions of *bazar* families, and the experience the education accorded to children of many urban merchant families.

Maraghihi highlights education as a theme in his work, as he reports in an autobiographical passage in the third volume of *Ibrahim Bayg*. Coming from a family with Kurdish roots who emigrated to the town of Maraghih to work as merchants, he was fortunate to have been raised in a family of some means. However, as he notes, his background was not a guarantor of access to good education.

> When I had passed eight years of my life, I was placed in school where I was occupied with training and education, For eight years I followed the path of this primary school. But what kind of school was this? And what teacher did we have? (May the Muslim never have to hear of nor even the unbeliever have to see such things!) Given the teaching at these schools, where the letter "alif" is not even distinguished from the letter "ba," after eight years I left school in absolute ignorance. I was fated to live in the shadow of the ignorance and lack of knowledge brought about by that cursed school . . . what is surprising is that despite my incredible ignorance, I was still stirred to seek knowledge. I would never be ashamed of what I have just reported, and now I truly believe my thoughts to be correct. To make a long story short, at the age of sixteen I was sent to the seminary, and at the age of twenty I was sent to Ardebil to work as a merchant.
>
> (*Siyahatnamih*, 2006, p. 540)

Yet, Maraghihi does not elaborate upon the specific circumstances that led to his interest in writing. Nor does he cite literary or other inspirations for the innovative writing he was to produce. Situated outside of the major social roles that enabled prose writing in this period, Maraghihi's mere decision to write *Ibrahim Bayg* is, perhaps, as remarkable as the book itself. While Maraghihi did not embody the concept of authorship either as a function of official service (such as with Mirza Salih, al-Tahtawi) or as a product of individual idealism (as with Hajj Sayyah), it can be said that his inspiration derived from all of these kinds of writing. At the same time he cannot be thought of as filling a particular position in what we have termed the field of literary production, as someone such as the literati and cultural elites of the time did. In their devotion to language, word play, education, and literary debate, major intellectuals such as al-Yaziji and Jurji Zaydan, can be seen as modern advocates of the classical legacy of *adab*—the Islamic literary humanities. Maraghihi's education and his vocational pursuits should not have prepared him for his success as an innovative author of a popular and influential work of literature—yet that is exactly what he was to become.

An examination of *Ibrahim Bayg* gives a glimpse into the cultural and social currents that made up Maraghihi's literary imagination. The first volume, while despairing of the deeply entrenched corruption and incompetence of the Qajar political system, finds hope in the possibility for its reform—importantly, in the first volume, attacks on the venality of the Qajar ruling system stop short of personal criticism of the Shah (although one cannot help but perceive Maraghihi's antipathy for Nasir al-Din in certain passages). Yet, despite the guarded hope the first volume displays, the narrative concerning the character Ibrahim Bayg finds a tragic conclusion by the middle of the second volume of the trilogy. Not long into the second volume, Ibrahim falls ill in exile in Istanbul—as no doctor can diagnose his condition, he is sent to Egypt. The illness worsens until it is discovered that his malady stems from the innate relationship he has with his homeland, thus his health is simply following along the contours of Iran's own state of well-being. Throughout his illness, he is cared for by his young Circassian wife (who he had met in the first volume, another of many gestures to an ideal of local cosmopolitanism), and some improvements occur—again, proving the relationship between his own health and the fortunes of Iran. For example, after hearing of the installment of the new shah, Muzaffar al-Din, in 1896, his health improves for a time (although Maraghihi goes to lengths to arrange the narrative in such a way that Ibrahim Bayg cannot have heard of the assassination of Nasir al-Din, so his improvement cannot be said to have been related to this divisive fact). Yet, shortly afterwards, after obtaining and reading an issue of *Habl al-Matin* containing a particularly depressing report about the situation in Iran, he falls ill again. Not long after this, a personal letter from Iran corroborates the dark view of the aforementioned article, and his health declines beyond repair. Stricken down by these two items—a newspaper and a letter—he dies. Overtaken by grief at his funeral, his Circassian wife collapses, and also dies on the spot.

Where the first volume of *Ibrahim Bayg* balances narrative elements against digressions and monologues concerning the state of Iran, the second volume is largely comprised of overtly political content. Ibrahim Bayg's sudden death removes the imperative for a narrative, and gives Maraghihi free reign to more directly present his social and political criticism. Unshackled, the text begins to meander, ebb, and flow. In the third volume, the material grows even more diverse and diffuse, mixing the autobiographical with excursa on poetry, historical questions, short semi-fictive accounts, and political diatribes, even revisiting Ibrahim Bayg as he ascends to heaven.

In this same period, in Egypt, the author and publisher Muhammad al-Muwaylihi (1858–1930) was struggling with innovating Arabic narrative fiction along lines not very distant from the efforts of Maraghihi. Muwaylihi was a figure born into the modernist and early nationalist ambience of a developing bourgeois intelligentsia in Cairo and Alexandria—metropolitan, but Ottomanist in their outlook and concerns. His father, Ibrahim Muwaylihi, was the publisher of newspapers and journals as well, and Muhammad was brought up in the fold of various salons and social circles of proto-nationalist intellectuals. This is not at odds with his own often pan-Islamist tendencies, as it would be incorrect to try to narrowly define the figures of this time with simple labels such as "nationalist" or "pan-Islamist." Often the two tendencies existed side by side in an individual figure, and the contradictions in the discourses were absorbed into the passion of their imagination, galvanized against perceived and real injustices, and hopes for the future.[22] In 1898, the younger Muwaylihi established a regular feature in the periodical *Misbah al-Sharq*, under the running title "Fitra min al-Zaman" ("A Period of Time"). This feature presented a serialized narrative concerning the adventures of an Egyptian Basha, reborn from the grave nearly a century after his death, and follows his confusion and bewilderment with the changes witnessed by Egypt over the course of the years since his demise. The journal in which "Fitra min al-Zaman" was serialized was established by his father, Ibrahim, and slowly came under the direction of Muhammad until its closing in 1903. The narrative, collected, edited, and published in 1907 as a book with the title *Hadith 'Isa ibn Hisham*, "the most important work of imaginative literature of its generation," is marked by certain resemblances to *Ibrahim Bayg* noteworthy in both form and content (Mitchell, *Colonising Egypt*, p. 115).

The frame story of each text concerns a character who identifies with his homeland in some essential sense, but who is also absolutely unfamiliar with its contemporary realities. Nor is either character able to make use of the social legitimacy and currency that he believes due him, as each represents institutions and sensibilities based on now-deteriorated social structures and legacies. In *Hadith 'Isa ibn Hisham*, the "narrator" is the polite 'Isa ibn Hisham, who devotes a great deal of time and patience to assisting the Basha through his various pitfalls. In Ibrahim Bayg, two characters to some extent fulfill this role; to a greater extent Ibrahim's traveling companion Yusef 'Amu, and to a lesser extent his unnamed friend in Istanbul who reads his travel notes and comments upon them in the frame of the text. These characters serve as intermediaries, markers of the intended readers' own identification. Yet through their interactions with the central characters, these intermediators come to see the logic of their madness. Also, both texts show a deep appreciation with classical belle lettrist traditions in each language—through widespread references to classical literature, but also in terms of form and genre identification.

Hadith 'Isa ibn Hisham has often been discussed within the framework of the nineteenth-century Arabic *maqama* revival. The transformation to the classical *maqama* form—a classical prose–poetic genre compiling relatively short episodic narratives often concerning a recurring cast of characters—in the nineteenth century shows the tenuous line the nationalist–novelist paradigm makes between tradition and modernity. This question has featured in literary histories concerning *Hadith 'Isa ibn Hisham* as an example of the Arab revival of interest in the *maqama* in the late nineteenth century. Muwaylihi is an author who has often been factored into the nationalist canon of Egyptian modern fiction—often described as perhaps the first author of an Egyptian novel, as M.M. Badawi states in his work *Qadiyyat al-hadatha* (Badawi, *Qadiyyat al-hadatha*, p. 102). Muwaylihi is, in a sense, representative of a generation of Arab intellectual figures, literate in both the classical literature and styles, but entirely devoted to new technologies and literary methods. This generation was largely ambivalent, however, showing an acerbic and often-nostalgic anti-modernism, a sense that classical literature and social organization was the pinnacle of Arab achievements, and that modern methods were leading to social corruption and disintegration. This ambivalence is carried out in Muwaylihi's serialization of *Hadith 'Isa ibn Hisham* in the newspaper *Misbah al-Sharq*. *Hadith 'Isa ibn Hisham* refers directly to the classical maqama form and specifically to the *Maqamat* of Badi al-Zaman al-Hamadhani.

The maqama form may well have appealed to Muwaylihi because of his deep appreciation of classical literature, but also its episodic form easily conformed to the serialized publication he envisioned for *Hadith 'Isa ibn Hisham*. Yet, the innovation in his work was to tie, much more so than in the classical idiom, the various episodes together into larger narratives. So, while each episode was largely self-contained, groups of episodes also carried threads of narrative that would resolve over longer periods or lead to further issues to explore. This innovation is what has led the work to be termed an early example of novelistic writing—disputes over this appellation have usually concerned the definition of "novelistic writing." The question that remains is how literary historians can reasonably evaluate the role of *Hadith 'Isa ibn Hisham*—is it more proper to see this text as a link within a chain of development culminating in the novel as the modern literary form par excellence, or is it better understood as exemplifying a unique achievement within a nexus of literary and social formations of late-nineteenth century Egypt? Put another way, is the text better considered as representing a beginning, an ending, or a seamless link in a larger continuity?

In scholarly studies of modern Arabic literature, Muwaylihi's text is most often viewed as a progenitor to the novel, that is, a kind of beginning. One scholar well summarizes the novelistic reading of the text, by asserting that, "when we say that *Isa 'ibn Hisham* was a splendid start to the novel, we are not suggesting that it managed to fulfill all the requirements of the genre, nor that it is free of artistic faults.... However, it is a move in a new direction toward a specific genre of literature" (quoted in Allen, *A Period of Time*, p. 69). In the Arabic, the term used is "riwaya"—which more literally means "narrative" but which has come to be popularly used as the modern term for "novel." The quote shows a double reification of the concept of *'Isa ibn Hisham* as novelistic. Another critic has argued that, "the main aim of many Arab writers during the 19th century was... to use the form of the novel for the purpose of social criticism. This was in fact, what

Muwaylihi was doing [with 'Isa ibn Hisham]" (Moreh, *Studies in Modern Arabic Prose and Poetry*, p. 112). Even postcolonial theorists have treated the text quite similarly, citing Muwaylihi as an author of novels (Makdisi, " 'Postcolonial' Literature in a Neocolonial World," p. 96). *Ibrahim Bayg* has been read in much the same way by scholars of modern Persian literature; the similarity in the appropriations of these two texts for novelistic genealogies is quite noteworthy. The most comprehensive study of modern Iranian literature has termed *Ibrahim Bayg* a "new direction in literature," terming the book a "novel" (*ruman*—the French term is used in Persian) as well (Mirabedini, *Sad sal-i dastan nivisi-i Iran*, Vol. 1, p. 20).

In these examples we see the retroactive cooptation of two innovative narrative prose texts by novelism in literary scholarship. By any measure of what constitutes the history of "the novel," these are texts that neither in terms of their own genealogies or their content can be considered part of a novelistic trajectory. In the case of the assessment of *'Isa ibn Hisham*, the concern that it does not fulfill "the requirements of the genre" follows on a sense of its being a failure in attempts by Arabic literati to join the modern literary field through the production of a novel. It is thus unsurprising that the earliest efforts at producing a self-identified Arabic novel were often a direct product of European education: the famous novel *Zaynab* was written by Muhammad Haykal in 1912 while living in Paris, as a conscious exercise in writing a novel along the lines of the European form (Smith, "Love, Passion and Class in the Fiction of Muhammad Husayn," p. 249). In Persian, the legacy of *Ibrahim Bayg* serves no less ambivalently in attempts to link the intellectual currents of late nineteenth century Iranians with those experiments in novel writing that were carried out almost exclusively by individuals who had been sent to Europe for higher education in the early twentieth century—individuals such as Muhammad 'Ali Jamalzadih who wrote much of his innovative prose in the early twentieth century while living in Switzerland.

This is not to say that the innovations represented by the work of Maraghihi and Muwaylihi were somehow anti-cosmopolitan. Indeed, the experience of travel and exile was constitutional to the literary imagination of each author—both Muwaylihi and Maraghihi traveled outside of their home societies, spending significant periods of time in exile. Muwaylihi's father's outspoken stance vis-à-vis the 'Urabi revolt of 1882, and the ensuing British occupation of Egypt, as well as his activity in domestic Egyptian politics involving political and social reforms under the Khedive Isma'il, who was compelled to abdicate in 1879, resulted in his expulsion from Egypt for some time. Yet rather than record their social and cultural critiques through the convention of an autobiographical travelogue, each chose to utilize a literary imagination involving fictive, even fantastic, elements within their texts. Muwaylihi experienced Italy and Istanbul while accompanying his exiled father in the early 1880s, and subsequently spent time in Paris (again with his father) in the mid-1880s, where the father and son worked on the journal *al-Ittihad*. Later yet, in London, they joined the pan-Islamic reformer Jamal al-Din al-Afghani for a period (Allen, *A Period of Time*, pp. 4–5). In 1900,

Muwaylihi returned to England and France, reporting on the Great Exhibition of Paris in that year (ibid., p. 10). This experience served as the basis for writing the second section of *Hadith 'Isa ibn Hisham,* called *al-Rihla al-Thaniyya* ("The Second Journey") where the protagonists travel to Paris in order to better understand the root causes for the immense changes the Basha has observed in Egyptian society.

Another commonality between *Ibrahim Bayg* and *'Isa ibn Hisham* is the fact that novelistic criticism has tended to valorize aspects of each text, while all but neglecting other aspects. For example, the "second Journey" of *'Isa ibn Hisham* rarely figures into discussions of the text, just as few critics have found much of value in the second and third volumes of *Ibrahim Bayg.* This somewhat peculiar oversight is indicative of the degree to which each of these texts fails to fulfill the presumptions of nationalist–novelist readings of the work of this period. One critic has argued that "the first volume is the most valuable of the volumes... its subject is coherent and to the point. But this textual coherence is less often perceived in the other two volumes" (Mirabedini, *Sad sal-i dastan nivisi-i Iran,* p. 23). Somewhat similarly, Roger Allen says of the "second Journey" of *'Isa ibn Hisham* that "the inclusion of the episodes from Paris alters the particularly Egyptian focus... and to a certain extent presents us with a work which has a wider focus than its predecessors and a lesser critical intensity" (Allen, *A Period of Time,* p. 42). As a translation of the third edition of the text—an edition that contained greater focus on Egyptian institutions than those that would later be prepared for use as a school textbook—Allen's English translation of *Hadith 'Isa ibn Hisham* is also missing this second part.[23]

However, the "second Journey" is arguably an important episode within the larger project of *'Isa ibn Hisham,* and represents its most deeply transactional element. The subject of the "second Journey" is intended as a resolution of the questions raised in the Egyptian episodes. In the final paragraphs of the first part, the Basha muses about the root causes for the chaos he observes around him. A friend explains: "The true reason for all of this is the sudden penetration of Western civilization into Eastern countries and the impersonation by Easterners of Westerners in all aspects of their lives, as if they were blind, since they are unenlightened by knowledge, have no capacity for comparison, can not benefit from experience..." (Muwaylihi, *Hadith 'Isa ibn Hisham, aw fitra min al-zaman,* p. 207). The friend continues, arguing that not only is the emulation of the West a problem, but more importantly the fact that only the most superficial aspects of Western culture are emulated. The Basha agrees, and yet desires for more particulars about the phenomenon. "If only I could research and observe the foundation of Western civilization, in both its material and spiritual aspects" (ibid., p. 208). 'Isa agrees and says "I have in mind to travel with you on a journey to Western countries to obtain from this experience the fruits of knowledge and research" (ibid.). To omit the Paris episodes from critical consideration results in a general disregard for the narrative imperatives of the text itself—regardless of the acuity of its critique of "Western culture," the "second Journey" is an integral part of the comprehensive vision of the text. The cause of this disregard may best be understood within the context of the contingencies of a reading of literary modernity framed by the nationalist–novelist paradigm.

During the course of the second journey, 'Isa and the Basha attend the Exhibition, experience the street life of Paris and meet a wide cast of Parisian characters, remarking upon the technological and organizational achievement they observe in France. The "second Journey" begins with this description of their first impression of Paris:

> Isa ibn Hisham said: All praise be to He without whom matters do not occur, and duties do not impress, without His allowing for them. God sent us on a journey to European areas, for us to see the spectacles of Western civilization. And we completed the journey allowed us, for we arrived in Paris, disposing of our walking sticks, and we found there public roads, and wide squares. We found no tribes calling out and flowing, no troops assembling and gathering, no living dead spreading out, and no creatures swarming. The people appeared crowded and confined, colliding and struggling, seeming to pour from the pathway as if in the rush of a flood, under lights wiping out the traces of the night, as if there was no night. One would be terrified of what was to be seen, fearing being blinded from the intense light . . . If you looked down upon the street from above, it would not be an exaggeration if you said it was a stormy sea, with two coasts of light bordering it on both sides.
>
> (Muwaylihi, *Hadith 'Isa ibn Hisham, aw fitra min al-zaman*, p. 211)

This introduction centers on the city as a field of vision. The rich mix of description and metaphor gives character to a new subject, a character that has been long missing from the "characters" of *Hadith 'Isa ibn Hisham*—that of the city. The passage begins by defining the city by what it is not. It is not a place where tribes or troops gather chaotically, nor the site for incredible creatures or the dead to emerge from imagination. Nonetheless, it is a place of strange wonders—the crowds, the lights, the flood of humanity all distinguish it from the qualities of Cairo at this time. In particular, the vantage point of "looking down" upon the streets of the city, implies an omniscience and objectification of this new subject. This is a new perspective in Arabic literature, perhaps the first time such a panoptic perspective is presented within a literary description. More fully than in any passage in the first part of *Hadith 'Isa ibn Hisham*, a panoptic vista is used to introduce the qualities of a social space. The very foreignness of Paris is the enabling element to the introduction of visuality in literary representation; nowhere does Muwaylihi bring a wide-angle perspective upon an Egyptian social space in the manner that he does in this introduction to the Second Journey. This follows Mitchell's observation that Arab travelers of this period were fascinated by the impulse toward spectacular representation inherent in European engagements with the orient, reporting on how these European spectacles "set up the world as a picture" (Mitchell, *Colonising Egypt*, p. 6). Here, Muwaylihi wrests this impulse to spectacle and directs it toward the subject of the European city instead.

From this point, the second journey charts the qualities of Paris through narrative, yet continuing still to emphasize the spectacular nature of the experience. These passages offer a translation of the visual register of Paris into poetic terms familiar to an Arab readership. With humor referencing the most grotesque fears of an Arab traveler—that the city would be full of incredible "creatures swarming" or militarized by "troops assembling and gathering," the text translates the spectacle of a late-nineteenth-century-European city, offering it as a new character for Arabic literature, a character key to its modern aspects. The "second Journey" exemplifies the textual transactions at the heart of *Hadith 'Isa ibn Hisham* as a whole, taking the travelogue genre—as it was codified by al-Tahtawi, for example—into a new register. At the turn of the century, at the time when Muwaylihi composed these lines about Paris, Hajj Sayyah had already completed his exploration of an interiorized, subjective narrative within the travelogue form. Muwaylihi, and Maraghihi—through differing aesthetic strategies—innovated upon available literary strategies to create new representations of a new subject, that of society itself. Both did so through comparative contexts—using the travelogue genre, but fictively charging it with a critical social component.

This reading repositions these texts as examples of modern writing that cannot be evaluated through the narrow framework of the novel. In a sense, rather than marking the beginning of novelistic writing, these texts are better understood as marking an end to the experimental and innovating forms of literary modernity charted over the course of the nineteenth century, forms that signaled the increasing autonomy of the act of writing, and reading within Arab and Iranian societies. The transactional nature of their texts—generated through intercultural contacts and travel—follows on the legitimacy accorded to the autonomous category of "literature" by antecedents such as *Alf layla wa layla*. Yet important distinctions between these two authors must be considered—in particular when considering the social roles inhabited by each as they came to produce these texts. As I have already discussed, Maraghihi's roots lie outside of the currents that predominated the supply of literary figures in the Iranian–Persian literary context at that time. Muwaylihi, on the other hand, was from a literary family with long-established ties to reformist political movements. However, despite these distinctions, both were to produce texts that would use certain formal elements common to the travelogue genre so as to explore and elucidate their home societies, articulating critiques that otherwise would have been nearly impossible to make. In this sense, they both were to be following a well-worn literary strategy employed by writers as distant as Montesquieu in his *Persian Letters*, by having foreign or defamiliarized travelers articulate wide ranging social critiques. It was for both of these authors an imperative that the naïve reporter of the ills of contemporary Egyptian and Iranian societies be a son of these societies, yet alien enough to retain a critical view on their surroundings. Through travel writing, in both its factual and fictive forms, emerges a new form of literary imagination carved from new social contexts. Muwaylihi and Maraghihi create a new measure for this mode of literary production, arriving at it through very different paths—one through the autonomous institutions of print media in Egypt and Europe, the other through the value of literary practise for the exilic Iranian merchant class—to set a framework for the emerging autonomous field of literary production.

5

ON NOTHING AND EVERYTHING

Travel, conversion, and the transformations of (Ahmad) Faris al-Shidyaq, Arab observer of Europe

In its entirety, chapter six of the second book of Faris al-Shidyaq's *al-Saq 'ala al-Saq fi ma hua al-Faryaq* (1855) reads:[1]

> On Nothing:
>
> I was thinking that if I abandoned Faryaq here and placed a point of respite within this description of Egypt, then it would be as this—indeed here it is. I must now rest for a while in the shadow of this brief chapter so as to shake off the dust of tedium, then to begin again—if God on high is willing.
>
> (al-Shidyaq, *al-Saq 'ala al-saq*, p. 246)

A brief two sentences in length, this chapter conveys the ironic tenor characteristic of Shidyaq's prose in this work, as well as evincing the self-reflexive dimension of the text as a whole. Despite its brevity, this selection expresses a great deal about both the book and its author. The title "On Nothing" (*Fi La Shay'*) introduces this chapter using a convention followed throughout the book, that of titling each chapter as an exposition upon a discrete subject (e.g. "On Describing Egypt," the preceding chapter). However, this title negates this convention, by describing its subject to be about nothing. The chapter contains a reference to the book's protagonist, "Faryaq," a shadow or an altered reflection of Shidyaq himself (the name quite clearly being a combination of Faris and Shidyaq). Furthermore, the selection is ostensibly related to travel writing (with the reference to the text's "description" of Egypt). While here the text employs the third-person to discuss its protagonist, it is also common for the author, Shidyaq, to address Faryaq in the second person. At times the two even carry out dialogues.

The previous discussions of "conventional" travel accounts such as those of al-Tahtawi, Flaubert or Hajj Sayyah, or the fictive travel frameworks for works by Marghihi and Muwyalihi show that the travel text set a fertile ground for the re-estimation of how the authorial or narrator's self could be represented in a literary framework. Here, in this passage quoted from Shidyaq, we find a new set of possibilities being opened—possibilities I intend to examine in greater detail over the course of this chapter. Shidyaq presents a quite radical departure from the modes of subjective exploration I have presented so far—instead of presenting a narrative that articulates the emergence of the subject (as narrator or author) into society, Shidyaq's text sets about examining the many ways the self cannot be accommodated by social frameworks the world around. By fragmenting the subjectivity of the author (or his shadow Faryaq) Shidyaq exposes the limits that exist in either narrating the self through representing a social framework, as well as the limits of literary representation to actually render the complexity of the modern self.

In the short chapter of *al-Saq* translated above, Shidyaq admits to a touch of weariness, as a result of the work of writing. He goes so far as to suggest "abandoning" his protagonist briefly in the hope of rejuvenating himself. But why does he write it out? This entry records what is most often effaced in a text, the temporal dimension of the work of writing, the space between sensation and its signification. Certainly, writing takes time; writing wears the author down. But to comment upon it, or to make it a subject of one's writing, is to raise the veil on the process, denuding it of its magical claim. We are here brought into an intimate and self-referential moment concerning the process of writing, captured in Shidyaq's declaration of the need "to shake off the dust of tedium." In this manner he loosens a possible claim to his authorial power, as he says in the first sentence, "then it would be as this; indeed here it is." This statement suggests he needs to write out a time and space of respite so as to recover from the wearying work of writing. At this point, as elsewhere in the text, Shidyaq intimates that it is the text that leads him in its writing. Through his writing, he redefines the structural and rhetorical outlines of the literary conventions available to him.

This brief but telling chapter from *al-Saq* is a small window on the work as a whole; a work that is the major achievement of a nineteenth-century Arabic literary figure instrumental in producing texts of a literary modernity framed by transactions between social, cultural and religious registers, as well as across linguistic boundaries. *Al-Saq* is, to say the least, an enigmatic work. Rather than following Lukács' formulation of the modern novel as directing the narrative toward a particular reconfiguration of a singular subjectivity, Shidyaq's text episodically and elliptically touches on a variety of perspectives on subjective transformations, with no holistic self emerging through the text. In considering the distinct literary imagination that produced this work, certain other paradoxes present themselves, with few inclinations toward resolution—in fact, it is very much these irresolute points that allow for the opening of a vista upon the textual and narrative innovation in his work.

Through its attention to classical forms and rhetoric, *al-Saq* embodies a consciousness of the coherence of the heritage of the Arabic literary humanities. Yet, through its undoing of the forms and conventions of the classical genres, and through the self-reflective and auto-critical mode of its autobiographical and travelogue-driven narratives, the book must be understood as fundamentally contending with questions about Lukács' "process of becoming." I have earlier discussed the transactional nature of translations such as *Alf layla wa layla*, which served as potent indicators of the new value for literature. I have also examined nineteenth-century factual and fictive travelogues with an eye toward understanding how they worked to innovate and transform literary practice through the cooptation of textual materials, the deployment of literary strategies such as subjective narrative development, as well as through contributing to the emergence of a new social value for authorship for such works. However, with Shidyaq's *al-Saq*, all of these issues, and many other ones, resonate within a single text. It may be natural that *al-Saq* has defied simple appropriation into any literary canon, or any simple genealogy of modern literature. While a continuing subject of interest among scholars for relatively minute issues such as the presence of several neo-*maqama* narratives within the book, few English-language scholars have explored the full depth of Shidyaq's literary imagination. Thus, Shidyaq's most formidable work is best viewed as being among the most complex of transactionary texts.

Al-Saq poses as biography or autobiography, but also follows many of the formal considerations of a travelogue—the coincidence of the two is not surprising given the unsettled and rootless life of Shidyaq in the period after leaving the Mount Lebanon region, through his travels in the region and in Europe, up to his eventual settling in the Ottoman capital. Mixing the genres of autobiography and travelogue with digressions into satire and reportage, composed in both prose and poetry, the text meanders around unanswered questions exploring the limits of narratives of subjective transformations, yet also fundamentally undermines the aim of creating a stable subjectivity as the resolution of such narratives. Thus the work is too idiosyncratic to be characterized by genre categorizations—many digressions and divergences serve to undo the coherence of considering the text as fitting any of the major literary forms encountered before (or indeed, since). Poems, linguistic discussions, wordplay such as lists of synonyms, and unrelated or incomplete narratives intervene on the chronology that otherwise serves as a framework for the text. Yet, the work as a whole does qualify as a narrative, with the character of Faryaq fulfilling a protagonist's role through the description of his life over a span of many years, from his childhood until his adulthood. For the most part, the digressions from the strictly narrative portions of the text are meant to serve an ancillary role in illuminating an aspect of the protagonist's story.

Perhaps because the characterization and categorization of *al-Saq* has preoccupied much of the scholarship concerning it, few scholarly works have endeavored to move much beyond the qualification of the text within pre-existing genres. The text has been termed, in turns, an autobiography, a travelogue, or an early novel.[2] The extent to which the autobiographical dimension of the text is accepted as legitimate is testified to by the number of scholars who have cited *al-Saq* as a reference for biographical details about Shidyaq.[3] Indeed it is quite surprising how comfortably the "historical" or factual potential of the text has been accepted, although it is widely acknowledged that a great deal of the text is deliberately fictional as well. Caught between the aforementioned categories, few have commented on the explanation supplied by Shidyaq himself in the introduction to his book, that the text simply is a series of reflections on two issues: illustrating the "strange and lesser-employed aspects of (the Arabic) language," and "describing the benefits and blameworthiness of women" (al-Shidyaq, *al-Saq 'ala al-saq*, pp. 65–7). Neither seems to fit the genre descriptions listed above—one makes the book out to be a grammatical treatise (a genre to which Shidyaq did contribute with his exploration of Arabic lexicography in *al-Jasus 'ala al-Qamus*) while the other may indicate a peculiar hybrid of gendered social commentary and the classical tradition of classificatory texts found within the Arabic humanistic traditions. But if we were to consider these claims as serious, we may have to construct an understanding of the narrative aspirations of the text in a manner that will eventually take us away from the question of form and genre.

In his introduction, Shidyaq delves into two subjects—in shorthand we may term them "language" and "women"—with some details concerning each. Over two pages Shidyaq introduces a theory that the recurrence of certain letters in the construction of certain words relates these words to certain categories of meaning; an esoteric theory, to be certain, but of a type not unheard of in the framework of classical Arabic linguistic discourse (ibid., p. 65). For example, he observes that words such as *al-ta'kid, al-ta'yid, al-jal'ad, al-jalmad, al-jamid, al-hadid, al-sahdad, al-sakhdud* and a list of 15 other words all end in the letter "dal" and all relate to concepts of power or intensity (ibid., p. 66). He then presents other sets of words relating to different letters and proposes other areas of meaning they may relate to.

Later and more briefly, Shidyaq suggests that the second goal of his text is to "note the good of women as well as the bad, and of the good is the progress of women in knowledge as a consequence of the changing of their conditions, as is apparent from what occurred with Faryaqiyya" (ibid., 66). The latter is the name of a female character in *al-Saq*, presumably the wife of Faryaq, of whom we hear that

> she used to be unable to differentiate between one who is beardless and one who is shorn of beard, or between salty sea water and fresh river water. She slowly gained knowledge so that she began arguing with intellectuals and the informed, and began to criticize political matters and social and material conditions in various countries, and on these subjects she offered excellent critiques.
>
> (Ibid., p. 67)

Those scholars who have read *al-Saq* as an autobiography tend to assume that Faryaqiyya is simply a name for the character of Shidyaq's first wife. Yet, while the noun is feminine, it is not simply a feminization of his name (which would be Faryaqah). Faryaqiyya should more correctly be translated as "Faryaq-ness," although as a grammatical formation it is feminine. Within the text, it is not always clear that it refers to his *wife* (although at times it clearly does). While certain correspondences do validate this claim, the role of Faryaqiyya within *al-Saq* is rather complex, and cannot be summarized simply as signifying a historical character; indeed at times she seems to displace Faryaq as the subject of the narrative, while at other times the two lose distinction in their dialogues on various subjects.

As puzzling as Shidyaq's foregrounding of the theme of women is the fact that the text of *al-Saq* also contains no actual return to his proposed linguistic theory—although linguistic issues are certainly at the centre of much of what is to follow. Thus generally speaking, the introduction to *al-Saq* deliberately mischaracterizes the contents of the text as a whole. However, the introduction does set the parameters for other, less transparent areas of inquiry. Through his discussion of both language and women, Shidyaq raises themes relating to the seeking of new forms of knowledge, and new forms of social organization, and relates these both to a concept of subjective transformation. In addition the introduction sets the tone for a blurring of lines between the author and his protagonist, as well as between the protagonist and his feminized companion, or alter ego,—for the confusion between them exists from the outset. For example, she suffers criticism more often leveled at Shidyaq himself for his reliance on (and delight in) the use of arcane linguistic formulations and obsolete phrases and terms. "For it was said that she conveyed strange utterances (*alfaz ghariba*) obscure, non-existent in speech, or in writing, which are impossible to be so articulated. And I responded that a transcription does not here need to be literal to convey the figurative meaning" (ibid., p. 67). Even the relation between the accusation about Faryaqiyya's arguments ("her strange utterances") and the defense ("I responded") seems to lessen the subjective distance between the author and his female character. Furthermore, here the theme of "women" also seems about to collapse into the initial topic, that of "language."

The introduction sets out a framework for a narrative concerning Faryaqiyya's transformation through her gaining of knowledge. However, with Faryaq, there is no corollary thread of personal development. Instead, the text outlines the question of Faryaq's irresolvable quest as a search for subjectivity through language and through dialogues with his feminine interlocutor. In the narrative episodes that make up much of the text, Faryaq does not follow a trajectory toward achieving a specific subjective position, nor does he transform himself within a particular subjective mould, but rather he struggles through different social contexts and settings rootlessly, reacting and commenting on these experiences, without developing them into a coherent or idealized image of himself.

Early in the book, Shidyaq goes on to clarify the distinction he wishes to make between his subject "women" and those classical literary texts that exist under the heading "Descriptions of Women" (*wasf al-nisa'*). He satirically compiles a list summarizing the kinds of categorizations such texts may be expected to contain, including:

> The ornament of existence. And the delight of the world and its splendor. And the beatitude of this life and fate. And the comfort of the soul. And the blood of the heart. And a refreshment for the eye. And the reviving of sentiment. And the soul of the soul. And the clearness of thought. And the stimulator of intelligence. And the object of desire. And the garden of emotions. And the kindness of nature. And the purification of blood. And the pleasure of the senses....[4]
>
> (al-Shidyaq, *al-Saq 'ala al-saq*, p. 81)

By listing at length these literary clichés concerning women, Shidyaq undoes the naturalized application of terms such as these through a conscious mastery of the linguistic constitution of such ideas, and clears the page for a different literary role for representations of women. He critiques the classical tendency toward embellishment and generalization, in particular as gender roles are conceived. He marks the distance between these supposedly immutable, trans-historical literary tropes associated with women—whether as social actors, or as romantic objects—and his own narrative of the transformation of Faryaqiyya and her gaining of knowledge, through the particular narrative exigencies of the text.

Still, it would be wrong to limit our reading of *al-Saq* to either an analysis of Faryaqiyya as a character, or to dwell too long on either the representational question of how Shidyaq chooses to address issues of gender, despite the relatively egalitarian position taken by him on the subject of social reforms and women's roles in society. Of the scholars of Shidyaq, al-Azmeh and Trablusi are perhaps the most attentive to the social implications of his views on the social roles of women in his writing, including *al-Saq*. They argue that in this text, the dialogues between Faryaq and Faryaqiyya—what they term his frank attention to women's desires, and his defense of women's rights in their intimate relations with men—are the centerpieces of his radical views on the social roles of women. Where figures in the Arab *nahda* such as Qasim Amin, Rifa'a Rafi' al-Tahtawi, and Butrus Bustani are credited with having called for women to be endowed with greater social responsibilities, Shidyaq asserted a need for the absolute equality of women in education as well as work. But going even further, Shidyaq was alone in utilizing the term "sexual repression" to critique the staid perspective these "reformers" held on the issue of women's sexuality, and called for the right to equal regard in matters relating to sexuality and desire. Thus al-Azmeh and Trablusi argue that he sees "respect for a woman's pleasure as the apex of respect for her" (Shidyaq, *Silsila al-a'mal al-majhula*, p. 34).

Beyond displaying a commitment to a reconsideration of gender roles and responsibilities, Shidyaq employs an obsessive concern with "women" as an axis from which to engage reflections upon Faryaq's own character. While Faryaqiyya is the subject of a great deal of his description, so too do the women in the various social settings he travels to serve as points of departure for the descriptions of his travels. However, in distinction with the voyeuristic treatment of women in European men's travel writing, the discussions of women in *al-Saq* tend to be openings by which Faryaq's character is subject to examination. This is somewhat similar to predominant trends in the travel genre in the same period in Europe, which was dominated by masculine tropes and perspectives, thus playing an explicit role within the more generalized idealization of masculinity as constructed by the colonial literary imagination.

> [In travel writing] masculinity is thus neither endorsed nor enhanced by the role of traveler, which displays a comparative sexlessness, certainly a lack of affectivity in personal relations. This absence of interiority allows the persona to embody European culture and its attendant urge to appropriate and erase, or, less dramatically, to categorize and comprehend; the evacuation of individuality enacts submission to the imperial mission. Again, the cost exacted is far more striking than any apparent rewards; the primary object of aggression is the self.
>
> (Clark, *Travel Writing and Empire*, p. 21)

This observation may be less universally applicable than its author intimates, passing over, as it does, the self-conscious application of sexual experiences as metaphors for travel within post-romantic travelogues. However, this statement does capture one affect of the "reportage" travelogue genre. From the European perspective, travel writing was often considered one of the duties of the colonial subject; the writing of the travel experience was a conscious self-interpellation of the productivity and scientific empiricism that the colonial project claimed for itself. Desire and sexuality have little of clear value to contribute to the colonial endeavor—thus these elements of the colonial dynamic are sublimated more often in travel writing than in other forms or genres. It is only within the anti-bourgeois gestures of post-romantic travelogues that we discover the sexual metaphor is unhinged—Flaubert's retreat from the bourgeois restrictions of Europe into a pacified yet sensuous orient is no better understood than when Kuchak Hanem envelops her body around him (Flaubert, *Flaubert in Egypt*, pp. 113–19).[5]

In this context, Shidyaq's obsession with sexual allusions and metaphors, and with the qualities of women in various societies, betrays something of the anxieties of the colonized male subject within the colonial metropole. His displacement of this anxiety into satire, and into a self-conscious performance of a mastery of Arabic, is one way he seeks to reconstitute a masculine subjectivity within the colonial encounter—language is one domain where his efforts are not to be challenged either by the cruelty of the church clergy of his childhood, nor by the arrogance of the missionaries who subjugated him during much of his life in Malta, Egypt, and in Europe. Thus the initiating concerns for his text: language, and women. The first is the domain where Shidyaq's mastery over rivals—Europeans as well as Arabs—is not to be doubted, the second is the site of a specific anxiety for the colonized male subject, one which is controlled through his recourse back to language.

Shidyaq uses innovating devices not only within the text of *al-Saq*—including self-reflexivity, a blurring of subjectivity between characters as well as the author, socially radical considerations of gender and religion—but also brings this innovating vision into the material elements of his production of the book. *Al-Saq* is a text *conceived of* as a printed book, and is organized with a clear conception of its form as the production of a printing press. Using this form, it assumes an artifice of balance, using chapters, pages, and typefaces to do so. Encompassing four books, each twenty chapters in length, with appendices and introductory materials balancing the text, this formal artifice takes on an exaggerated role within the text itself. For example, Chapter 19 of Book 2—that is, nearly the "middle chapter" of the work—is titled "On the Circle of this Universe, and the Center of this Book." While the title has nothing in particular to do with the content of the chapter (which continues a narrative episode concerning Faryaq's illness in Egypt and his relationship with his physician's family), it ironically creates a parallel between the book and the universe (*al-kawn*, also "existence"). The title calls attention to the conceit of the text to represent, or even to become, the known universe. By continuing in his discussion on an unrelated narrative, Shidyaq creates a gap between the titular imperative—captured well in the construction of each title as "On…" (*Fi*…) and its claim to an exposition of the subject that follows, and the narrative, which has nothing at all to do with the title. In another example of a similar auto-critical reference, Chapter 15 of Book 2 consists entirely of only three lines of ellipses spaced widely apart, which end with the words "…on that matter" (al-Shidyaq, *al-Saq ʻala al-saq*, p. 322).

These disjunctions occur throughout the text, at each turn refusing to allow the reader to lose a sense of the artifice of the work, indeed perhaps of the artifice of texts in general. Chapter 16 of Book 3 similarly creates a disjuncture within the narrative, although in this case it follows from the narrative itself. The chapter preceding this relates Faryaq's experience travels from Syria to Egypt—returning from his travels he arrives in Alexandria. There, he contacts Faryaqiyya to join him in quarantine—typically, she initially responds contrarily by saying "I neither enjoy isolation, nor idleness," but eventually goes to meet him. Faryaq then "rested from the pains of travel, and breathed in the odour of a woman…" (ibid., p. 491). The chapter ends, and Chapter 16 follows on the next page, a brief few sentences in its entirety:

On the intoxicating fragrance

> It is the fragrance of the mother, pungent. All that crawls and flies, matures in it, as well as that which follows a path in the seas. And its quality is expressed in the title [of this chapter]. Have you [o reader] committed this to heart?
>
> (Ibid., p. 492)

The sensual implications of their reunion are thus highlighted by a focus—delegated to an entire "chapter"—on one element, pushing to excess the experience of this reconciliation for Faryaq. Shidyaq brings exceptional focus to a rather minor and fleeting element within the larger narrative, disrupting its otherwise restrained tone with a short and somewhat jarring exposition of the sensuality of this single moment. He intensifies this by also addressing the reader directly, either feigning instruction or edict—the final sentence even has something of a religious tone of compulsion achieved through its construction as a rhetorical question. Again, in the organization of the text, Shidyaq brings his experience in typography and publishing to bear, by presenting this and the other faux-chapters separately, starkly drawing distinctions in layout between each of them and the other chapters.[6]

Through circumstances alone, Shidyaq lived through a period witnessing the transformation of Arabic textual production, from scribal technologies to those of the printing press. These transformations, and their effects upon the imagination of Shidyaq, play a large role in the conception and formulation of *al-Saq*. In this, while the text is self-consciously about language and its intricacies, about travel, and about the subjectivity of its protagonist Faryaq, it is also more fundamentally about the textuality, about writing, about the creation of a book. Shidyaq consciously links these material activities to the imaginative process of engaging a text. At times this process is treated reverentially, at other times it is laid open for a critical view. In both impulses, Shidyaq attempts to create a text that brings about a creative bridging of the obsessive and meticulous approach of the scribal reader or writer with the possibilities and challenges offered by the new technology of printed texts. From these formal questions, which guide the reader to the physicality of the book, to the constant dialogue that occurs between author and character, author and reader, and between characters, *al-Saq* achieves its singularity through its deliberate destabilization of the subjectivity of all involved: reader, author, and character.

Shidyaq's biography, that which is known of it, often figures importantly within discussions of this work, and also relates to *al-Saq* given the presumed inclusion of autobiographical elements in this work.[7] Shidyaq was a prolific writer, editor, and publisher—in addition to *al-Saq*, he was the author of two travelogues, composed several influential texts on Arabic linguistics and grammar, produced a number of translations, and was the editor of the influential newspaper *al-Jawa'ib* (and its related publishing company, al-Jawa'ib Press).[8] Yet in comparison to many of his contemporaries, Shidyaq has perhaps been the subject of greater controversy concerning his significance as a literary and cultural figure. This, in some part, may be due to the fact that to speak of Shidyaq is to find limits to the conventional idioms signifying identity; religious, national, or otherwise. It is unfortunate that discussions of his life and work have often been based on less than justifiable attempts to resolve Shidyaq's paradoxical identities.

A Muslim Christian. A sedentary traveler. An ascetic sensualist. A modernist classicist. A literary gutter-mouth. A pious unbeliever... these and other paradoxes in what Shidyaq *was* seem to affect his social reception to this day, when a public memory of Shidyaq—who is widely known among Arab historians and literary enthusiasts, but may hardly be considered famous—is subject to debate and dispute given the complexities of his biography and literary work.[9] Faris Yusif Shidyaq was born in the village of ʻAshqut in the Mount Lebanon region, in 1804.[10] Of moderate means, the family was provided for by his father's work as a scribe. As Maronite Catholics, and thus part of the largest of the diverse religious communities of the Mount Lebanon region at the time, the family was well known for providing local clerics and political leaders with several generations of highly regarded scribes and clerks. Even in his youth, Faris distinguished himself by composing praise poems for his father's patrons—a talent that was to come to be of some use to him in later years, as we will see.

Yet despite their respectable position in the community, the Shidyaq family came to be accused of entertaining traitorous inclinations, during a period when communal tensions in the Mount Lebanon region manifested in sporadic violence between the Maronite Christians and neighboring Druze.[11] During one episode of this conflict, as a result of making common cause with the local Druze community, Shidyaq's father was compelled to flee the region, and his home was destroyed. He died shortly afterwards in exile in Damascus. While this deeply affected the family's fortunes, and made a critical impression on Faris (who was still a child at the time) the death of his brother Asʻad some years later would leave an even greater imprint upon him. Asʻad was imprisoned within the Maronite patriarch's compound as a result of embracing Protestantism after working with British and American missionaries in the region. He died an untimely death in a dungeon on the patriarch's property—missionaries publicly made accusations of his having been tortured and abused, and termed him a martyr in their publications.[12] During his brother's imprisonment, Faris fled to Beirut, and then escaped to Malta under the protection of the evangelical missionaries who had earlier motivated his brother's conversion.[13]

While the exact circumstances of his departure from Beirut are unclear, Faris possibly also confessed to Protestantism in 1825 (Karam, *Encyclopedia of Islam*). However, it seems that where Asʻad was moved by sincere religious convictions, Faris—if he did convert at all—more likely was motivated by his disdain for the traditional Maronite religious authority. Over the course of his life, this critical position was reapplied to other forms of authority and orthodoxy. Where Asʻad left letters and documents, which also are confirmed by personal testimonies, indicating the depth of his convictions in embracing evangelical Protestantism, Faris was to produce satirical manifestoes undermining the sacred claims of clerics in general.[14] He then settled in Egypt for nine years (1825–1834), where he was employed tutoring missionaries in Arabic. At the same time, Faris gained exposure to the new field of journalism and newspaper publishing (ibid.). In Cairo, Shidyaq also had occasion to pursue studies of rhetoric, grammar and other literary arts with educators affiliated with al-Azhar University. During his period in Egypt, "he also spent some time studying, and copying, Arabic literature with Muslim scholars in Cairo . . . Faris himself was a scribe and calligrapher, and copied for his own use many of the texts which he owned" (Roper, "Ahmad

Faris al-Shidyaq," pp. 233–4). Having married a Syrian Christian woman in this period, Faris became a father with the birth of his first son, Salim. He then moved to Malta to work for the Protestant Evangelical Mission as a teacher, writer, and editor.

Solicited by English evangelicals to assist in a full translation of the Bible into Arabic, Shidyaq later visited Britain, eventually settling with his family in a village near Oxford for much of the duration of the project. Yet, Shidyaq's temperament apparently did not fully compliment those of his patrons, and he found himself frustrated and often at odds with them in the work of the translation over "their excursions into etymology to decide the precise meaning of a word and their suspicion of stylistic flourishes suggestive of the Qur'an" (Cachia, "Translations and Adaptations," p. 31).

His application for a position in Arabic at Oxford resulted in rejection, and so a disillusioned Shidyaq made his way to Paris to pursue other work. Al-Azmeh and Trablusi argue that his stay in France during the culturally and politically tumultuous 1840s "liberated" him, not only from his reliance on the evangelicals who had long been his primary patrons, but also from the internalized limitations of one so enveloped by the legacy of Arabic classical literature.[15] Certainly, living in France during the events of 1848 must have had a significant impact on an observer as sensitive as he. It was in Paris, in 1855, that Shidyaq completed and published *Al-saq 'ala al-saq*.[16] During this period a praise poem composed to commemorate the visit of the Tunisian Ahmad Bey to Paris resulted in an invitation for Shidyaq to visit and work in Tunis. An earlier elegy to Queen Victoria, perhaps coinciding with his search for an appointment in England, had elicited no response from Her Majesty (Stetkevytch, "Some Observations on Arabic Poetry," p. 10).[17]

It was in Tunis in 1857 where his conversion to Islam is recorded, and where Faris al-Shidyaq became known as Ahmad Faris (al-Shidyaq, *Silsila al-a'mal al-majhula*, p. 21). By now, Shidyaq had publicly broken not only with the Maronite clerical hierarchy—which, as mentioned, are subject to vicious and often hilarious attacks in *al-Saq*—but also with the Protestant missionaries and evangelicals, his former patrons, who fare little better in the same text. Indeed, one may say that his rejection of both confessional approaches is a recurring theme in *al-Saq*, and that certain elements in the text may also anticipate his later conversion to Islam. Within a short period after his conversion, he was invited by the Sublime Porte to Istanbul, where he was given the charge of initiating an Arabic newspaper, the first to be based in the Ottoman capital. Thus began the run of *al-Jawa'ib* newspaper (1861–1884) and al-Jawa'ib Press. *Al-Jawa'ib* gained prominence as one of the most influential Arabic newspapers of its time. Encountering readers of *al-Jawa'ib* in his travels in India, Charles Doughty reported that the "news-sheet is current in all countries of the Arabic speech; I have found it in the Nejd merchants' houses at Bombay," and further attributes the "erudition of these Arabian politicians" to the newspaper, which he terms an "excellent Arabic gazette" (quoted in Hourani, *Arabic Thought in the Liberal Age*, p. 99).

While gaining repute as an advocate of pan-Islamism, Shidyaq's writing in this period is noted for his attention to social issues and institutions, and for his participation in debates on Arabic linguistics with other luminaries of the Arabic *nahda* movement. For occasionally asserting too much his independence from the Ottoman court, Shidyaq suffered periodical interference from authorities. These problems increased in particular after the suspension of the liberal Ottoman Press Law shortly after the accession of Sultan 'Abd al-Hamid and the onset of the Russian-Ottoman wars (Cioeta, "Ottoman Censorship," pp. 170–1). His son, Salim, had assumed many of the managing duties of the press in the final years of Ahmad Faris' life, and *al-Jawa'ib* newspaper was eventually ordered closed by the Ottoman authorities in 1884. Shidyaq spent the remainder of his life in Istanbul, active in publishing books (including reprintings of *al-Saq*) through his press, and occasionally traveling to neighboring Arab regions, including a visit made to Egypt in 1886 only months before his death. Ahmad Faris Yusif Shidyaq died in 1887, and was buried in the Mount Lebanon region, his birth-place: he had fled it as a young man, only to return in his death.

The purpose of the preceding biographical sketch—offered at some length, yet hardly comprehensive—is to foreground the complexity of approaching the question of the social circumstances of the authorship of a text such as *al-Saq*, and the need for an understanding of the material and historical framework surrounding its production. As it contains autobiographical elements, and as it partially fulfils the category of travelogue, a familiarity with the broad outline of Shidyaq's life informs an understanding of the text in important ways.

Prior to composing *al-Saq*, Shidyaq produced two travelogues. In these, *al-Wasita fi ma'arif ahwal Malta* (A Description of the Known Conditions of Malta) and *Kashf al-mukhabba fi funun Uruba* (A Discovery of the Hidden in the Arts of Europe), Shidyaq shows a perceptivity to detail, as well as a critical position that make the works exemplary if not especially innovative examples of the reportage style of the nineteenth-century *adab al-rihla* (travelogue) genre. Following the common format of this style, the texts have little authorial evidence other than to note his presence in specific locations and occasional personal details that may be necessary, for example, for describing meetings with specific individuals. In *al-Saq*, despite incorporating elements of travelogue writing, Shidyaq makes a dramatic shift from the style followed in the previous two texts. Indeed, *al-Saq* retells certain events and travels already described in the first two travelogues, and yet does so in an entirely original manner.[18] Thus, in Shidyaq we have the rare example of a *litterateur* who is the author of works both in the traditional, reportage mode of travel writing, and also of fully interiorized, subjective form of writing. Intentionally obscure, Shidyaq's work by no means anticipates a singular readership, which may be why some scholars have somewhat plaintively seen him to have "*almost* achieved greatness" (emphasis added, Haywood, *Modern Arabic Literature*, p. 71).

Yet few scholars—especially outside scholars—have devoted significant attention to Shidyaq; no monographs devoted to his work have been produced to date in English. Although he is often included in general surveys and thematic studies of nineteenth-century Arabic literature, references to Shidyaq tend to be divided into two general areas. The first are references to his experimentation with the *maqama* form. The second are references to Shidyaq's journalistic achievements—an area which has been the focus of attention for modernists, given Shidyaq's regard for and experience with European periodicals before beginning his influential newspaper *al-Jawa'ib*. Yet by focusing solely on these issues, scholars tend to advance the narrow evaluation of Shidyaq common to many literary scholars, be they traditionalist or modernist in disposition. These two modes of scholarship have over-emphasized his small body of work in the *maqama* form, and tend to cite the prestige of his work on *al-Jawa'ib*, with little reference to the innovations involved in his writing for this publication, much less the remainder of his literary output.

For example, even in his references to *al-Saq*, Sabry Hafez only discusses the four excursa/ chapters of *maqama*-style composition, presenting but few general comments on the rest of the text. In this, Hafez's analysis of Shidyaq's standing in modern Arabic literature hardly differs from those of preceding literary historians, who have been drawn to his passing interest in neo-*maqama* style as a kind of missing link between classical writing and modern novelistic prose. In this way, Hafez does afford an approach to thinking about Shidyaq that breaks with the two major approaches that he critiques, while still using him in very much the manner both the traditionalist and modernist schools of criticism have long done. This results in his making only passing references to Shidyaq's work in poetry, travelogue writing and essay writing, and offering little analysis of *al-Saq* as a whole. When endeavoring to show how "narrative discourse" emerged—we may think of this as roughly analogous to the emergence of literary modernity—it is puzzling that a figure such as Shidyaq is neglected, except for those instances where his work has fitted the mould that novelistic or short-story writing has set. At times, there seems to have been confusion over the very essential issues of the text: even Roger Allen performs a kind of metonymy in his discussion on *al-Saq*, terming Shidyaq's satirical character Haris ibn Hitham, who appears only in the four chapters in *maqama* form, the "hero" of the book (Allen, "The Beginnings of the Arabic Novel," p. 181). The limits in this approach leave open the question of in what manner an evaluation of innovative, modernist writing that falls outside of the trajectory of novelism can be effectively made.

Conversion as transactional: religion and Shidyaq and Malkum Khan

In his writing it is evident that Shidyaq inhabited his various religious identities (as either a Maronite or Protestant Christian or as a Muslim) with a particularly critical perspective, explicitly and implicitly addressing matters—such as the authority of religious leaders—rarely directly touched upon publicly. This critical element seems quite closely linked to his public conversions between these creeds and faiths. The question of religious conversion also factors centrally in the identity of a late-nineteenth-century Iranian literary and political figure, Mirza Malkum Khan, an Armenian Iranian and a convert to Islam active in the period's reformist movements. But how did conversion function as an individual or as a social category for these two figures? This question may be examined through a comparison of selected texts written by Shidyaq and Malkum Khan where religious identity plays a central role, as well as by looking at defamatory texts that were written attacking each of them at particular junctures of their lives.

Much of the scholarly work on these two figures has largely viewed their conversions solely as a tactic for social gain. Hamid Algar, for example, identifies Malkum Khan's religious identity as belying a "tactical desirability of the use of Islam for the promotion of westernizing reform" (Algar, *Mirza Malkum Khan*, p. 15). He is even more blunt when he terms Malkum Khan's attitude toward religion as "opportunistic" (ibid., p. 18). Being somewhat more subtle in his report of Ahmad Faris al-Shidyaq's conversion, Albert Hourani writes of the latter's "steadfastness" in religious identity, in accepting the rumors of his having reverted to Maronite Catholicism on his deathbed (Hourani, *Arabic Thought in the Liberal Age*, p. 36). This sentiment implies, again, a solid and immutable element to Shidyaq's religious identity as a Maronite that was not to be affected by surface claims of being Muslim. In the end, the biographical and historical scholarship on these figures has failed to fully address the issue of how the adoption of Muslim identities, or indeed any religious identity, were employed or occupied as generative spaces for these figures and others of their time.

However, within the context of colonialism and the emergence of anti-colonial nationalist discourses, the issue of religious identity played a profoundly ambivalent role for intellectuals in Muslim domains—particularly those of non-Muslim backgrounds. As Gauri Viswanathan has suggested, by conceiving of conversion within relational terms that identify religion with power, we may say "conversion is defined not as a renunciation of an aspect of oneself (as it is in the personal or confessional narrative form), but as an intersubjective, transitional and transactional mode of negotiation between two otherwise irreconcilable world-views." (Viswanathan, *Outside the Fold*, p. 176). Furthermore, the idea of religious conversion was not merely a question of being "opportunistic" nor a matter of the "steadfastness" of innate, immutable, social identities—religious categories were largely more fluid and in many contexts Arab and Iranian individuals of minority backgrounds felt that the reformulation of communal identities was not only an instrument for participation in discourse upon social reform, but also of reconceiving social subjectivities.

Scholarship on Shidyaq often terms his conversion to Islam as yet another turn in an already disjunctive and meandering trajectory of religious identity. Given his earlier associations with Protestant missionaries in Malta and Egypt, and by dint of his work in England translating the Bible into Arabic, Marwan 'Abbud, Luis Shaykhu and Albert Hourani have asserted his association with American and English missionaries as proof of his conversion to Protestantism along the lines of his brother As'ad (Hourani, *Arabic Thought in the Liberal Age*, p. 36). This may be the case, however none of these assertions are made on the basis of testimony of any sort on the part of Shidyaq himself, but more likely result from a logical presumption that his escape from Lebanon and his long association with missionary institutions evince his own religious conversion. Missionary reports reproduced in Butrus al-Bustani's recounting of As'ad's "martyrdom" paint a vivid portrait of an independent-minded and rebellious Faris, struggling to read the gospels (which had been supplied by the missionaries in translation) under angry threats by his brothers (al-Bustani, *Qissa As'ad al-Shidyaq*, p. 56). Yet even these reports do not make the claim that Faris followed his brother in converting. This is quite significant as As'ad was the first Maronite Catholic to convert, and news of his conversion spread quickly through evangelical publications in England and the United States—had his brother Faris also joined the faith, it seems likely that it would have been similarly announced as well. As'ad, in the period before he was to be incarcerated in the patriarch's compound, sought public venues for describing his conversion, and wrote a public letter to the patriarch, challenging him on several points of Maronite liturgy and practice. Faris often attacked the patriarch and other Maronite figures, but never in the context of a defense of protestant tenants.

While it is possible that Faris al-Shidyaq may have privately converted while among the missionaries it is nonetheless clear that over the course of his work with them he increasingly adopted a skeptical position toward religious institutions in general, including those of the missionaries. His studies of rhetoric and grammar in the premier institution of Islamic religious education, al-Azhar university in Cairo, also certainly exposed him to Islamic jurisprudential and theological traditions in a way that he most likely would never have had an opportunity to, in his family's traditional community in the Mount Lebanon region.

In a satirical poem on Paris, placed within a group of poems that are included in *al-Saq*, Shidyaq engages in rather impressive display of *balagha* (rhetoric). Dividing the page in half, he presents two poems simultaneously—the first in praise (*fi madh*) of Paris and the second critiquing it (*fi dhanb*) (al-Shidyaq, *al-Saq 'ala al-saq*, p. 655). The poem, in keeping with the framework of classical *balagha*, has little to do with the actuality of Paris—but rather describes the city through tropes relating to either heaven or hell. The achievement of *balagha* is measured by the skilful way in which Shidyaq matches rhyme and even entire couplets across the two variations of the poem, while expressing opposing ideas about the heavenly or hell-like aspects of the city and its inhabitants.

What is striking is that the terms for heaven and hell described in the poem are derived almost entirely from Qur'anic sources. Although the poem is dated 1270 (AH) (1854 or so), meaning some three years before his conversion to Islam, it shows that Shidyaq's thinking was directed within or toward an Islamic context or aspect, and utilized themes and tropes that derive from that context for the expression of his ideas. Perhaps we can better understand his use of Qur'anic sources if we see his engagement with a literary modernity as one that related closely to a reinvigoration of classical themes and concepts. The use of Islamic motifs in classical literature undoubtedly enriched the literary vocabulary of Arab Christian *litterateurs* such as Shidyaq, Jurji Zaydan or Butrus al-Bustani, and set the landmarks of the literary domains they inhabited. Yet in this, an entirely *balagha*-oriented "critique" of Paris—a critique which only deploys literary and religious concepts in a non-material "description" of Paris—the use of classical Islamic terms and motifs serves to both alienate the real Paris from the Arabic reader's imagination while rendering it intelligible through the use of familiar literary terms. This use of Islamic themes as a valuative field by which to render a representation of Paris, allows a *litterateur* of the Islamic world to juxtapose himself against the presumed "Christian" essence of Paris, while using heavenly images to also identify with it. The poem itself, as a split and self-contradicting literary act, foreshadows Shidyaq's later ambivalent inhabitation of a Muslim identity. The framework is Islamic, yet the poem's references to the European metropole are simultaneously double-edged—the bad is represented through the worst of the Islamic imagination, while the best occupies a vaulted seat imagined through Qur'anic tropes.

While *al-Saq* makes religion an explicit object of critique in its constant satirical excursuses on the clergy of the Maronite church as well as the Protestant missionaries of Shidyaq's early adulthood, there are few specific references to Islamic clergy, institutions or rituals. Traditionally, texts written by Muslim authors begin with an introductory series of dedications, including passages that may acknowledge the authority of God before the author, or acknowledge the inspiration of the example of the Prophet Muhammad in their work, etc. This formality may be as brief as a sentence or two, or developed across several pages. Often dedications to contemporary patrons follow these statements.

Al-Saq's concluding page is in some sense just such an "introduction." Satirically, however, rather than beginning the text it appears at the end. The irony of this is emphasized through the use of the phrase "Bi-ism Allah al-Rahman al-Rahim" the conventional Islamic phrase of introduction of a text (and the first phrase of the Quran). To "end" a text with this phrase would certainly displease a pious believer beholden to the legitimacy of the invocation. The following text is written in Egyptian colloquial dialect (unlike the entirety of the book preceding it, which is written in a high classical literary Arabic), and begins with a dedication to the text's motley crew of ostensible patrons: Shaykh Muhammad, Matran Butrus, Abuna Hanna, Abuna Minqiryus, Sir Abraham, Mister Neckton, Herr Schmidt, Signor Juzbi Hadini.

> I made this book, meaning I wrote it—[but] didn't print it, didn't bind it—and put it between your hands, I know well that my lord Shaykh Muhammad would laugh at it if he would read it. Because he knows that he himself would be able to do better than it, but he thinks that it is something empty [of value] [. . .] However, our lord and our father and our sir will not and even cannot understand it because of this, I request

> of them that they, before they light up the fire so as to burn it, ask about what is good in it, and about what is not good, and should the good be more weighty, release it to me, or burn it with its cover. And if they find in it some error, it would not be just for them to burn it, for each one of us has many errors, and God on high does not burn us in the hellfire [solely] for this reason [.] Oh Father Hanna, I swear to you that I don't hate you, however I hate your arrogance and ignorance, for when I greet you, you offer up your hand for me to kiss, how can I kiss it when you are ignorant, and in your life you did not either produce a single book nor even a simple spiritual poem? [. . .] My Sayyid, Shaykh Muhammad, I know that books on jurisprudence and grammar are more sublime than my book here, because readers, knit their brows and scowl when they read one of those books, if only in order to try to understand its meaning, and as you know, veneration and glory is not achieved but through a knitting of the brows. Yet books of jurisprudence do not claim that laughing is forbidden or hateful, and you—praise God!—are reasonable and intelligent [. . .] And you have read more in books in the humanities than our lord Bishop Butrus has eaten roasted chicken, and in each study of humanistic discourse (*al-adab*) you will find a special section dedicated to humor and cleverness, for if cleverness was against humanistic discourse, it would not be included in them [. . .] And by the grace of God we are at peace, but as for Monsieur and Mister and Herr and Signore, they are not obligated to print my book because my words are not for the sheep and the donkey and the lion and the tiger, but rather are for humans, the descendents of Adam. And this is all. And God alone knows the true reason for your anger with me. End the book.
>
> (al-Shidyaq, *al-Saq ʻala al-saq*, p. 709)

This satirical diatribe, addressed to patrons of various identities (Muslim, Maronite, Protestant, Arab, British, German, etc.) is an apologia for his work. Anticipating criticism by each, Shidyaq sets out to pre-empt the terms of their presumptive dismissal of his work. He begins with a statement claiming authorship, but foregrounds the particular aspect of its production that is his own labor, *writing* it, not "print[ing] it" or "bind[ing] it." This act—of writing—is what defines the book's creation, and his authorial role in its production.

The most vehement passages seem directed at a certain "Father Hanna," likely an Arab Christian priest, who he derides for "arrogance and ignorance." Yet Shidyaq marvels at the possibility of Father Hanna demanding a position of respect or authority because he "did not either produce a single book nor a spiritual poem." This follows on a common theme throughout *al-Saq* concerning the illiteracy of priests, their lack of knowledge of literature or indeed proper use of Arabic grammar.[19] This is, perhaps, a less than conventional manner by which to satirize a social class whose legitimacy hardly derives from the ability to compose poetry, or to write books. Indeed, Bishop Butrus fares even worse, where his consumption of roasted chicken allows a point of comparison for Shidyaq's command of the works of the Arabic literary humanities. While the jurisprudent Shaykh Muhammad escapes such infamy, clearly Shidyaq anticipates his displeasure of *al-Saq* for its satirical tone, and its reveling in the material world. And yet Shidyaq does not simply dismiss this interlocutor, and instead extols him to not allow his apparent austerity (manifested in the furrowed brows he has developed) to distract him from the value of texts of humor and satire. Shidyaq argues that pleasurable texts are not subject to prohibition by Islamic law or literary traditions. One senses a slight anxiety, as if of these various "patrons" he has the highest hopes that Shaykh Muhammad will—if he is able to overcome his predilection for the serious over the satirical—possibly find *al-Saq* a text endowed with some value. And so he admits that the latter is "reasonable and intelligent," even if he is uncertain, even apprehensive, of the response he will receive from him.

The final lines are also telling—here Shidyaq makes a reference to a variety of Europeans, and assumes a pose of abject indifference concerning their reception of his text. Where English and American missionaries had previously acted as his patrons, in a few words he shows that he by now has no further interest in such a relationship—if they cared to print his book, it would be for "the sheep and the donkey and the lion and the tiger," and not for true humans. The animals of his allusion are perhaps a reference to the orientalists, religious scholars, colonial officials and others with whom Shidyaq was compelled to work (and who, outside the small exilic Arab population, were the only possible audience for an Arabic text published in Europe). They are by no means the audience for his book, he intimates, and somehow, somewhere, he hopes "the descendents of Adam" will find and make use of his work. If, in the end, Shidyaq could identify with any of these communities comfortably, it seems it is this abstraction, humanity, he wishes to be his audience.

This appendix to *al-Saq* gives us a complex look into both Shidyaq's sense of himself vis-à-vis the various religious and social forces he found himself caught within, as well as opening a discussion concerning his idealization of an audience for the text. Following on themes developed through the text, he takes one last opportunity to settle his scores with his presumed adversaries—primarily those he fled as a young man, those who he felt were responsible for his brother As'ad's death. Yet, the Americans and Europeans, who earlier in his life had perhaps enjoyed his gratitude for their support, are irrelevant, even antagonistic to him. No longer seeking their approval, Shidyaq dismisses them out of hand, looking for a new community, a new audience. The references to Shaykh Muhammad betray an unresolved sense of desire for his gaining of some legitimacy within the Muslim community. Cautiously, Shidyaq hopes for the approval of Shaykh Muhammad, and anticipates his criticism with references to Islamic jurisprudence as well as classical Islamic *adab* literature. Perhaps all he wanted was a sign indicating the possibility of his acceptance within their ranks. It would seem he found it, in his invitation to visit Ahmad Bey in Tunis in 1857.

As I have already noted, after Shidyaq converted to Islam he found employment in Ottoman Istanbul as the publisher of *al-Jawa'ib*. Eventually, Shidyaq came to establish and oversee al-Jawa'ib Press, which published various books in addition to the newspaper, and had established himself as an articulate advocate for pan-Islamist projects as well as the institution of political and social reforms. In April of 1868, a rather marginal set of articles in *al-Jawa'ib* give evidence of the limits and boundaries Shidyaq faced on the subject of his religious identity. Over the course of two issues, Shidyaq devotes two articles to defiling the publisher and poet Rizqallah Hassun, in response to an offence he has taken from him. Shidyaq is here responding to Hassun's book *al-Nafathat*, which was essentially a translation of a number of Russian folk tales into Arabic.

In the first of these articles, Shidyaq notes that Hassun had composed a vitriolic attack on him in *al-Nafathat*, by satirically applying Shidyaq's name to a pseudo-numerological formula of letters (which he apparently attributes to Shidyaq himself), and deriving from this experiment a statement that Shidyaq is a "Kafir" (unbeliever) guilty of "eating pig and drinking wine" (*al-Jawa'ib*, 1868, p. 3). What is most intriguing about this charge is that Rizqallah was himself an Armenian Christian, and an author of a polemical disputation of Islam (Shaykhu, *Tarikh al-Adab*, p. 176). To better understand this attack, we must know that these two men almost certainly perceived the other as a literary competitor; for example, each claimed to have been the first author of a poem in blank verse in Arabic (Moreh, "Blank Verse in Modern Arabic Literature," p. 482). Both also published influential journals, taking opposing positions on the reformability of the Ottoman empire. In addition, Hassun, who at this time was living in Paris, had emerged as a vocal critic of Ottoman policies after having spent some time in Istanbul. It is to be expected that he felt disappointed by Shidyaq's success in the Ottoman capital—a success which was likely to some extent enabled by the latter's conversion to Islam.

A week later, Shidyaq continues his defense by writing an article titled "A Response to Rizqallah Hassun." Here he engages in a discussion on the category of *kufr* (unbelief), suggesting that an erroneous accusation of *kufr* proves that the accuser is in fact guilty of *kufr* (al-Jawa'ib, "Tabi 'al-Radd," p. 2). He uses the same pseudonumerological formula, concluding that the letters that make up Hassun's name can be used to show that Hassun is the same author of the book *Hasr al-Litham 'an al-Islam* (Lifting the Veil from Islam). This is the title of Hassun's aforementioned polemical text, which Shidyaq terms "the most atrocious defamation" of Islam and the Qur'an. In this response, Shidyaq uncharacteristically sheds his satirical restraint, instead lunching an *ad hominem* attack terming Hassun an anti-Muslim. The excessive tone, for one who was more often known for his creative and subtle powers of satire, gives a sense of the anxiety that Hassun's accusations had given rise to. Clearly, Shidyaq felt compelled to respond forcefully to this attack on his character, and to perhaps forestall further circulation of such rumors about him.

Even before his conversion to Islam, in Shidyaq's literary work, exemplified by the *qasida* on Paris, his identification with an Arabic–Islamic literary heritage that has been unselfconsciously and completely made to be his own is quite evident. This poem, which precedes his actual conversion by several years, also complicates the idea of conversion itself. We may actually say that Shidyaq's *literary* conversion is in a sense documented in this poem (although it may serve as the first sign of such a "conversion") and his public "social" or "religious" conversion was to come later. Yet this open field of inter-religious identification in the literary arena had limits in the social sphere. The debate between Shidyaq and Hassun shows how a notable Christian Arabic-literary figure felt it plausible to attack Shidyaq's credentials as a Muslim in an attempt to undermine his public standing. In return, Shidyaq finds it appropriate to respond by citing Hassun's polemical critique of Islam as a sign of the latter's own questionable position, as a non-Muslim. Both make their critiques through use of the very serious charge of *kufr*, which would place each outside a community of believers.

It is useful to reflect upon the issue of Shidyaq's tenuous religious identity with consideration of how this impacted on the work of Mirza Malkum Khan, another reformist intellectual, albeit one from a different linguistic and social context. In the mid-nineteenth century, Malkum Khan's father, an administrator in the Russian legation to Iran, had converted from Armenian Christianity to Islam. In his youth Mirza Malkum was educated in France as well as Iran, and as a young man was employed to work as a translator to European instructors at the new *Dar al-Funun*, the first institution of higher education in Iran. Later, he worked in the Qajar court in various administrative positions, gaining the favor of Nasir al-Din Shah. He used this position to advocate for reforms, and eventually ran afoul of conservative forces in the court; these intrigues climaxed with allegations of financial impropriety connected with a scheme he was involved in to introduce a national lottery in Iran. Other allegations were raised in connection with his involvement in freemasonry. In 1872 he left the country and accepted a post as the Iranian consul to England. By 1889, tensions between his views and that of the court boiled over, and he was dismissed from this post (Balaghi, "Constitutionalism and Islamic Law in Nineteenth-Century Iran," pp. 333–4). He remained in London and established the Persian-language newspaper *Qanun*, which became a forum for him to forcefully argue for the institution of a transparent system of law—in the form of a constitutional monarchy—in Iran. While largely avoiding direct criticism of the figure of the Shah, Mirza Malkum rendered all other official figures as corrupt and incompetent, squanderers of the natural potential and resources of Iran. These themes were reiterated in pamphlets and books he also wrote during this period. Although officially banned, his writing reached a relatively wide audience in Iran, and he is credited with introducing a spare, economical prose style to the Persian language, politically potent, yet innovative in its form.

It would seem that Mirza Malkum's particular inhabitation of his religious identity continued to raise questions during his lifetime, in particular due to his continuing links with the Armenian community, for example, the fact that he chose to marry an Armenian Christian woman. This should not necessarily call into question his conversion to Islam, but this choice indicates the complexity of religious and ethnic identity and conceptions of community in this period. In his own writing, Mirza Malkum does not deviate from an Islamic identity, and makes constant reference to Islamic religious unity and to religious themes and issues. His political disposition can be generally termed pan-Islamist, while retaining a more narrow specialization on the specific issues of corruption and injustice in Iranian society. In this sense, he exemplifies certain prevalent tensions inherent in the political imaginations of many reformist intellectuals of his time—with the apparent paradox of embracing of both pan-Islamist and proto-nationalist positions. In this context, his religious identity is enabled through the discourse of pan-Islamism, and finds its full articulation in this project.

One example of this is to be found in an exchange that occurred in *Qanun* newspaper in 1890. "A question arrives from Herat," states the title of a short piece concerning the ideal of Muslim unity (*Qanun*, "so'ali az herat miresad," No. 17, p. 3). The segment begins with an editor's note describing the correspondence as having been written "by one of the learned clerics of Afghanistan." The question follows: "Certain useful publications place a priority on unifying the Muslim nations. What circumstances will allow for this blessing, meaning the unity of Muslims, and if possible, where on the face of the earth will the center of such a union be located?" Mirza Malkum responds by writing "Recently, concerning this very issue, investigations have been carried out in the majority of the Muslim nations. In response to the question of the learned Afghan, some of the theses of these investigations, each of which is the outcome of the work of a major *'alim* (religious intellectual) of our age, will be presented here in brief" (*Qanun*, "so'ali az herat miresad," No. 17, p. 3). Thereafter, nine bullet points—an innovation characteristic of Mirza Malkum's typographical style—are listed constituting various aspects of the answer to this question. The arguments present the core stipulations of pan-Islamist discourse. For example, one bullet states: "The majority of those peoples who find certain commonalities between them come to agreement [concerning their community]. The unification of the Muslim peoples, who by definition are a single nation, should not find this to be an impossibility" (ibid., p. 4). Further points elaborate that Istanbul is the natural location for the capital of these domains. The last point states that Islam "represents the desires of the spirits of all the prophets" and thus Islamic domains should be the "center of the light of progress" for the entire world (ibid., p. 4).

In the next issue, Mirza Malkum reports that new responses to this question have arrived, and he prints several of them—each one takes issue with the centrality of Istanbul to the Islamic nation, and each suggests other locations as a more appropriate capital. An Indian suggests Mecca, a Turkistani suggests Bukhara, an Egyptian insists on Cairo, another insists on Najaf, an Iranian deems Mashhad most appropriate, etc. After listing these letters, Malkum Khan admits that this is a matter for *ulama* (religious leaders) to hash out—but he insists that "what is clear from this is that Baghdad, Egypt, Isfahan, Islambul and all nations of Islam are the property and sovereignty and rights of the Muslim people of the world" (*Qanun*, "Dar bab-i ettehad-i millal-i Islam," No. 18, p. 1). The developing tensions between the proto-nationalist assertions inherent in the letters cited, and the pan-Islamist discourse which had by now been appropriated by reformists in the Ottoman court around the concept of the caliphate, are clear in this symbolic discussion concerning the proposed capital of the Islamic polity.[20] Yet, Malkum Khan is aware of the dangers of overstating the pan-Islamist case to his audience—an adjoining note has him returning to his own voice, by stating that "in the midst of all of this, what is most important and closest to us is the issue of the worries and concerns of our Iran" (ibid.). Two points may be of interest in our investigation here; the first is the manner by which Mirza Malkum delegates and directs these debates—he does not claim a position from which to deliberate over the issue of pan-Islamism. Rather, he presents himself as an arbiter of various legitimate positions, paying respect to the various concerns raised by the numerous contributions to the debate, but trying to focus the debate on the elements he deems to be essential. He is respectful of dissenting views in the debate over which location would better serve as a capital for the ideal Muslim nation. These can be boiled down to advocacy of the social cohesion of Muslims, but Mirza Malkum wishes to carry this out through a specific concern for Iran's unique maladies.

There is a confidence in how Mirza Malkum engages in discussions pertaining to pan-Islamism, which does not dilute the care with which he positions himself—as a conduit for debate, but not as an authority on religion. Despite this, his contemporaries were often quick to use the issue of his religious identity in their criticism of him. Noteworthy is the attack directed to him by I'timad al-Saltanih printed in *Ittila'at* newspaper in 1891. Huma Natiq terms this scathing attack on Malkum a semi-official court response to the provocations of *Qanun* newspaper, which had only been circulating for a little over a year at this point (Malkum Khan, *Ruznamih-yi Qanun*, p. 15). In the climax of his defamatory article, I'timad al-Saltanih writes "everyone will agree that for an Armenian—the root and material of whose religious beliefs are unclear, and who seeks personal gain, finding sympathy or antipathy with any religion—how can this individual, who is not a Muslim, claim to speak for a Muslim nation like Iran, in advocating for the establishment of laws? Which laws exist that are better than those of the Qur'an brought down by the Prophet, which are the normative laws of the [Iranian] government and nation!" (ibid.).

In ideological terms, this attack differs little from the analysis of scholars who deem Mirza Malkum's conversion simply a tactical choice for social gain, although it does not make the claims to objectivity that they make. In the context of I'timad al-Saltanih's attack, these questions about Mirza Malkum's religious identity play a central role—they are his most damaging pieces of evidence, or at least they are what he deems to be the points that will go farthest in damaging the credibility of Mirza Malkum in the face of the widespread popularity of his views. Here, the tenor of the attack is much blunter than that of Rizqallah Hassun against Shidyaq. Where in the latter, the allegations of *kufr* are an ironic claim against the quality of Shidyaq's conversion (in effect, mocking his claim to conversion), in the case of I'timad al-Saltanih the legitimizing principle is rather purely chauvinism, indeed an ethno-nationalist and religious chauvinism.

The accusations that Malkum Khan and Shidyaq faced as converts indicate the instability of these new religious identities for prominent social and cultural figures in the nineteenth century, and leads us to view their intermedial identity—either and both Christian and Muslim—as posing a threat to the intuitive nature of religious identity adopted by their opponents. An examination of their own use of religious identity problematizes the general assumption advocated by some scholars that their conversions were reflections of a simple desire for a higher social status. No doubt this analysis has an element of truth to it—but the preceding episodes show how this higher social status was a very tenuous one, and how little protection they were afforded from attacks by either Muslims or Christians, who could not accept the use of conversion as a transactional position to offer innovations or challenges to either ruling concerns or to the use of religion within colonial discourses in the West.

In the case of both individuals, the act of conversion was part of their development of conceptions of modern Arab and Iranian subjectivities, partially as a result of European hegemony and colonialism, and as a part of their own experiences in traveling between Islamic societies and Western Europe. Furthermore, and more importantly perhaps, conversion functioned as a challenge to the normative social categories within their own original societies, at a time when the valuing of various kinds of communal and individual identities was undergoing serious reconsideration, and indeed the relationship of the individual to society was being re-evaluated. Gauri Viswanathan notes that within the context of colonial modernity "the power of conversion as an epistemological concept is that it reclaims religious belief from the realm of intuitive (non-rational) action to the realm of conscious knowing and relational activity" (Viswanathan, *Outside the Fold*, p. 176). We may view Shidyaq and Malkum Khan's conversions as attempts to create a divide between a pre-modern intuitive relationship to religious belief, transferring religious identity to a conscious and even performative social event, one that is relational as well.

The preceding examples offer somewhat different perspectives on the motivation for and identification with conversion on the part of these two figures. In the context of the political advocacy that Malkum Khan and Shidyaq were to become engaged in, and in the context of their disillusion not only with ruling systems in the Arab–Ottoman and Qajar–Iranian contexts, but also their ambivalence with the offerings of a Christian-identified Western Europe, the relational position of a convert allowed for them to occupy just such a "transitional and transactional" social role. The threat that they were viewed as, by both elements of the Christian and Muslim communities, illuminates the challenge that conversion posed to both identities as "intuitive" ones, and propelled religious identity into the field of engaged public activity.

* * *

Shidyaq lived through a period of significant transformation in Arabic textual production, from scribal technologies to the increasing use of those of the printing press. These transformations, and their effects upon the imagination of Shidyaq, play a large role in the conception and formulation of his book *al-Saq*. This book is presented as an illumination of an obscure theory of language (one not to be taken up, although it sets the stage for the rhetorical and linguistic games to be featured in the remainder of the text), but when Shidyaq discusses the second "topic" of the text—the gaining of knowledge by women, as exemplified by Faryaqiyya—the issue reverts back to language, a defense of Faryaqiyya's "obscure utterances" and collapses into a point on language and representation. How can meaning be conveyed . . . ? We return to the domain of language.

This discussion highlights a question unresolved by reading *al-Saq*—what is its intended readership? Previous discussions here have shown that many innovating nineteenth-century texts followed from either institutional considerations, such as court institutions, addressing the audience of a political elite, or in some cases were works of a personal nature, gaining a measure of autonomous value through modern institutions such as the press or the educational system. Yet, with *al-Saq*, it is difficult to link its production or publication with these institutional imperatives. Instead, the text may either be seen to be synchretic (working between and combining considerations from different institutional bases) or simply exceptional to this framework.

Shidyaq consciously links these material activities to the imaginative process of creating a text. At times this process is treated reverentially, at other times it is laid open for a critical view. With both impulses, Shidyaq is attempting to create a text that brings about a creative bridging of the obsessive and meticulous approach of the scribal reader or writer with the possibilities and challenges offered by the new media of printed texts. Where some *al-nahda* intellectuals chafed at the restrictive limits these "traditions" imposed, Shidyaq found them a necessary respite from the bleak choices of identity within the new social and institutional formations emerging at this time. From the colonial foundations of Evangelical missionary activity, whose primary disruptive force was to make the sacred Christian texts legible to its followers in the orthodox churches, to the inhibitions of the capitalist social strata of England, Shidyaq could not reconcile himself to any of the various positions he was expected to inhabit. In this sense, *al-Saq* is a pre-testament to his conversion to Islam in that his conversion was an act of claiming agency, and idealizing community from the elements which he drew his consistent points of reference—Arabic literature, language and its related categories of the humanities. Islam, then, served hardly as a creed for Shidyaq, as much it was a mode of creative, even idealist, agency toward the foundation of something less settled, less restrictive, and more able to articulate the relationship of an Arab past and its capacity to recreate the present. This, for Shidyaq, was an Arab modernity, as much as for Malkum Khan a recourse to an Iranian essence—coded Islamic, but again hardly as a creed—could be an opening to a similar, indigenous articulation of modernity. In both cases, conversion was among other things, an act of will and imagination as an outcome of contending with the limitations of religious identity in a modern world.

6

TRANSACTIONS AND TRANSLATIONS

Hajji Baba Ispahani's value between English and Persian readerships

> He announced it as his intention to make a present to us of a certain produce of the earth, unknown in most parts of Asia, but much cultivated in Europe, which would not fail to be of incalculable benefit to the people of Persia; and he requested the vizier to assist him in his undertaking, promising shortly to send him a specimen of the intended gift.
>
> (James Morier, *The Adventures of Hajji Baba Ispahani*)

In the previous chapter I have explored how Ahmad Faris Shidyaq's exploration of the limits of subjective representation in modern literary work also sets in relief the limits of the nineteenth-century travel text's conventional ambitions to articulate the emergence of the self into society through the representation of the experience of travel. The following chapter will look at how the confluence of travel writing and translation came to bring about a text imbued with a similar fertile ambiguity as that which made *Alf layla wa layla* such an important text in modern Western European, Arab and Iranian contexts. Here, I will discuss the writing and publication of a marginal (if commercially successful) English faux travel-text, and will follow how this text came to be re-evaluated in its translation into Persian. Here, I hope to bring together discussions that emerge from part two of this book—touching on issues such as the changes to the notion of literary value in this period, and the role of these changes in producing a concept of literary modernity—into conversation with the discussions of the previous two chapters—those concerning changes to literary approaches to the question of character and subjectivity as articulated in nineteenth-century travel writing. As read through the shifting value of a nineteenth-century colonial text, which through translation was implicated into revolutionary and anti-colonial contexts, the following discussion will present a case study for understanding how this complex mosaic of issues relates to our comprehension of the categories of both literature and modernity.

Readers, texts, and their values

What follows is an attempt to examine how the authority of the text tenuously engages the agency of a readership, and to see if the common primacy of the text in the generation of "a reading" of itself can be interrogated. Garrett Stewart, writing of the conscriptive "Dear reader" so often stumbled across in the nineteenth-century British novel, argues persuasively that the textually invocative moment reveals the texts' "tactic for the annexation of receptive consciousness into subjectivity," which he later calls "the conscriptive event" (Stewart, *Dear Reader*, pp. 27, 397). The move from Althusser's interpellative "hey, you" to the polite presumptions that belie the "conscription" of the "dear" reader's consciousness is, however, a short one that implicates the author–text–reader relationship into a general framework of an apparatus of ideology and its subject. The authority of the text in this relationship, it is true, is clearer to establish than the possible agency of the reader that is raised in my introductory statement. However, there is a place for an accounting of the complicity of readerships—that is to say, a social imagination—as being less predetermined than the call to the "dear reader" may make it seem. The exercising of this kind of agency may be called "deliberate mis-readings" or "counter-interpellations," and may span a range of justifications, including "incompetent" readerships or overly-competent ones, semi-literate readerships or communities of writers, etc. The translated text may offer a particularly valuable point of entry for an examination of this question, if the argument of the invocative power of the text is made on the basis of a discussion of socially delimited values. Translations, those that cross social boundaries, are prime arenas for the engagement of a readership on a basis unrelated to the aura of authorial intention. This chapter will examine just such a setting, that of a translation which in its birth had an uncertain social value, and which through a variety of interventions was refigured as containing a certain potential for the counter-interpellation of a secondary readership vis-à-vis the original-language text.

In early 1824, John Murray, an English publisher, released an anonymously-penned volume by the title *The Adventures of Hajji Baba of Ispahan*. But in some sense, the story of Hajji Baba begins some time before: in 1807, a 24-year-old by the name of James Justinian Morier was deployed into the relatively hermetic social sphere of Qajar-era Iran as the private secretary of Harford Jones, the special envoy from King George to the Qajar Fath Ali Shah. By the time of his return to England, Morier had already begun to capitalize on his experiences by writing memoirs of his travels and work, which were released in the two volumes *Journey through Persia, Armenia and Asia Minor* and *Second Journey through Persia*. While pleased with the quiet acclaim these works attracted, he then set his sights on the larger market offered by the novel. Thus was the character of "Hajji Baba of Ispahan" introduced to a British readership.

One British literary historian has remarked that, "it is not surprising that [Morier] should have decided to exploit his exceptional knowledge of a little-known country"—thus confirming the value that a certain knowledge of distant cultures might bear in the market of fiction writing at that time in Britain. Furthermore, the same critic continues, this was "an age in which novels were so much in demand and there was . . . [a] keen an interest in the East" (Jack, *British Literature*, p. 245). This interest in the East, borne out in the accumulation of numerous translations and pseudo-translations of oriental texts, also may have influenced Morier to stretch his facilities from bureaucratic writing and intelligence reportage to the whimsical style he conjures in *Hajji Baba*. Perhaps the novel, a relatively new and ascendant literary form in the English literary market by the mid-1820s, beckoned too strongly to a middle-aged and sedentary ex-diplomat living somewhat beyond his means. Morier may have come to appreciate the cultural value of literary representations of his experiences in a part of the world that was now a source for the British public's literary fantasies.

Some decades later, perhaps some thirty-odd years after Morier's death in 1849, Mirza Habib Isfahani (183?–1893), an exiled Iranian man of letters, translator, instructor and author of two books on the grammar of Persian, sat down to put his pen to translating Morier's *The Adventures of Hajji Baba of Ispahan* into his native tongue. A Persian translation of the book was first published in 1906, but it was somewhat later before it became recognized as a major landmark in the reworking of Persian prose from the previous courtly and highly ornamented style into a written vernacular, a common and widely understandable prose. The timing of the publication of Mirza Habib's translation may seem to legitimize what was to become its inclusion into the discourses of anti-colonialism and reform which were part of the Iranian Constitutional Revolution of 1906–1911, the set of events culminating from over a half-century or so of social- and political-reform agitation which resulted in the establishment of a constitutional monarchy, the first such constitution in the Middle East.

That Mirza Habib's *Hajji Baba* continues to be read in Iran is a result of the coincidence of a variety factors, both literary/aesthetic and political.[1] *Sargozasht-e Hajji Baba-yi Isfahani* has been put on lists including Talibof's *Kitab-i Ahmad* and Maraghihi's *Siyahatnamih-yi Ibrahim Bayg*, which, as has been discussed, are often considered canonical within the political texts of modern Iranian literature (Bakhash, *Iran*, p. 305). Given the fact that *Hajji Baba* is a translation of a British novel of the oriental tale genre, and that Mirza Habib was never known for overtly political writing on the order of Talibof or Maraghihi, one may ask how it was that *Hajji Baba* came to be integrated into this canon. Indeed, to this day, none of the other numerous translations of this period are endowed with the literary or social value of *Hajji Baba*. How could an orientalist text be mis-read as supporting a nationalist and largely anti-colonial movement such as Iranian constitutionalism? What counter-interpellations signified the move of *Hajji Baba* from orientalist to constitutionalist imaginations?

As I have suggested above, the crossing of the paths of Morier and Mirza Habib marks also the intersection of what have been termed fundamentally opposing discourses: orientalism and national constitutionalism. I will outline the connections of Morier to an orientalist discourse, and Mirza Habib to nationalist constitutionalism, but what is more suspect, perhaps, is the claim of a fundamental opposition of modernist constitutionalism to orientalism. In investigating the cultural economies within which the two versions of the text circulated, this question arises over and over. Is it that Mirza Habib's very able and literate translation (deemed by many Iranian critics, not surprisingly perhaps, as superior to Morier's original text) "transformed a colonialist text into an anti-colonialist one," as one Iranian literary historian has put it? (Natiq, *Az mast ke bar mast*, p. 102). Or, literary "value" notwithstanding, was there more at play in the transference of an Englishman's attempt at a popular "oriental tale" into a cultural sphere where, as I will discuss later, *Hajji Baba* was to be identified with the martyred leaders of the constitutionalist movement?

The issues of the authorship of Hajji Baba, as they are both historically and theoretically constituted, suggest reasons for the misidentification of the translator of *Hajji Baba* by orientalist scholars, and to understand the implications of this misidentification for later engagements with the text. In addition, the character of Hajji Baba offers readings of the characteristics of this fictive personage within the context of both an orientalist discourse and an aspiring nationalist–reformist discourse, and the cultural economies of the readerships of each. Last will be a discussion of readerships—both imagined and documentable—of these texts, with a specific interest in showing the relationship of the development of a new narrative tradition (and a readership for it) as part of a political and social reform movement, in the Iranian context, to the already-established fantasies of the British novel-reading public, supplied by the developing orientalist discourses of the nineteenth century. The question of the reader, mis-readings and counter-interpellations will then again be raised, although these concerns will lurk between the lines as I unravel the issues I have outlined above.

Mis-recognition and authorship

Confusion over the authorship of *Hajji Baba* was to follow the book for decades after its initial publications, in both the English and Persian versions of the book. In 1824, James Morier contracted with John Murray for the publication of his book—and as was not uncommon, the book was released with no stated authorial credit. The introduction, a clearly satirical letter to one "Rev. Fundgruben," was signed "Peregrine Persic," a false editorial moniker, as the book was in its own fictional claim the work of Hajji Baba himself, and was only translated by the former diplomat "Persic." The first British review of *Hajji Baba*, published in *Blackwood's Edinburgh Magazine*, misidentified the text as a sequel by Thomas Hope to his popular novel, *Anastasius*, and argued that *Hajji Baba* was significantly inferior to the latter ("Hajji Baba," *Blackwood's Edinburgh Magazine*, p. 51). None other than Sir Walter Scott was to later step in to rescue the literary reputation of *Hajji Baba* and its author, repositioning the text and arguing for its placement among the highest productions of the oriental tales genre. The debate that Scott was to enter concerned the kind of value *Hajji Baba* was to be endowed with. Scott describes Hajji Baba as "a lively and entertaining history of the hero... an easy and humorous introduction...to the oriental manners and custom, but especially to those which are peculiar to the Persians" (Scott, *Sir Walter Scott*, p. 357). Despite the harsh criticism of *Blackwood's Magazine* for the book on literary and other counts: what was to emerge from the critiques of the book in the mid- to late-nineteenth century is an estimation of an *ethnographic* value (such as Scott's) of the book, which was to drive any regard for its possible "literary" value. It is noteworthy that over the course of the mid- to late-twentieth century, British and American literary critics, perhaps uncomfortable with the use of a purely ethnographic reading for assessing the book's ultimate value, have begun to find ways to argue that the book's appeal may be more "literary" than previously considered, perhaps simply to justify its enduring popularity, even as it continues to be read with an eye to its ethnographic value.[2]

Not only did Hope briefly replace Morier as the identified author of the text, but so was Mirza Habib Isfahani later to be confused with his friend and associate Shaykh Ahmad Ruhi, whom any reader of E.G. Browne's *A Literary History of Persia 1500–1924* would have to conclude to have been the translator of *Hajji Baba.*[3] Furthermore, a full generation of Iranian literary scholars debated passionately whether or not Morier could have been the author, or if he himself had absconded the glory from an actual "Hajji Baba" (i.e. taking the introduction of the text to be, albeit satirically phrased, a sort of admission of the truth) which led to an entire area of inquiry that focused on the possible identification of this person.[4] What can be concluded from this is that the social identification of the authorship of *Hajji Baba* was for a period of time (longer in the Iranian case) an issue of confusion in both languages. How this confusion impacted the reception of the text in any particular time and social setting is something that must be very delicately examined.

The mis-identifications that have muddied an understanding of the Persian translation of *Hajji Baba* may have had a large role to play in a certain kind of association it was given to constitutionalism. The origin of this confusion is to some extent Mirza Habib's association with the group of Istanbul-based Iranian constitutionalists led by the charismatic Shaykh Ahmad Ruhi Kermani, who were related to the pan-Islamic ideology of the Muslim modernist/revivalist, Seyyed Jamal al-Din al-Afghani. These two figures were implicated in the assassination of Nasir al-Din Shah in 1896, a fact which led to Shaykh Ahmad's eventual expulsion from Ottoman domains, and his brutal murder by Iranian agents as he was being transported to Tehran (ostensibly to stand trial). Mirza Habib's death is recorded in the Persian-language constitutionalist newspaper, *Akhtar*, in May 1893 ("Mirza Habib," Akhtar, p. 206). His obituary emphasizes his distinguished standing within the Iranian intellectual community in Istanbul, stating that "in his literary writing in knowledge or erudition he had few peers" (ibid.). It is significant that the often-polemical newspaper does not speak of any particular political associations or of a legacy of activism when remembering the life of Mirza Habib. However, it would be incorrect to assume that Mirza Habib was untouched by the political turmoil in Iranian society, or that he was uncommitted in the highly charged atmosphere of an expatriate community which at that time was central to the fomenting of social discontent. He himself described his flight from Iran as motivated by a personal (but politically tinged) conflict with Muhammad Khan, who was then the commander of the royal bodyguards in Tehran (Aryanpur, *Az Saba*, Vol. 2, p. 395).[5] His choice to remain in Istanbul for the rest of his years may or may not have been due to continuing intrigues related to the court.[6] Mirza Habib, fluent in Arabic, Persian, Turkish, and French, apparently had little difficulty employing his erudition to live comfortably under a more hospitable Ottoman government (although, even there, Mirza Habib was expelled from the academy *Anjuman-i Ma'arif* and from his teaching job for a period, until the Sultan was moved to reinstate him—exactly why, we do not know) (Aryanpur, *Az Saba*, Vol. 2, p. 395). During this time, he is known to have written at least two books on the instruction of Persian, one for use by foreigners and one directed at young Persian-speakers, as well as having published poetry (often in *Akhtar*).[7] In addition he edited a book on calligraphy in Turkish.[8] He was also a prolific translator, producing renditions of *Gil Blas* and plays by Moliére.[9] We may assume that he did other work of this sort, but it does seem as if most of his translation work only became publicly known after his death. Given this biographical information, can we assume that his motivation in translating *Hajji Baba* was either purely "literary" or "political" in nature? The scarcity of detail on Mirza Habib's life makes any conjecture that definitively emphasizes one motivation over the other largely irresponsible, but we can see that both are aspects of his life's work and course, and while it is possible that his translation of *Hajji Baba* was carried out for more "literary" reasons than not, it certainly was done in such a way and in such a social context so as to make available a "political" reading of the text.

The "political" label affixed to the translation of *Hajji Baba* was initially largely a result of the confusions over its translator's identity. It is perhaps ironic that this confusion was an outcome of the misidentification of the translator by orientalist scholars. The misidentification of Shaykh Ahmad Ruhi for Mirza Habib apparently occurred first in the mind of Major D.C. Phillott, a one-time British counsel in the city of Kerman, who was given a manuscript of the translation of *Hajji Baba* by the associates of Shaykh Ahmad after the latter's murder. Phillott, assuming that the manuscript was Shaykh Ahmad's work, took it with him to Calcutta after leaving his diplomatic position in 1906. He oversaw its publication there in Calcutta—not an entirely noteworthy fact, given the presence of a small but active community of Iranian exiles in that part of India, as well as the persistence of an Indian readership of Persian texts. However, Phillott's edition is a rather peculiar effort: the book contains an English introduction, and the text is supplemented with a critical apparatus with helpful definitions of certain Persian colloquialisms, in English. The intended audience of this edition is therefore apparently an oddly limited one: perhaps English-speaking students of

Persian, or orientalists for whom the colloquialisms were unfamiliar, or else perhaps Indians who wished to increase their knowledge of contemporary Persian. Phillott notes in the introduction that another publisher in Calcutta was at the same time preparing the publication of the same book.[10] Sadeghi reports that another edition was published in Calcutta "shortly after" Phillott's, by the *Habl al-Matin* Press, and edited rather liberally by Mu'ayyid al-Islam Jalal al-Din Hussayni—it seems likely this is the edition Phillott mentions. This second edition was meant for a solely Persian-reading audience, either in India or Iran, and thus lacked the critical additions made by Phillott (Morier, ed. Sadeghi *Sargozasht*, p. 10).

That Phillott was incorrect in his presumption that Shaykh Ahmad was the translator of *Hajji Baba* is to some extent understandable: the manuscript was, after all, among the possessions of Shaykh Ahmad. What is curious is that Phillott does claim that "assisted by Mirza Habib, a poet from Ispahan [Shaykh Ahmad] translated several French and English works, including Haji Baba [sic] and Gil Blas," and in a footnote to a claim that Shaykh Ahmad had once lived in Isfahan he concludes: "hence the erroneous idea held by many Persians that the translator [of *Hajji Baba*] was an Ispahani" (Morier, ed. Phillott, *Sargozasht*, p. vii). Clearly, Phillott should have had reasonable cause to think that Mirza Habib (the Isfahani) was more than simply "assisting" Shaykh Ahmad. However, one has the sense that Phillott is overwhelmed by a need to associate the book with the turmoil, contemporary to his efforts, which was enveloping Iranian society. A reason for the desire of orientalists to politicize this book may be found in an examination of the ambivalence some felt for the constitutional movement. Phillot's introduction for *Hajji Baba* mixes praises for the constitutionalists and bitter lamentations over the brutal death of Shaykh Ahmad with a high esteem for Morier's "insights" into Iranian society—going so far as to say that "*Hajji Baba* must, in fact, be regarded as serious history and not as burlesque" (ibid., p. ix). This mixture, of a support for constitutionalism mixed with a deeply orientalist perspective on the "character of this composite people," is one that is present from this very first edition of Mirza Habib's translation (ibid., pp. ix–x). What is even more curious is the manner in which Phillott blithely characterizes Shaykh Ahmad as a Babi, which he goes on to term an "obnoxious sect" (ibid., p. vii). Although Shaykh Ahmad likely had once found the Babi movement to resonate with his discontentment with the Qajar monarchy, he had to a great extent disassociated himself from Babi politics in his later life (Amanat, *Pivot of the Universe*, p. 443). While this is not an entirely appropriate place to discuss the intricacies of Babism and the British colonial opinion of the sect, it is important to understand how un-nuanced Phillott's understanding of the constitutionalists must have been. The evidence of such misunderstanding is manifold: in his introduction, Phillott goes on to term Jamal al-Din al-Afghani "a Babi leader," an astounding overstatement even if Jamal al-Din did have contacts with Babi thinkers, which shows a surprising ignorance of either Jamal al-Din's politics, Babism, or likely both

(Morier, ed. Phillott, *Sargozasht*, p. vii). What emerges is a mindset in which constitutionalism is conflated with Babism, which, as nothing more than an "obnoxious sect" reifies the colonial orientalist perspective of Iran: no political movement in Iran could be established on anything but what was considered by colonial officials as an irrational esotericism, and thus the constitutionalists were confused with Babis in their mutual antipathy for the Shah. The political possibilities of the text, "proven" through its identification with Shaykh Ahmad, are amplified through the latter's history as an activist. Yet, this political reading of the text must also be substantiated by the then-dominant British reading of the text, which viewed Morier's work as a pure documentation of the irrational "decadence" of the Persians—thus we can understand the collapse of all constitutionalism into Babism. Of course, 1906 also marked the beginning of the Constitutional Revolution. Phillott's edition was being sent out into a tumultuous social climate, and its introduction identified its publication with the constitutional movements, even as it mis-characterized their leaders.

E.G. Browne, one the most nuanced of the orientalist scholars of his day, wrote an introduction to an 1895 English edition of *Hajji Baba*, and also made mention of the Persian translation of the book in at least two separate volumes on Iranian literature and society. In fact, Browne would have been the best-suited individual to establish the identity of *Hajji Baba's* translator: in July 1892, Browne received a letter from Shaykh Ahmad, which was part of a long-standing correspondence between them on literary and political matters. In this letter, after discussing other concerns briefly, Shaykh Ahmad writes:

> The admirable literary man, Mirza Habib Isfahani has translated the book *Hajji Baba* from the French[11] . . . he wanted to publish the book in Istanbul, but permission was not given by the censor; if you would be agreeable to it, I can send you a copy of the manuscript, and if you would oversee its publication in London, I know of the fact that in Iran a great market and interest exists for it, and Habib Effendi would give his rights for such a publication.
>
> (Morier, ed. Jamalzadeh *Sargozasht*, p. 15)

This note is perhaps the strongest evidence to establish Mirza Habib as the primary and sole translator of the book. However, even after having received this letter from Shaykh Ahmad, Browne went on to cite Phillott's introduction to the Calcutta edition in identifying the translator as Shaykh Ahmad in his 1920 work *The History of Persian Literature 1500–1924*. Browne also failed to identify Mirza Habib as the translator in his 1910 text, *The Persian Revolution of 1905–1909* (Browne, *Persian Revolution*, p. 93). Whether this was a result of a faulty memory, bad notes, or due to a mistrust he felt for Shaykh Ahmad's word (in favor of the opinion of a fellow-Englishman) is unclear. However, the latter possibility seems unlikely, given Browne's propensity to cite Iranian and other non-European sources, more so than many of his colleagues. We may only speculate about Browne's motivations in these almost deliberate mis-identifications, and to offer a clear answer we will have to look at Browne's relationship to the constitutionalists a little more closely than the limited scope of this chapter will allow.

While Browne had long been an outspoken supporter of constitutionalist reforms, he was to allay that support somewhat as the populist and anti-colonialist aspects of the revolution were to gain momentum, even as he went on to advocate for the constitutional movement as a whole years after its collapse. As part of this move, he may have found it more plausible to imagine that a firebrand such as Shaykh Ahmad undertook the translation of *Hajji Baba* for purely political, polemical reasons, and to repress the potential of a literary man such as Mirza Habib having had more complex motivations for the translation of the text. The difference would purely be in the nuance that the authorial aura produces in each case. However, for Browne, reading the translation of *Hajji Baba* as primarily the product of Shaykh Ahmad's politics would likely simplify the question of its audience, drawing into harmony an orientalist critique and the constitutionalist critique of Iranian government and society (which in itself would serve nicely as a reflection of his own position as a British orientalist with strong sympathies for the constitutionalists). In this view, for an Iranian to read *Hajji Baba* would be an education in the orientalist perspective, placing a pre-eminent orientalist critique as the source for constitutionalist politics. On the other hand, Mirza Habib's involvement would tend to have to complicate the picture in the manner I have just discussed, thus complicating the possible readings of the text available to an Iranian readership.

The debates outlined above concerning the part orientalists had to play in the ascribing of a social value upon the Persian translation of *Hajji Baba* touch upon questions of textual invocations of a readership, and the possibilities for willful mis-readings of a text. For, in the view of orientalists such as Phillott and Browne, the understanding of the currency of the translation of *Hajji Baba* into Persian could be rationalized through either of at least two moves: the text's use of an orientalist critique fit into the aspects of the constitutionalist movement that engaged in social critique, as opposed to materially anti-colonial discourse—Browne, for one, in his discomfort with the latter aspects of constitutionalism, would exemplify such a perspective. So, as he and others valorized Morier's work as an accurate critique of then-contemporary Iran, they anticipated that the Iranian reading of the book would be a sort of education of an Iranian public in the orientalist critique offered by the text. The other possible explanation may be that for other critics, the text's orientalist critique is simply "history and not burlesque." Nonetheless from this perspective, the Iranians, while admirable to orientalists in their efforts to utilize the text for social reform, were doomed to some extent to mis-applying it, as even their reformist leaders were implicated in "obnoxious" sects that used irrationalism as their ideological basis. This reading reifies a potential for the mis-reading of the text, while valuing it negatively.

The character of Hajji Baba

The complex history of the various misidentifications of and debates around the author(s) of *Hajji Baba* should not obfuscate a careful reading what is in any case a largely a remarkable work. Here I will advance a reading of the character of Hajji Baba that will examine the manner in which the imagining of a character invested with incredible powers of social mobility and transience is significant to a text that has circulated in both British orientalist and Iranian reformist imaginations.

Hajji Baba is first of all, born of low means ("the son of a barber"); a factor of clear significance in his circuitous journeys that span from Central Iran to the border of Persia and Russia (present-day Armenia) to Turkmenistan to Baghdad and even Istanbul. The book ends as his journeys are about to continue on to England. The characterization of him as "a rogue," which is the term most used by British reviewers to describe him, is based on the fact that Hajji's moral qualities are largely, as an issue of narrative, unformed. At any given moment, his response to a specific situation may be based on criteria that are more central to developing certain qualities of the narrative than to developing a "round" character of Hajji.[12] That he will act on the basis of respectable intentions on one page and of an amoral selfishness on the next is a quality that largely allows for the imagination of his social mobility. Deidre Shauna Lynch has argued that this model of character conforms to a trend in eighteenth-century literary character production that

> is supposed to be a means for producing a sense of social context (rather than the social context counting as a means for producing our sense of a character): this character is the prosthetic device that enables readers to apprehend the comprehensive, impersonal systems that bind them together.
> (Lynch, *Economy of Character*, p. 87)

That Hajji is more or less simply a "prosthetic device" for an investigation of Persian Culture and Society is borne out by the manner in which critics and reviewers have been able to legitimize their generalization of his story to an understanding of this "culture" at large. This ethnographic reading of Hajji Baba is very greatly bolstered by his "flat" and unformed character (both in a moral and a physical sense).

Hajji is himself unidentifiable, bereft of characteristics, while the characters he meets are charged with an adjectival fecundity. For example, Osman Aga, Hajji's first mentor, is described as "a short squat man, with a large head, prominent spongy nose, and a thick, black beard" (Morier, *Adventures*, p. 18).[13] Noses, ears, beards, and body shape are a part of what distinguishes each character from the other, thus outlining a continuity of differences in a coherent social environment. Conversely, Hajji is identified only through detailed descriptions of the changes of costume his many social transformations require: from a merchant's assistant to a Turkmen slave-fighter, from a mendicant qaliyan-vendor to a wealthy merchant, from an assistant to the court physician to being one of the royal executioners.

Morier details at length the costume Hajji's new position assumes, and often goes so far as to describe the price and manner of its purchase. Chapter XVII, which is subtitled, "He puts on new clothes, goes to the Bath, and appears in a New Character" is entirely dedicated to one such transformation. The detailed description of not only the clothes required for Hajji's new station in society but also the act of shedding his old ones and enrobing in the new attire, locates the development of Hajji's character on the empiricization of this act. At the end of the above-mentioned chapter, the act of enrobing is explicated in tedious detail—I will quote it at length in order to draw attention to the mode of its description:

> As soon as it [the bath] was all over, the dalak brought me some dry linen, and conducted me to the spot where I had left my clothes. With what pleasure I opened my bundle and inspected my finery! It appeared that I was renovated in proportion as I put on each article of dress. I had never yet been clothed in silk. I tied on my trousers with the air of a man of fashion, and when I heard the rustling of my vest, I turned around in exultation to see who might be looking at me. My shawl was wound about me in the newest style, rather falling in front, and spread out large behind, and when the dagger glittered in my girdle, I conceived that nothing could exceed the finish of my whole adjustment. I indented the top of my cap in the true *Kajari*, or royal style, and placed it on my head considerably to one side....
>
> (Morier, *Adventures*, pp. 93–4)

Hajji's pleasure at the sight of his new clothes is commensurate to the "renovation" the clothing leads to. When he "turns around in exultation" to catch the eye of an admirer, it is to appreciate the "finish of the whole adjustment" made to his character. That in the chapter sub-title the author (who, solely in this aspect of the text, is *not* Hajji) proclaims the end to this process to be the creation of a "New Character" is an over-admission of the utility of such a character for the aims of the narrative: while Hajji exits the bath invested with the history of the narrative, he is easily rewritten as new in his entrance into a different social sphere. Thus the various social spheres are imagined as interrelated in an imaginary whole that is subsumed under the conception of a society's "Manners and Mores."

While distinguishable in his costume, Hajji is in other ways unmemorable to his companions, for in nearly every reunion with a previous friend, he must remind his friend of his identity. However, most often the tendency toward his mis-recognition is a cause for Hajji's success: in one episode Hajji is unfairly implicated in the death of the royal court's head theologian and thus deems it necessary to flee Iran (Chapters LVII–LXII). In the course of his escape, Hajji meets up with a caravan and only later realizes that one of the enshrouded bodies the caravan is taking for burial near a Shi'a shrine is none other than that of the deceased mullah, and that the latter's entourage is traveling in the caravan as well. However, despite his terror at being discovered, at first Hajji finds that no one recognizes him, even as they curse his name before him. The simple act of changing costume has transformed him so much that even the Mullah's servants, who once knew Hajji personally, cannot recognize him. In this, his tendency to not be recognized is one of the causes for his surviving adventures that lead to the death of others around him who are physically distinguished (i.e. Mulla Nadan, his companion in the above-mentioned episode, who miscalculates and is executed after choosing the incorrect clothes to present himself in). Later, when he is finally discovered, it is for having swindled one of the travelers out of some money. However, he is quickly saved by the coincidental attack of a Kurdish tribe on the caravan, which allows him to escape unnoticed. His recognition, linked not to characteristics but "character" (as in a moral character), differentiates between the (in)visibility of Hajji's characteristics and his internalized roguish tendencies. So, despite his ability to adopt multiple visual significations within the social fabric, his *character* remains unchangeable.

A tendency toward Hajji's misrecognition allows for the mapping of an Iranian/Persian social space as a unified, comprehensive, and knowable system. As I will discuss later in more depth, this mapping follows developments in the popular British imagination of the orient. These developments move from an emphasis on the fantastic and incommensurable aspects of the orient to a rationalization of it on the terms of an increasingly penetrating mode of colonialism. Mapping the social space created a sense of the potential for its dominance and more importantly, a moral justification for desires to do so. What is more difficult to settle is the issue of whether the character of Hajji Baba was to be a suitable vehicle for the deployment of an imagination sympathetic to the Iranian constitutionalist discourse, albeit through translation. While, as I have argued, certain evidence leads to the conclusion that the translation of *Hajji Baba* occurred as a result of myriad reasons with rationales that could be coded both "social/political" or conversely "literary," there is no doubt that its circulation and endurance was brought on by the an ever-increasing interest on the part of a politically-awakened audience in Iran for new forms of writing. Entwined in this is the simultaneous conceptualization of a "national literature" for a modern nation, Iran, which would rely on one language, Persian, for the linguistic unification of the nation. In this context, there are several ways to interpret the attraction of the character of Hajji Baba to an Iranian audience. To begin with, the mode of character employed for *Hajji Baba* is not necessarily one "foreign" to Iran; the socially mobile and "flat" character has certain corollaries in traditional literary modes such as epic poetry and oral tales, as well as in certain written genres. In any case, a simple (and not illegitimate) approach would argue for the reading of the character of Hajji Baba as somehow related to "traditional" characterization in Persian literature.

However, there may be more convoluted issues at stake in the character of Hajji Baba as he was read by an Iranian readership. This topic is perhaps one location where possible affinities of Iranian constitutionalism to nineteenth-century British orientalism may be theorized. These affinities will likely be loose and ambivalent, more a byproduct of these discourses than a feature of them. A mis-reading of

Hajji Baba's bereft-of-characteristics-character may offer us various allegorical spaces for imagining the interpellation of an Iranian reformist reader into the "dear reader" conversation (annunciated in the final paragraph of the book in the words "gentle reader!"). The characteristic-less protagonist is, notably, a quality of Maraghihi's *Siyahatnamih-yi Ibrahim Bayg*. Ibrahim Bayg is as thinly-constituted a character as is Hajji Baba, even though his "flatness" is more a result of an exceeding naiveté, where Hajji's is due to his moral vacuity. What is similar about both characters is their ability to traverse social boundaries, so as to "apprehend the comprehensive, impersonal systems" that constitute the Iranian nation, itself a conception of a recent history.

That the characters Hajji Baba and Ibrahim Bayg were empowered, through their lack of characteristics, to not only detail the contiguity of social classes, but also to contain these within an imagination of a unitary national space, was something of great importance to constitutionalists; in previous Iranian literature, nowhere were there examples that could so effectively map a seamless national space where a narrative would run its course. This is most clear in the text when Hajji Baba travels to Ottoman Turkey; the events that befall him there (particularly the ill fated marriage he proposes with a Turkish woman, Chapters LXVI–LXXI) largely work to reinforce not only his identity in terms of its difference from that of a Turkish or Arab identity, but it also develops a similar difference in terms of the imagination of a social space, and link his identity to the social space and geography of Iran.

While in the British context it is possible to see the character of Hajji Baba as not only continuing a mode identified by Lynch as one that maps the circulation of cultural value through a social space, it furthermore developed a fictional narrative on the basis of penetrating and mapping Persian society in keeping with developing trends in British colonial discourse. While the old oriental tale emphasized an exotic otherness about the orient, Morier was able to innovate the genre in such a way so as to reflect the change which occurred in colonial discourse from a discourse of *othering* to one of *knowing*. Hajji Baba's social mobility and lack of identity allow the reader to imagine the Persian social space as knowable, quantifiable, and definable. This desire had certain affinities with the discourse of Iranian constitutionalism: the desire to quantify and map the nation were parts of the imagination of reformist Iranians who wished to pursue nationalist models which were part of earlier reform movements. Not only did *Hajji Baba* necessitate a skilful translator such as Mirza Habib to render it readable, but also the readers of *Hajji Baba* were historically-positioned so as to be able to render the text un-readable, so as to translate for themselves the imaginary spaces of the book as relating to the material struggles they were engaged in. Thus the character of Hajji Baba—which in the Iranian context was a cousin of other characters in the contemporary fiction of the time, such as Ibrahim Bayg—was able to simultaneously operate within the seemingly contradictory discourses of mid-nineteenth-century orientalism and *fin de seicle* reformist constitutionalism in Iran.

Receptions and readerships of *Hajji Baba*

The English version of *Hajji Baba* was to become "enduringly popular," and Patrick Brantlinger argues persuasively that part of this popularity relates to the book's reproduction of ideals of social advancement which relate directly to Britain (*Rule of Darkness*, p. 144). This is quite plausible, given Hajji Baba's eventual association with British diplomats, and his selection as part of the Persian diplomatic delegation to England. However the popularity of Hajji Baba was not at first a foregone conclusion, and despite the redemptive plot, the initial review of "Hajji Baba of Ispahan" in *Blackwood's Edinburgh Magazine* offers an view of British reception of the text that would argue that the book fell very closely on the cusp of a change in the relationship of the reading public to the "orient." This is born out by comparing the basis of value established by this review to the manner in which later reviewers valued the text. *Blackwood's* review of the book as on one hand ethnographical, and on the other hand fantastic, remained the measure for most reviewers. The anxiety contained in the *Blackwood's* review reflects concerns touched upon in the previous discussion on the character of Hajji Baba; indeed, the character is the locus for the reviewer's dissatisfaction with the book. As Britain's colonialist discourse developed in line with changes in the material aspects of colonialism, so did literature begin to re-imagine the orient to reflect these changes.

Blackwood's Edinburgh Magazine devoted seven pages to its rather detailed review of *Hajji Baba* which appeared in the January 1824 issue of the influential publication. The review, while largely unfavorable to the book, outlines, in a comparison with *Anastasius* the qualities of an oriental tale that are considered valuable to the anonymous reviewer, who invokes public taste as his or her measure.[14] Where *Anastasius* is "a work of immense genius, and natural power," displaying "an extraordinary acquired talent for drawing MAN, as he is in one particular country; but still more extraordinary intuitive talent for drawing man, as he is in every class, and in every country," *Hajji Baba* is an abject failure ("Hajji Baba," *Blackwood's*, p. 51). This glorification of the *talent* that is associated with the outlining of national characteristics, is one part of the *intuition* that will generate a universalizing representation of "man" outside the bounds of social and cultural "characteristics." It is of course the presumption of the reviewer that the goal of all literature, including the oriental tale, is the achievement of such a universal perspective on man—presumably primarily the European man. Thus, while Anastasius is an Eastern character riddled with "vices" and thoroughly distinguishable from the reader's own experiences, he nonetheless "never thoroughly loses the sympathy of the reader" because:

> There is a rag of good feeling—a wretched rag it is, and it commonly shews itself in the most useless shape too (in the shape of repentance)—but there is a remnant of feeling about the rogue [Anastasius], (though no jot of moral principle,) and a pride of heart, which, with romance

> readers, covers a multitude of sins; and upon this trifle of honesty, (the very limited amount of which is a curiosity,) joined to a vast fund of attractive and unpopular qualities—wit, animal spirits, gay figure, and personal courage—he contrives, through three volumes, to keep just within the public estimation.
>
> ("Hajji Baba," *Blackwoods*, p. 52)

This "public estimation," is, however, not to be well-engaged by the qualities of Hajji Baba, which the reviewer finds "materially" at odds with the public's ideal. "starting as a barber, is starting rather low; and it is one material fault in our friend Hajji Baba, that, from the beginning to end, he is a low character" ("Hajji Baba," *Blackwoods*, p. 53). While the prejudice of class-origin is a barrier to the reviewer's empathy for Hajji Baba, this prejudice is one that is aggravated by his inability to shun the characteristics of his class: "Obscure birth is no bar to a man's fortune in the East; nor shall it be any hindrance to him among us; but we can't take cordially, East or West, to a common-place fellow" (ibid., pp. 53–4). Furthermore, the issue is not merely class-characteristics, but also the projection of these qualities onto the character's very immaterial self. This marks the crucial difference between the empathetic Anastasius and the un-likable Hajji Baba. "Anastasius is meanly born, but he has the soul that makes all ranks equal." Thus, even Anastasius' roguish qualities are mitigated by the fact that he is a "rascal like a gentleman," an "advantage" denied Hajji Baba. The difference between them, however, is the irreconcilability of Hajji's "common-place" characteristics, characteristics that were to eventually be valued as ethnographic. That the "common-place" Persian was no fair topic for a novel reflects the desires of a public for a tale with "exceptional" characters, not for representations of what was felt to be no more than the oriental norm. This quality of Hajji Baba was to be that which endowed the character and book with a lasting value through the course of late colonialism and even afterwards.

In the language cited above, another question arises: the relationship of the reviewer to the "public." The public is cited at other important points in the review— "[the book] falls so very far below what the public expected" ("Hajji Baba," *Blackwoods*, p. 52). But it is also implicated in the reviewer's reading of text itself, when the reviewer claims that "profiting by the example of the Persian story-tellers, he pauses in his tale at the most interesting point, and says to the public, "Give me encouragement, and I will give you more" (ibid., p. 57). This is an expansion on the ideal of the "dear reader" statement, and here the reviewer clearly reads the statement as one intended to address the public-at-large. This collapse of the notion of an individual reader with specific characteristics—that is, the Literate Gentleman, or the Young Scholar, etc.—into a readership that involves the entire "public" points to the manner in which the oriental tale's readership was not to be envisaged within the singular terms of the "reader" but rather was considered to be part of an imagination which is part of the rights and expectations of *the public.*[15] This notion of the public relates to a sense of the unity of the British social environment, and reflects the manner in which a book like *Hajji Baba* cannot but be implicated in the national aims as they were articulated in colonial discourse.

Given this concern with the public/nation, it is not surprising that the reviewer's strongest criticism of *Hajji Baba* is reserved for a discussion of the ending of book, where Hajji Baba begins his association with the British consular officials and the Shah's Vizier, and eventually is assigned to a delegation that is to travel to Britain. Here, the comic digressions between Hajji, the Vizier and others, that are meant to display the comic ignorance of the Persians of anything European, arouse great displeasure in the reviewer, for whom it "is, to speak the truth plainly, very wretched stuff indeed" ("Hajji Baba," *Blackwoods*, p. 57). The anxiety here is with any representation of England through the eyes of an oriental, even if they are meant to signal the oriental's ignorance. This anxiety leads to the final assessment of the text, which argues that "seriously, Hajji Baba should be cashiered forthwith. As far the public is concerned, the journey of the 'pilgrim' should be at an end. And indeed, England to be described by any foreigner, is a subject just now not the most promising" (ibid.). The reviewer's anxiety concerning the depiction of England by a foreigner is thus complicated by the alleged desire, once again, of the public, for whom and to whom the reviewer claims to be speaking. Here the conception of the public's desires is linked to the integrity of the nation (and the empire), for in reading Hajji's take on "the Franks," the reviewer exhibits anxieties over a possible critique of English society emerging from "any foreigner"—which by its saying confuses Morier with his character, Hajji, who is the foreigner mentioned. The undeniable irony of such an anxiety (i.e. the currency of a description of Persia by Morier not matching the "promise" of the latter's *character* describing England) is not to be registered by the reviewer and is subsumed within the concerns of what is claimed to be the public's desires.

What this concern with the "public" betrays is a concern with the growing power of novels to impact collective imaginations—this despite the relatively modest circulation of the first print run of *Hajji Baba* at 1,250 units (Johnston, *Ottoman and Persian Odysseys*, p. 213). Even though the first edition was to sell out within a few months, the reviewer's estimation of the novel, and the constant references to "the public," would intimate an emerging confluence of the power of novelistic writing over public imagination and national identity which seems far out of proportion to the small initial circulation of the novel. Later reviewers attempted to re-evaluate the novel and assess its cultural value on the basis of criteria not used in the *Blackwood's* review. Some complain of the fact that the novel is rather long, or that many passages appear irrelevant to the narrative and seem to function only to describe specific cultural or social scenarios that Morier appears to find of personal interest—however, the rereading of *Hajji Baba* as literary *ethnography* imparts an entirely new kind of value upon the novel as a genre. And so, by 1895, E.G. Browne could without pause claim that "every cultivated Englishman who has not read *Hajji Baba* (if, indeed the Englishman who has not read it can, in the full meaning of the term, be described as cultivated) should at once proceed to remedy this defect in his education" (Morier, *Hajji Baba* 1896, p. ix). That Browne equates the reading of Hajji Baba to "education" is quite telling within the conception of role of this kind of oriental tale. Browne can further distinguish where the *Blackwood's* reviewer cannot, when he states that "considered merely as a piece of fiction, *Hajji Baba* has many rivals; considered as a faithful picture of the living East (as opposed to the purely imaginary and unreal East of Moore and Southley), it has none" (ibid.). The valuing of *Hajji Baba*, which may not have shone in the ranks of the oriental literature of its day was to be rethought by the time of Browne's writing, and Browne very transparently delimits the new assessment of the text's value as a "faithful picture of living East" in opposition to the flights of fantasy constructed by the likes of Moore and Southley. The distance between Browne and the *Blackwood's* reviewer is formidable, but is one that may be plotted along the lines of the development of British colonial discourses over the nineteenth century. So while both may claim to reflect the desires of the public, it is possible to read these claims as arising from the trajectory of colonialism, as mentioned, from othering, to knowing. What drives the *Blackwood's* reviewer's anxieties is the transition from the mode of oriental tale (e.g. *Anastasius*) which others the orient, to that of *Hajji Baba*, which aims to know it. The valorization of *Hajji Baba* by later reviewers, particularly orientalists such as Curzon and Browne, is largely a reflection of the ascendance of the colonial discourse of knowing in the public sphere.

The issue of the readership of *Hajji Baba* in Persian is a matter that may require more conjecture than one would prefer, but there are specific points of interest that would tend to create a framework for understanding it. Iranian society in the early part of the twentieth century was of a great majority illiterate. While by the early part of the century, a number of small exclusive schools offered secondary education, the great preponderance of students received their primary education in the religious *madrisa* system. This system was largely closed to women, who could only gain education in informal settings, or from family members—although this policy was already challenged by the nascent secular education system in Tehran. The system of the religious educational institutions nonetheless bred the majority of the reformist Constitutional Revolutionaries, who were by and large highly educated in Persian, Arabic and often Turkish literary history. Many also were self-educated to some degree in French, German, and/or English. The knowledge of Persian literature that this class of men had gained was a result largely of private and informal efforts or through studies they had undertaken in cities in areas neighboring to Iran. However, beyond oral transmission of poetry, the great majority of people were not literate. Given these facts, one may ask is why Shaykh Ahmad had asked E.G. Browne for assistance in having *Hajji Baba* published? We know that, as with others in his milieu, Shaykh Ahmad was deeply committed to introducing social as well as political reforms to Iran; and yet mass literacy was a very distant goal. How then would the publication of *Hajji Baba* fit into these concerns?

We do know that the newspapers that Shaykh Ahmad and Mirza Habib were involved in the production of, *Akhtar* central among them, reached audiences through public readings and the circulation of used newspapers and pamphlets.[16] Memoirs from these times do contain references to the public reading of both newspapers as well as books, and these were largely carried out in the setting of clandestine meetings of banned political organizations, where issues of the day were to be discussed. These secret gatherings constituted the local and grassroots educational institutions engaged in the replication and reproduction of the political themes of reformists and constitutionalists. Na'im al-Islam, a historian contemporary to the constitutionalist period, recalls meetings where selections from *Ibrahim Bayg* were read out loud, drawing the participants to tears, and notes also that some of the participants had most of the book memorized (Maraghihi, *Siyahatnamih*, p. 16). These meetings provided the settings for the reading of texts such as *Hajji Baba* within the context of a political reformist discourse. While we do not have specific citations of *Hajji Baba* as being a book of choice for such circles, what can we make of Shaykh Ahmad's claim to Browne that "I know of the fact that in Iran a great market and interest exists for it?" The market and interest alluded to by Shaykh Ahmad is possibly a market of such reading-circles, where the interest of politicized Iranians for new literary forms to reflect their desire for political and social reforms came together with a translation of uncommonly innovative use of Persian colloquial to generate deliberate mis-readings of Morier's book. Thus can we begin to reconcile the divisions between political and literary value that came to enshrine Mirza Habib's work as one of the most notable achievements in Persian of his era, and also locate a readership for the book, within the clandestine reading-circles of the constitutionalists, which would resolve the question of the reader called to in the final paragraph of the book: "And here, gentle Reader! the humble translator of the Adventures of Hajji Baba presumes to address you, and, profiting by the hint afforded him by the Persian storytellers, stops his narrative, takes a bow, and says 'Give me encouragement and I will tell you more'" (Morier, *Adventures*, p. 456). Mirza Habib had only to smile as he finished his translation, for his own postscript was already written. He had only to reread it.

A circle of readers...

While the readerships of *Hajji Baba* were clearly differently constituted in the British and Iranian contexts, there are affinities between the prevalent political discourses of each readership that allowed for its migration through the act of translation. Complicated by mis-recognition, the ideological basis of *Hajji Baba* was initially as overdetermined as its readership was unrecognizable. When the *Blackwood's* reviewer of the book assumed the reflection of public desires, he or she was mis-recognizing the development of the fantasies of the public through the desire for knowledge of the orient. In the Iranian context, Mirza Habib's able translation was given cultural value through Shaykh Ahmad's attempts to have it published. That he was only successful in this through death confirms the potential for its finding value within the constitutionalist imagination, even as it led to the mis-recognition of the translator.

These mis-recognitions affected the critical conceptions of the two texts, and affected later readings of them. Twentieth-century critics of the English edition moved away from the assessment of the value of the text as relating to its ethnographic scope, and thus attempted to deflate the book of its initial value, which in the nineteenth century closely related it to the colonial discourse of a particular historical moment in British colonialism. Critics of the Persian text, however, led on by the mis-recognition of the translator by the orientalists, read the book within a highly political context, greatly reducing the complexity of that text. When looked at through the context of deliberate mis-readings and counter-interpellations, the Iranian readership of *Hajji Baba* could not have been drawn into the orientalist critique of their society presented by Morier. The critique they were drawing from the book, enervated by the character of Hajji Baba, was a critique that reflected the ambivalences of Iranian constitutionalism, which was at once nationalist, and yet anti-colonialist, and thus nativist in its self-conception. Brought back to the final paragraph of the book (and now the final paragraph of this chapter), a question resurfaces: can the polite "gentle reader" addressed by the "author" of *Hajji Baba* have been so directly interpellated into the ideological imperatives of the text? A historical and textual investigation would lead, rather, to our having to imagine readers in part filling the book, just as they were expected to fill the character of Hajji Baba, with their own imaginations and desires, and thus deflating the power of the call of the text and reconstituting it for their own reading needs.

CONCLUSION

Toward critical philology[1]

In this study I have endeavored to present readings of a series of texts that go against the conventions of many literary histories on nineteenth-century English, Arabic, and Persian literatures, and to complicate our understanding of the development of the category of "modern literature" within these contexts. In simple terms, I have argued that these conventions generally fall under the rubrics of novelism and nationalism—through making the novel and the nation the presumptive culmination of literary and intellectual developments in the nineteenth century. The problem these conventions give rise to are the limitations they set in valuing much of the innovative narrative prose writing from the nineteenth century—a problem that has been followed here through English, Arabic and Persian literatures, but which relates in fact to any discussion of literature and modernity. Through limiting the terms of modernity to valuative terms that are derived from the conventions of novelism and nationalism, most of the literature discussed in this study has been subject to what may be termed a hermeneutic injustice. I have instead offered an alternative framework for evaluating the categories of literature and modernity, attempting to show how the intersections between these literatures—isolated from terms of "influence" or "impact"—played an important role in the development of literary modernity.

By foregrounding texts that arise from and are formed through their circulation between social and linguistic arenas, this study has argued that textual transaction is an important marker of cultural modernity. The transaction of texts occurs as collisions of cultural fields with differential value systems. Yet the transactionability of certain texts is directly related to their increasing estimation within autonomous systems of cultural value. Autonomous cultural systems both allow for, and are generated by, textual transactions.

The system of this study has also worked against certain methodological conventions common to previous scholarship on the texts and contexts discussed here. Rather than limit readings in these texts to narrow expositions of the theoretical claims of this study, the texts themselves have tended to direct the analyses offered here. The complexity of interpretive bases for many of these texts has been the very object of the analysis. Through hinting at these complexities—which admittedly at times threaten to overwhelm the analysis—this study has sought to bring to the fore the problem we face in subjecting them to interpretation. In also foregrounding the social and cultural circumstances around the production of the text, this study has focused attention on the codes of value and legitimation that initially made intelligible the text to its contemporary readers. Through illustrating the interplay between the recovered social– and cultural–historical context of the production of these texts, and the aesthetic strategies of their authors—that is, the *textuality* of these texts—it is possible to begin to understand the contingencies each text represents in charting a genealogy of literary innovations and influences, or understanding the disjunctures and, as Foucault has termed them, epistemological ruptures, around the texts. This is work that is philological, yet situated within a critical historical approach; we may term it critical philology.

Many of these choices have been made in part as a response to a set of questions most poignantly argued by Edward Said in his posthumous collection of lectures, *Humanism and Democratic Criticism*. As a graduate student at Columbia attending the lectures presented in a later book, I must admit that the call for a return to philology as articulated by Said in these lectures was one that at that time was one that I was initially rather unwilling to consider very seriously. The discipline of philology had not only been identified by many readers of *Orientalism* as the structural framework for the development of orientalist discourse (as at least two generations of students and professional academics had often argued in their seminars and conferences) but also had come to be associated with a form of academic practice hardly appealing to those of us who saw our academic work as an extension of our social engagements with the world around us, and not simply a fetishization of the world of books. Despite this, it would be the work involved in this research—and the progression from research to writing—that would bring me to embrace the urgency of Said's instruction that a "return to philology" was an imperative for humanists within the academy. The methodology of this study—the movement between the close reading of a text and the reconstruction of the social context for the production of the text—is precisely that which Said has called for in arguing that a humanistic return to philology requires a rethinking of the act of reading.

> Reading involves the contemporary humanist in two very crucial motions that I shall call reception and resistance. Reception is submitting oneself knowledgeably to texts and treating them provisionally at first as discrete objects (since that is how they are initially encountered); moving then, by dint of expanding and elucidating the often obscure or invisible frameworks in which they exist, to their historical situations and the way in which certain structures of attitude, feeling and rhetoric get entangled with some currents, some historical and social formulations of their context.
>
> (*Humanism and Democratic Criticism*, p. 61)

The "movement" articulated by Said from the text to its context, is one that may require a training that literary scholars have less often sought out or been offered in our studies. To read over the contextual criticism of a text in its time often requires an engagement with archival work: be it in researching manuscripts of contemporaries of the author, or through reading over dusty collections of periodicals and pamphlets that extol or condemn the reading of a text, or by evaluating biographical materials concerning the writers one is reading (no less than those of their colleagues, followers, and enemies). They may also require charting the reception and readership of a single text over time—much as botanists who chart years of drought and rain through the rings of a tree trunk—or, following the movement of a text across the globe and through different languages. These contextual studies require the literary scholar to adopt interdisciplinary methods of research—ethnology, sociology, history all inform them. Yet, Said's idealization of a return to philology is not simply fulfilled by the expansion of the terms of research and linking texts to reception (which Said provocatively relates to the hermeneutics of *ijtihad*—the principle in Islamic theology allowing for the reinterpretation of a religious text to suit contemporary needs), and the contexts of their production and to surrounding historical and social trajectories. From this new vantage on the text, Said argues for a scholarship of resistance, which involves "the ability to differentiate between what is directly given and what may be withheld" (*Humanism and Democratic Criticism*, p. 76). In other words, this involves a consciousness "that two situations are at play: that of the humanistic reader in the present and that of the text in its framework" (ibid., p. 74). Resistance begins with a self-reflective position, yet one that is not self-defeating, carrying out work that is both critical and idealistic.

What is at stake in this kind of work is quite simple; it is a reconsideration of the terms of that which has long been sacred for the secular Enlightened imagination. The critical component of this methodology is the enactment of an analysis of the discursive context for the production of texts, and of readings of texts over time. The idealistic component suggests a rethinking of these discursive contexts toward the production of ones that more sufficiently address the essential terms of humanism: social justice, democracy, dignity for individuals and their communities. The narratives of modernity suggested through the readings of these texts, and constructed by this reconsideration, tend away from a view of the modern as a historical, temporal, or ideological configuration, eschewing technological and material bases for the conception of modernity. Instead, a conception of modernity as a state of cultural autonomy, a condition of autonomous values and systems of legitimation in literary and other cultural spheres, may be addressed. This conception idealizes atemporal manifestations of modernity, intimating that the category of the modern may relate to a wide body of texts emerging from varying historical periods and conditions. But this point, so intriguing, will have to be unfulfilled here and left for later investigation and exploration. So, this study cannot be said to follow what have been termed anti-humanist academic trends of cultural and social theory, as work of these schools has had little reference in this study. A closer look may show that while retaining some categorical terms from the aforementioned schools of theory, this study has tended more toward arguing for a radical positivism—even the insistence on the concept of "modernity" as a humanistic endeavor, a positive one, would very deeply run against the deconstructive or "new historical" approaches to literature.

So it is that this study focuses on the many ways in which transactionary texts were instrumental in innovations and transformations in literary practise over the course of the nineteenth century. The models often taken for granted in many studies of the effects of colonial discourse often utilize a framework of center–periphery relations based on uneven power relations between colonizing and colonized societies—while often perfectly legitimate for the study of certain issues, this kind of framework tends to be insufficient in addressing the complexity of literary relations both between colonial centers and outposts, as well as between societies subject to the effects of colonialism. By focusing on transactionary texts, this work also challenges the nationalist-novelist paradigm that defines much of twentieth-century criticism, and which limits and distorts our perspective on nineteenth-century literary practice, through appropriating the works of this period for national-literature models. So, for example, when 'Ali Asghar Hikmat attempted to recover *Alf layla wa layla* for use within an emerging Iranian nationalist framework that he was invested in, he violently distorted the perspective of his audience upon a wonderfully complex text that confounds both nationalist and novelist systems of value. By returning our perspectives to the conflicted debates and circumstances that surrounded the production of the text for nineteenth-century English, Arabic, and Persian readerships, we may begin to assess the damage done by nearly a century of erasure and denial.

NOTES

1 THE LITERARY ABACUS: TRANSACTIONS IN NINETEENTH-CENTURY ARABIC, ENGLISH, AND PERSIAN LITERATURES

1 The argument of modernity as a self-legitimating article of faith has been strongly advanced by Bruno Latour in *We Have Never Been Modern*. In addition, Marshall Berman similarly argues an idealistic basis to modernity in his definition of the term: "world-historical processes have nourished an amazing variety of visions and ideas that aim to make men and women the subjects as well as the objects of modernization, to give them the power to change the world that is changing them, to make their way through the maelstrom and make it their own" (Berman, Marshall. *All That is Solid Melts into Air: The Experience of Modernity*, New York: Penguin Books, 1982, p.16).

2 Emphasis added. Raymond Williams points to this passage from *Persuasion* as a turning point in usage of the term "modern," arguing that after this, the word was used "without [Austen's] irony, as indicating updating and improvement" (*The Politics of Modernism*, New York: Verso Press, 1989, pp. 31–2).

3 This points to the limits of a periodizing theory of modernity. See: Donald Wesling, "Michel Serres, Bruno Latour and the Edges of Historical Periods."

4 For more on the problematic nature of theorizing non-European modernities, see: Julio Ramos, *Divergent Modernities: Culture and Politics in Nineteenth-Century Latin America*, Durham, NC: Duke University Press, 2001. Ramos follows genealogies of Latin American modernities (through the figure of the "enlightened *letrado*"), as well as the representation of European modernities in the "migratory" literature of Latin American thinkers.

5 The experience of colonial modernity has been described by Gregory Jusdanis as "belated modernity"—a term from which Jusdanis has argued that the development of non-Western European national literatures, functions within the imperatives of a national culture very differently than in eastern metropoles. See: Gregory Jusdanis, *Belated Modernity and Aesthetic Culture: Inventing National Literature*, Minneapolis, MN: University of Minnesota Press, 1991.

6 The alliance between the imagination of the novel and the political imperative of the nation is a thesis advanced by Franco Moretti, who argues, "the nation-state found the novel. And vice versa: the novel found the nation" (Franco Moretti, *The Atlas of the European Novel, 1800–1900*, New York: Verso, 1998, p. 17).

7 For analyses of the role of the novel in the articulation of European colonial discourse in the nineteenth century, see Edward W. Said, *Culture and Imperialism*, New York: Vintage Classics, 1994, pp. 62–80. Also see Suvendrini Perera, *The Reaches of Empire: The English Novel from Edgeword to Dickens* (New York: Columbia

University Press, 1991) and Patrick Brantlinger, *Rule of Darkness: British Literature and Imperialism, 1830–1914* (Ithaca, NY: Cornell University Press, 1988).

8 See: J. Brugman, *An Introduction to the History of Modern Arabic Literature in Egypt* (Leiden: E.J. Brill, 1984); Pierre Cachia, *An Overview of Modern Arabic Literature* (Edinburgh: Edinburgh University Press, 1990); and Roger Allen, *An Introduction to Arabic Literature* (Cambridge: Cambridge University Press, 1984), as well as Hilary Kirkpatrick, *The Modern Egyptian Novel: a Study in Social Criticism* (London: Ithaca Press for the Middle East Centre, St. Antony's College, 1974).

9 In the case of Luwis 'Awad, the nationalist case for a nineteenth century development of Egyptian literature is made in several texts. See: Luwis 'Awad, *Dirasat fi adabna al-hadith* (Cairo: Dar al-Ma'arifa, 1963). Also: Luwis 'Awad, *Tarikh al-fikr al-misri al-hadith: min 'asr Isma'il ila thawra 1919* (Cairo: Maktabat Madbuli, 1986). For other systematic and influential texts setting the terms for the assessment of literary values along the lines of novelistic writing concerning nineteenth-century Arabic literature see: 'Abd al-Muhsin Taha Badr, Tatawwur al-riwaya al-'Arabiyya (Cairo: Dar al-Ma'arif, 1968). Also: Ahmad Haykal, *Mujaz al-adab al-hadith fi Misr (ila qiyam al-harb al-'alamiyah al-thaniyah)* (Cairo: Maktabat al-Shabab, 1989).

10 Ali Gheissari offers a nuanced overview of modern Iranian intellectual history in *Iranian Intellectuals in the Twentieth Century*, including in his study a chapter on late nineteenth-century work as well. Kamran Talaatof's *The Politics of Writing in Iran, a History of Modern Persian Literature* presents a general theory for "modern" Persian literature through the contemporary period, through a periodization of literary work into several episodes enframed by political and ideological developments in Iran. Somewhat more of a cultural history, but much more critical in its analysis, is Mohamad Tavakoli-Targhi's *Refashioning Iran: Orientalism, Occidentalism and Historiography*. Each of these texts can be examined to understand the general outline of recent approaches to Iranian intellectual history of the nineteenth and twentieth centuries, in addition to modern Persian literary history. In the area of Arabic literature, Sabry Hafez's *The Genesis of Arabic Narrative Discourse* presents an alternative to predominant trends in scholarship on Arabic literature along somewhat different lines, by outlining sociological and empirical data to make more socially-oriented arguments concerning the production and consumption of Arabic literature in the late nineteenth and early twentieth centuries. Aziz al-Azmeh's *Islams and Modernities* provides a suggestive template for approaching the intellectual history of this period, including a critical conception of the category of modernity, through episodic and essayistic interventions on histories and theories of nineteenth- and twentieth-century Islamic intellectual productions. The neglected presence of women authors in the innovations of late nineteenth and early twentieth-century Arabic writing has been subject to new investigations, showing a wealth of texts requiring further scholarly attention. In particular, Joseph T. Zeidan's *Arab Women Novelists: The Formative Years and Beyond* has opened this area with new discoveries, as have important studies by Beth Baron (*The Women's Awakening in Egypt: Culture, Society, and the Press*) and Marilyn Booth ("Woman in Islam: Men and the 'Women's Press' in Turn-of-the-20th-Century Egypt"). As an innovation on the conception of literary historiographic work, Muhsin Jassim al-Musawi's *The Postcolonial Arabic Novel: Debating Ambivalence* works against the mould of chronotropic genealogies of literature, as it undertakes to locate recurrent themes and underlying tensions in Arabic writing from the nineteenth and twentieth centuries without relying upon simple periodizations. As noted, an important intervention in the predominant scholarship on the Arabic novel has come from Roger Allen in his article "Literary History and the Arabic Novel." One may wish to view Samah Selim's study *The Novel and the Rural Imaginary in Egypt, 1880–1985* as a kind of exemplar of the sort of rethinking of scholarship on the Arabic novel that is called for by Roger Allen.

11 For examples of this approach, see: M.M. Badawi, *Modern Arabic Literature and the West* (London: Ithaca Press for the Board of the Faculty of Oriental Studies, University of Oxford, 1985); Hilmi Budayr, *al-Mu'athirat al-ajnabiyya fi adab al-'Arabi al-hadith* (Cairo: Dar al-Ma'arif, 1982) and Mohammed Ali Shawabkeh, *Arabs and the West: A Study in the Modern Arabic Novel, 1935–1985* (Amman: Mu'tah University, 1992).

12 Examples of scholarship focusing on women readerships in Victorian England include: Mary Poovey, *Uneven Developments: The Ideological Work of Gender in Mid-Victorian England* (Chicago, IL: University of Chicago Press, 1988); Kate Flint, *The Woman Reader (1837–1914).* (Oxford: Oxford University Press, 1993); Nicola Diane Thompson, *Reviewing Sex: Gender and the Reception of Victorian Novels* (New York University Press, 1996); Jennifer Phegley, *Educating The Proper Woman Reader: Victorian Family Literary Magazines And The Cultural Health Of The Nation* (Columbus, OH: Ohio State University Press, 2004); Valerie Sanders, *Eve's Renegades: Victorian Anti-Feminist Women Novelists* (London: St. Martin's Press, 1996). The scholarship on Victorian travel writing is similarly rich and varied, some examples would include: Indrepal Grewal, *Home and Harem: Nation, Gender, Empire, and the Cultures of Travel* (Durham: Duke University Press, 1996), Laura Franey, *Victorian Travel Writing and Imperial Violence: British Writing of Africa 1855–1902* (London: Palgrave Macmillan, 2004); Amanda Gilroy (ed.), *Romantic Geographies: Discourses of Travel, 1775–1844* (Manchester: Manchester University Press, 2000). Reconsidering the definition of the literary text, recent scholarship has also begun to consider other forms of textuality as literary practice. See, for example, Amanda Gilroy and W.M. Verhoeven (eds), *Epistolary Histories: Letters, Fiction, Culture* (University Press of Virginia, 2000).

13 See Maggie Kilgore, *The Rise of the Gothic Novel* (New York: Routledge, 1995); Kelly Hurley and Gillian Beer (eds), *The Gothic Body: Sexuality, Materialism and Degeneration at the Fin de Siécle* (Cambridge: Cambridge University Press, 2004); Julian Wolfreys, *Victorian Hauntings: Spectrality, Gothic, the Uncanny and Literature* (Palgrave Macmillian, 2001); Cannon Schmitt, *Alien Nation: Nineteenth-Century Gothic Fictions and English Nationality* (Philadelphia: University of Philadelphia Press, 1997).

14 Richard Altick, *The English Common Reader* (Chicago, IL: University of Chicago Press, 1957).

15 In terms of Persian language sources, these would include: Yahya Aryanpur, *Az Saba ta Nima*, 2 vols (Tihran: Intisharat-i zaddar, 1994); Muhammad 'Ali Sipanlu, *Nivisandagan-i pishrau-i Iran: az mashrutiyat ta 1350* (*Tarikhchih-i ruman, qissah-i kutah, namayishnamih va naqd-i adabi dar Iran-i mu'asir*) (Tihran: Nigah, 1366 [1988]); Muhammad Isti'lami, *Adabiyat-i daurih-i bidari va mu'asir* (Tihran: (n/a) 2535 [1976]); Manzar Imam, *Adabiyat-i jadid-i Iran* (Tihran: Kitabistan, 1996); Hasan Mir 'Abidini, *Sad sal-i dastan-nivisi dar Iran* (Tihran: Nashr-i chishmih, 1380 [2001]); Muhsin Zulfaqri, *Tahlil-i sayr-i naqd-i dastan dar Iran* (Tihran: Atiyih, 2000); Muhammad Ja'far Yahaqqi, *Chun sabuy-i tishnih: tarikh-i adabiyat-i mu'asir-i Farsi* (Tihran: Jami, 1995); Muhammad Riza Shafi'i Kadkani, *Adabiyat-i Farsi az 'asr-i jami ta ruzgar-i ma* (Tihran: Nashr-i nay, 1378 [1999]); Ya'qub Azhand, *Kitabshinasi-i adabiyat-i dastani-i Iran* (Tihran: Armin, 1373 [1994]). In English these sources would include: Hassan Kamshad, *Modern Persian Prose Literature* (Cambridge: Cambridge University Press, 1966); Jan Rypka, *A History of Iranian Literature* (Dordorchet: D. Reidel, 1968); Edward G. Browne, *A Literary History of Persia* (Cambridge: Cambridge University Press, 1956) (in particular, Vol. 4); M.R. Ghanoonparvar, *Prophets of Doom: Literature as A Socio-Political Phenomenon in Modern Iran* (Lanham, MD: University Press of America, c.1984); M.R. Ghanoonparvar, *In a Persian Mirror: Images of the West and Westerners in Iranian Fiction* (Austin: University of Texas Press, c.1993).

16 This issue—the autonomy of the spiritual domain—has been subjected to sympathetic criticism. Joseph Massad accepts Chatterjee's theorization of a "spiritual" domain that distinguishes anti-colonial nationalisms from those of European origin but argues "whereas nationalists are agents in the construction of national culture, or what Chatterjee calls the 'spiritual', this domain is hardly 'sovereign' or independent from productive colonial machinations. The colonial state, through its institutions, is, in fact, instrumental in the production of national culture" (Massad, *Colonial Effects*, p. 7).

17 For more on the predicament of the limitations of both traditionalist and modernist modes of social analysis in the Arab world, see Abdallah Laroui, *The Crisis of the Arab Intellectual: Traditionalism or Historicism?* (Berkeley, CA: University of California Press, 1977).

18 Shafi'i Kadkani describes his interest in and study of modern Arabic literature in the introduction to his collection of translated modern Arabic poetry. See: Muhammad Safi'i Kadkani, *Shi'r-i mu'asir-i 'Arab* (Tehran: Intisharat-i Tehran, 1977).

19 In Iran, after the 1979 Revolution some study of Arabic became compulsory in the public schools, yet the training has been pedagogically poor and very elementary. The learning is also directed largely to grammatical issues that relate solely to religious study and the reading of the Qur'an. In comparison, the training is much less rigorous than the required English studies that are also a part of public school curricula. In Egypt, Cairo University does maintain a chair in Persian literature, and as of 2001 this position was held by Professor al-Saba'i Muhammad al-Saba'i. The major teaching duty of this chair is an undergraduate course on non-Arab contributions to Islamic culture.

20 By focusing largely on Levantine and Egyptian Arab literary figures, to the expense for example of writers from North African or Persian Gulf Arab, this study itself inevitably contains inherent limitations that must be acknowledged.

21 Along these same lines, Srinivas Aravamudan, argues "we should seek to make visible the limitations imposed by nationalist boundaries on scholarship by different pedagogical innovations that perpetrate an alienation effect…rather than accept borders as the lay of the literary landscape" (*Tropicopolitans*, p. 330).

22 This expansion on Bourdieau's terminology shares with his work a certain ambivalence with regard to Marxist analyses, which also foreground the economic role of cultural productions, but which often overstate the relations of "base and superstructure" in understanding the configuration of cultural capital within the capitalist economy. Frederic Jameson has attempted to offer a degree of compromise from the strict Marxist position, admitting that "exchange value, then, the emergence of some third, abstract term between two incomparable objects (an abstraction which, by way of the historical dialectic narrated by Marx…ultimately takes the form of money), constitutes the primordial form by which identity emerges in human history" (*Late Marxism*, p. 23).

2 BIOGRAPHIES OF THE *ARABIAN NIGHTS*, AN ENGLISH CHAPTER

1 I will use "the *Nights*" as a generic title in discussing the European phenomenon of texts produced ostensibly on the basis of the Arabic *Alf layla wa layla* tradition. Actual given titles of different published editions will be cited as they are referred to.

2 The earliest known possible reference to a text of a similar name (under the Persian title "Hizar Afsanih") occurs in Ibn al-Nadim's (d. 955) canonizing survey of Islamic literary and cultural works, *al-Fihrist*. See: Muhammad ibn Ishaq ibn al-Nadim, *Fihrist*, Gustave Flugel (ed.) (Bayrut: Khayats, 1964), Vol. 1, p. 304. Fragments of this text are found on the papyri presented in Nabia Abbott, "A Ninth Century Fragment of the 'Thousand Nights': New Light on the Early History of the *Arabian Nights*" *Journal of Near Eastern Studies*, July 1949: 129–64. Abbott's transcription only includes 16 lines

of text found on several scraps of papyrus, but nonetheless makes clear that in the ninth century the frame story for the *Nights* was used in Arabic scribal literature.

3 Of these, Robert Irwin's *The Arabian Nights: A Companion* complements several other works: in particular the research of Muhsin Mahdi on the various recensions of the *Nights* in the introduction of his Arabic edition, and the earlier comparative analysis of the translations of the *Nights* carried out by Mia Gerhardt. For more on the British criticism of the Nights, see: Jassim Ali, *Scheherazade in England*. Washington DC: Three Continents Press, 1981.

4 A concise account of Galland's construction of the *Nuits* from this manuscript appears in Muhsin Mahdi, *The Thousand and One Nights* (Leiden: E.J. Brill, 1994), pp. 10–49.

5 The context within which Hole presented his thesis is important to consider; even by the late eighteenth century, the *Nights* had become a lightning rod in disputes between the neo-classical ideal and the emerging turn toward a romantic imagination, which availed itself of orientalia.

6 "The Arabian Nights Entertainments, carefully revised, and occasionally corrected from the Arabic," *The American Quarterly Review*, December 1829: 295.

7 See: Muhsin Mahdi, *The Thousand and One Nights* (Leiden: Brill Press, 1994) pp. 17–20, 27–34 for a thorough accounting of how Galland obtained both "Sindbad" and his manuscript of "Alf Layla wa Layla" and how he came to decide to include the former in his *Nuits*. Mahdi also shows that Galland inserted another story "Qamarazzaman" from yet another source into his *Nuits*. Before Mahdi's important tracing of the origins of Sindbad, no clear consensus existed among scholars as to its legitimacy as part of the *Nights*. For example, in the same year as the publication of Mahdi's study, Robert Irwin would be led to presume that Galland had access to another *Nights* manuscript containing the several tales shown by Mahdi to have been imported from other sources (Irwin, *Arabian Nights*, p. 47). For more on these issues, also see Dwight Reynolds discussion of the *Nights* in his entry "Arabic Literature in the Post-Classical Period" in the *Cambridge History of Arabic Literature* (2006, pp. 270–91).

8 In this, it follows on the concerns by British elites for the dangers a mass reading public was thought pose to established class and gender roles. For more on this subject, see: Patrick Brantlinger, *The Reading Lesson: The Threat of Mass Literacy in Nineteenth-Century British Fiction* (Bloomington, IN: Indiana University Press, 1998), pp. 49–68. Also, for an account of the gendering of reading in nineteenth century England see: Flint, *The Woman Reader (1837–1914)*, pp. 209–30.

9 Also known as the Breslau Edition, edited by the German orientalist Joseph Freiherr von Hammer-Purgstall. The review refers to its translation, rendered into English by George Lamb. See: George Lamb (trans. and ed.), *New Arabian Nights' Entertainments* (selected from the original MS by Jos. von Hammer) 3 vols (London: H. Colburn, 1829).

10 Al-Musawi also notes that in Arab societies the *Nights* suffered "centuries of neglect by the classicists." Muhsin Jassim al-Musawi, *The Postcolonial Arabic Novel: Debating Ambivalence*, p. 4.

11 For a critical biography of Lane, see: Leila Ahmed, *Edward W. Lane*, London: Longman, 1978.

12 Quoted in Richard Burton, *Supplemental Nights*, Vol. VII, p. 494.

13 Sigma, "Pantagruelism or Pornography?" *Pall Mall Gazette*, September 14, 1885.

14 See: Sir Richard Burton, *The Book of the Thousand Nights and a Night* (London: H.S. Nichols), 1897. However, for ease of reference all citations from the Burton introduction will be to the following, more widely-accessible, edition: Sir Richard Burton, *The Arabian Nights, Tales from a Thousand and One Nights* (New York: Modern Library, 2001).

15 This of course marks another difference in perspective between Burton and E.W. Lane, whose work continuously returned to the idea of the *Nights* as providing an essential view on the ethnographic peculiarities of the Arabs. Where Burton saw the text as part

of an active engagement with Arab society, Lane utilized it as a transhistorical window onto the typical characteristics and qualities of the Arab. See in particular: E.W. Lane, *Arabian Society in the Middle Ages; Studies from the Thousand and One Nights* (London: Chatto and Windus), 1883.

3 MODERN ARABIC AND PERSIAN BIOGRAPHIES OF THE *ARABIAN NIGHTS*

1 Mahdi, Muhsin *The Thousand and One Nights*. Leiden: E.J. Brill, 1994.

2 It is not possible to sufficiently explore this point here. For a more general discussion concerning Egyptian reform projects and their relation to the emergence of new modes of consumption of literature in the eighteenth and nineteenth centuries see: Gran, *Islamic Roots of Capitalism: Egypt, 1760–1840*, pp. 151–64.

3 For more on this history, see Muhsin Jassim al-Musawi, *al-Riwaya al-'Arabiyya: al-nasha wa al-tahawwul* (al-Qahira: al-Hay'a al-Misriyya al-'Amma lil-Kitab), 1988.

4 *Alf layla wa layla* (Beirut: 1895).

5 It may be telling that in the issue of this publication available at the Princeton University library, it would appear the original owner of the journal has crossed out "Alf layla wa layla" in both instances of its appearance, and has written in "Kalilah wa Dimnah" over it. The marking may be from a later reader, but one may read this intervention upon the text as a possible sign of the early confusion over the history of *Alf layla wa layla*, and of a further sign of the general lack of information about this supposedly canonical text.

6 Ulrich Marzolph reports "although Turkish translations from the Arabic already existed before Galland's French adaptation, Persian translations apparently were not prepared before the beginning of the nineteenth century." Other than fragmentary translations, Tasuji's translation appears to be the first attempt at a complete edition, and was the first to be printed as a book. See: Ulrich Marzolph, "Persian Translations of the 1001 Nights," *Mipaku Anthropology Newsletter*, No. 16 (2003). Also, Muhammad Ja'far Mahjub, "Tarjumih-yi Farsi-yi *Alf layla wa layla*," *Sokhan*, Vol. 11. No. 1 (1962): 34–53.

7 See Amanat, *Pivot of the Universe*, pp. 46–57 for more on the struggle over the appointment of the young Nasir al-Din to the position of crown prince (*vali 'ahd*).

8 The cultural legacy of 'Abbas Mirza, and his program termed *nizam-i jadid* (the new order) is described in: Monica Ringer, *Education, Religion and the Discourse of Cultural Reform in Qajar Iran* (Costa Mesa, CA: Mazda Publishers, 2001), pp. 15–51.

9 In his biography of Nasir al-Din Shah, Amanat makes no mention of Tasuji having gained this title, although he notes that Tasuji had been a tutor for Bahman Mirza's children. Instead he states that Tasuji was "part of Nasir al-Din's literary ensemble" (Amanat, *Pivot of the Universe*, pp. 59–66). Indeed, a variety of sources agree that previous to Tasuji, Mulla Mahmud Nizam al-'Ulama was known as the *Mulla-Bashi*. However, I am inclined to follow Mahjub's account that Tasuji came into the title later, and having carried the Hajj pilgrimage to Mecca, gained the title *Hajj Mulla-Bashi* (Mahjub, *Tarjumih*, p. 36). This is corroborated by M. Qazvini, "Wafiyat-i ma'asirin," *Yadgar*, Vol. 5, Nos. 8–9 (1949): 69.

10 This point is corroborated M. Qazvini, "Wafiyat" 70. Qazvini's information comes from Yahya Dowlatabadi, another distant relative of Tasuji who had met him as a child.

11 Zill al-Sultan became a noted supporter of modern educational institutions in Isfahan, including schools for girls (Ringer, *Education*, p. 127).

12 Amanat cites the date 1845 (Amanat, *Pivot of the Universe*, p. 66) although Mahjub views that date as improbable.

13 No significant attempt has been made to carry out a close comparative study of Tasuji's translation and the Bulaq edition—reading both, I have found significant divergences between the two. Unfortunately a fuller discussion of this cannot be carried out here and will require further study.

4 THE INNER SUBJECTS OF ARABIC AND PERSIAN TRAVEL TEXTS ON EUROPE

1 This triumphalism lies at the core of Horkheimer and Adorno's critique of one template for the epic imagination—Homer's *Odyssey*—in *Dialectic of Enlightenment*. Horkheimer and Adorno present a multifarious critique of the *Odyssey* and so illuminate several key tropes of enlightenment thought. In opposition to Lukacs, they outline resonances between the enlightened novelistic and mythic epic imaginations, both of which can result in what they term totalizing conceptions of subjectivity. Early in their discussion of the epic, they propose reading Odysseus' journeys as a narration of man's conquest of the world of gods—"the flight of the individual from the mythical powers." This individual is however situated centrally to the Enlightenment's development, as Odysseus is "a prototype of the bourgeois individual, whose concept originates in [his] coherent self-affirmation." In this, the *Odyssey* presents a "protohistory" of subjectivity and the attempts of subjectivity to escape "prehistory." Beyond this central theme of the subject's relation to myth exist several sub-themes, key among them being: the translation of sacrifice into cunning (what might be called the relation of rationality to myth), the quest for identity in non-identity, and the relation of subject to authority. These themes are central to the process of enlightenment, particularly in its "fundamental" stages, where the *Odyssey* is located, and directly implicates canonical novelistic writing in these totalizing processes. See: Max Horkheimer and Theodore Adorno, "Odysseus or Myth and Enlightenment." Robert Hullot-Kentor, trans. *New German Critique*, Vol. 56 (1992): 109–141.

2 An example of this would be Mohammad R. Ghanoonparvar, *In a Persian Mirror: Images of the West and Westerners in Iranian Fiction* (Austin, TX: University of Texas Press, 1993). A groundbreaking study of the impact of travel writing on Arab intellectual history is Ibrahim Abu-Lughod, *The Arab Rediscovery of Europe: A Study in Cultural Encounters* (Princeton: Princeton University Press, 1963).

3 Some of these seventeenth-century travelogues have been translated in excerpts in Nabil Matar, *In the Lands of the Christians* (London: Routledge Press, 2003). Some have also appeared in recent editions in Arabic, such as: Ilyas al-Musili's *al-Dhahab wa al-'asifa: awwal rihla sharqiyya ila al-'alam al-jadid (1683–1668)*. Nouri al-Jarrah (ed.), Bayrut: al-mu'assissa al-'Arabiyya lil-dirasat wa al-nashr, 2001.

4 Shirazi's travelogue is later than another important text, which cannot be discussed in detail here: *Masir-i Talibi* by Mirza 'Abu Talib Khan (1752–1806). This is a travelogue chronicling a journey from Calcutta to Europe in 1799–1803, written by a Persian clerk from Northern India in the first decade of the nineteenth century. 'Abu Talib's text is not within the genre of "official" travelogue writing—that is, he was not responding to an official sanction, nor was he acting in diplomatic or other capacities. Instead, it represents a hybrid form between the subjective and the empirical modes of travel-writing. See: Mirza Abu Talib Khan, *Masir-i Talibi ya safarnamih-yi Mirza 'Abu Talib Khan*, 2nd edn, Tihran: Saziman-i entisharat va amuzish-i enqilab-i islami, 1363 [1984].

5 A later travelogue of similar merit to al-Tahtawi's, Khayr al-Din al-Tunisi's *Aqwam al-masalik fi ma'rifat ahwal al-mamalik*, pursues a similar function from the perspective of a North African functionary of the Tunisian Bey. See: Khayr al-Din al-Tunisi *The Surest Path: The Political Treatise of a Nineteenth-Century Muslim Statesman,*

A Translation of the Introduction to The Surest Path To Knowledge Concerning The Condition of Countries, Brown, Leon Carl (trans.) Cambridge, MA: Center for Middle Eastern Studies, Harvard University, 1967.

6 Beyond serving as works of textual transaction, both travelogues also serve as starting points for activities that distinguished their authors in later stages of their lives and work. In this sense, these textual transactions serve as the basis for the transactional lives of their authors. For example, Shirazi's fascination with the periodical press in England, to which he devotes considerable attention in his *safarnamih*, is no doubt a factor in his later occupation as publisher of the first Persian newspaper in Iran (Shirazi, *Guzarish-i Safar-i Mirza Salih Shirazi*, Humayun Shahidi (ed.), Tihran: intisharat-i rah-i nou, 1983, pp. 10–15).

7 Al-Tahtawi's work as a translator has been examined by several studies: Brugman includes a bibliography of these works. See: J. Brugman, *An Introduction to the History of Modern Arabic Literature in Egypt*, Series in Arabic Literature, M.M. Badawi (ed.) (Leiden: E.J. Brill, 1984), pp. 18–24.

8 Rifa'a Bayg Badawi Rafi' al-Tahtawi, *Takhlis al-ibriz fi talkhis bariz* (Cairo: Maktaba al-Kulliyya al-Azhariyya, Dar Ibn Zaydun, n/d). Translation: Rifa'a Rafi' al-Tahtawi and Daniel Newman, *An Imam in Paris: An Account of a Stay in France by an Egyptian Cleric (a Translation of Takhlis al-Ibriz fi Talkhis Bariz)*, trans. Daniel Newman (London: Saqi Books, 2004), pp. 195–205.

9 On this topic, see: Gran, *Islamic Roots of Capitalism: Egypt 1760–1840*, in particular chapters 4 and 5. Gran argues that the inspiration for al-Tahtawi's innovations, and indeed some of the innovations themselves, should be credited to al-'Attar.

10 Brugman places it under the heading "Beginnings of the Renaissance" (Chapter 1) and Hourani calls al-Tahtawi "the writer who first made articulate the idea of the Egyptian nation" (Brugman, *Introduction to the History of Modern Iran*, p. 68).

11 See: Mohammad Sawaie, "Rifa'a Rafi' al-Tahtawi and his Contribution to the Lexical Development of Modern Literary Arabic," *International Journal of Middle East Studies*, Vol. 32 (2000): 395–410.

12 For information on the translation programs under Muhammad 'Ali, see: Matti Moosa, *The Origins of Modern Arabic Fiction*, Boulder, CO: Lynne Rienner Publishers, Inc., 1997, pp. 98–9. Also see: Brugman, *An Introduction to the History of Modern Arabic Literature in Egypt*, pp. 215–18.

13 James Justinian Morier, *A Journey through Persia, Armenia, and Asia Minor, to Constantinople, in the Years 1808 and 1809 in Which Is Included, Some Account of the Proceedings of His Majesty's Mission, under Sir Harford Jones, Bart. K.C. To the Court of the King of Persia*, microform, Philadelphia, PA: M. Carey, 1816.

14 The work was titled *Mawaqi'al-aflak fi waqai'i' Tilimak* and is also discussed at some length by Albert Hourani (*Arab Thought*, pp. 73–5).

15 For more on Sayyah's attaining of American citizenship, see: Ali Ferdowsi, "Eating Corpse: The Deplorable Asylum of Hajj Sayyah at the US Legation in Tehran," *Annales of the Japan Association for Middle East Studies*, Vol. 11 (1996). For more on his experience under the protection of the American Legation in Tehran, see: Ali Ferdowsi, "Hajj Sayyah," *Encyclopedia Iranica*, Ehsan Yarshater (ed.), November 19, 2004. Columbia University Press. www.iranica.com/articles/v11f5/v11f5046.html Accessed June 2006.

16 He reports feeling near death after some 48 hours without food, something that appears to be a slight exaggeration given the fact that individuals have been known to carry out hunger strikes for many days and as much as several weeks before approaching death. The fictive dimension of this narration simply affirms thesis of this reading that the inclusion of this episode provides him with a transitional point for describing a personal transformation rather than serving as a simple report of events.

17 An excellent biographical essay on Maraghihi appears in the critical introduction to an edition of *Siyahatnamih* edited with an introduction by M.A. Sepanlu (Zayn al-'Abedin Maraghihi, *Siyahatnamih-yi Ibrahim Bayg*, M.A. Sepanlu (ed.), Tehran: Agah Press, 2nd edn, 2006).

18 Two Persian editions of *Siyahatnamih* have been prepared in recent years; one is a heavily abridged edition prepared by Muhammad Amin, while M.A. Sepanlu's text is authoritative and complete. It should be noted that differences exist over the pronunciation of the protagonist's name—Bayg, or Bayk, is an honorific title in currency throughout the Ottoman world, and in both Arabic and English is often rendered as Bey. Amin's edition uses the term "Bayk" while Sepanlu uses "Bayg." As all references here are to the Sepanlu edition, I have also followed his preference in the transliteration of the title as Bayg.

19 By way of an example: we are told that Ibrahim Bayg refuses to utter the name of the city of Alexandria, for the legacy of Alexander's pillaging of Persepolis pains him too much. Instead he calls it "an Egyptian harbor" Maraghihi, *Siyahatnamih-yi Ibrahim Bayg*, p. 36.

20 See: Huma Nateq, "Mirza Aqa Khan, Sayyid Jamal al-Din et Malkum Khan à Istanbul (1860–1897)," in T. Zarcone and F. Zarinebaf (eds), *Les Iraniens d'Istanbul*, Paris: Institut Français de Recherches en Iran & Institute Français d'Etudes Anatoliennes, 1993, pp. 45–60.

21 For more on Chihrinama, see: Mohammad Yadegari, "The Iranian Settlement in Egypt as Seen Through the Pages of the Community's Newspaper Chihrinama (1904–1966)" *Middle East Studies*, Vol. 16 (May 1980). For details concerning the Iranian community in Cairo, see: Anja Luesnink, "The Iranian Community in Cairo at the Turn of the Century" in T. Zarcone & F. Zarinebaf (eds), *Les Iraniens d'Istanbul*, Paris: Institut Français de Recherches en Iran & Institute Français d'Etudes Anatoliennes, pp. 193–202. I am thankful to Houshang Chehabi for directing me to these sources.

22 For more on the development of and competition between pan-Islamist and nationalist movements in Egypt, see: Israel Gershoni and James P. Jankowski, *Egypt, Islam, and the Arabs: The Search for Egyptian Nationhood, 1900–1930* (Oxford: Oxford University Press, 1987).

23 It should be said that all the first three book editions collecting the "Fitra min al-Zaman" articles into book form leave out the Paris episodes. Yet, the omission of the "second Journey" on the basis of their later inclusion in the book editions is a matter for greater discussion than may be possible here—suffice to say that the Paris narrative is an important part of the original serialized episodes offered in *Misbah al-Sharq*.

5 ON NOTHING AND EVERYTHING: TRAVEL, CONVERSION, AND THE TRANSFORMATIONS OF (AHMAD) FARIS AL-SHIDYAQ, ARAB OBSERVER OF EUROPE

1 The title is notoriously difficult to render into English—it follows a classical Arabic literary practice, as yet common in the nineteenth century, for preference of rhyme and wordplay in titles, over those that literally transmit an intention or summary of the text. One may render the title fairly literally as "A Leg Over a Leg, On He Who is Faryaq"—the full title also includes a secondary phrase: "Or, the Days and Months and Years in Arab and Non-Arab Lands." The phrase " 'al-Saq 'ala al-Saq" (A Leg Over a Leg) is often imputed to contain a sexual connotation, as well as possibly referring to the act of travel. But the title is full of ambiguity; as Roger Allen has pointed out, the first phrase of title could also be read as "The Pigeon on the Tree-Branch," although the implications of this reading are perhaps less provocative than the sexual or travel-related allusions cited above ("Literary History and the Arabic Novel," p. 207). No doubt

al-Shidyaq wished to invoke the layers of meaning these various interpretations present by using this ambiguous title for his work.

2 *Al-Saq* has only been rendered into one other language, that being a 1991 French translation of the text by René Khawam. It is noteworthy that this edition is titled *La Jambe Sur la Jambe: Roman*—a textbook example of novelism: Ahmad Faris Shidyaq and René R. Khawam, *La Jambe Sur La Jambe: Roman*, Domaine, Étranger, (Paris: Phébus, 1991).

3 Haywood terms *al-Saq* an "autobiographical work" (Haywood, *Modern Arabic Literature*, p. 20). Even Trablusi and al-Azmeh follow the trend of using the text as a biographical reference in their otherwise critical writing on al-Shidyaq. See: al-Shidyaq, *Silsilat al- amal al-majhula.*

4 The litany continues for another 1/2 page.

5 The episode of Kuchak Hanem forms a central point of Edward Said's analysis of the relationship of the centrality of sexuality in the romantic imagination to orientalist discourse in Edward W. Said, *Orientalism* (New York: Vintage, 1994), pp. 186–9.

6 One of the shortcomings of the French translation of *al-Saq* is its inattention to the layout and general organization of the original text. *La Jambe Sur La Jambe*, Faris Chidyaq (Paris: Phébus, 1991) René R. Khawam (trans.), p. 519.

7 It must be said here that it is not the object of this study to offer insights into the biographical information available on Shidyaq. Indeed, in Arabic several studies of his life are available, among them the are: Marun 'Abbud, *Saqr Lubnan: Bahth fi al-nahda al-adabiyya al-haditha wa ajuliha al-awwal Ahmad Faris al-Shidyaq* (Beirut: Dar al-Kashshaf, 1950). Also: 'Imad Sulh, *Ahmad Faris al-Shidyaq: Atharuhu wa 'asruhu* (Bayrut: Dar al-Nahhar lil-Nashr, 1980). In English the most comprehensive effort in this direction is the unpublished doctoral dissertation of Muhammad Bakir Alwan, "Ahmad Faris Shidyaq and the West," PhD Dissertation, Indiana University, 1970.

8 A complete bibliography of Shidyaq's work can be found in Alwan ("Ahmad Faris Shidyaq" appendixes).

9 Speaking anecdotally, I found this ambivalence quite clear in experiences I had in 2001 speaking with booksellers in Cairo while attempting to locate copies of his work. I found that to even mention Shidayq's name sometimes led to a raised eyebrow, or a sarcastic comment on the part of the members of the community of used and antiquarian book vendors in Izbikiyya Gardens area of the city. Some booksellers half-jokingly insinuated that my attraction to his work was possibly based on its supposed sexual content—it seemed a common conception that at least some of his work is pornographic. Another vendor opened a discussion by asking, "so what do you think? Did he really convert to Islam?" Then he commented that Shidyaq was no longer read by anyone. "Perhaps no one reads him because no one knows what religion he followed?" Yet this same question also seemed to be the reason for a continuing interest in him in other establishments. I eventually found a copy of *al-Saq 'ala al-Saq* in a back storeroom of a well-known bookshop in Cairo. I was led to this back room with an enthusiasm and interest roughly equal to the disdain or disinterest my inquiries had raised for some other booksellers—here I spoke with the young bookseller for some time as he rather lovingly dwelled on the complexities of *al-Saq* and the legacy of Shidyaq. Admittedly, the question of the contemporary consumption of and discourse on Shidyaq is certainly more complex than this anecdote may address. A related issue is the history of the republication of editions of Shidyaq's works—after the 1855 Paris edition, and subsequent al-Jawa'ib press editions, *al-Saq*, two subsequent editions were produced in Cairo, one in 1919 by Yusif al-Bustani's Maktabat al-'Arab press, and the second is an undated copy of al-Bustani's edition, published by Maktabat al-Tijariyya. Since then, the text has been republished in Beirut by Maktabat al-Hayat in 1966 (and also, it is likely, in new runs of this edition, with the date unchanged, since then), not counting

an abridged edition: Ahmad Faris al-Shidyaq and 'Imad Sulh, *I'tirafat al-Shidyaq fi kitab al-saq 'ala al-saq*, 5 edn (Bayrut: Dar al-Raid al-'Arabi, 1982). This trend—a shift in republications from Cairo to Beirut—may further indicate a possible waning of interest in Shidyaq in Cairo in the latter part of the twentieth century, as interest in him in Beirut has apparently increased somewhat during the same period.

10 The year and exact location of Shidyaq's birth have long been in dispute. A.G. Karam's entry on Shidyaq in the *Encyclopaedia of Islam* rejects any date but 1804. See: A.G. Karam, *Encyclopedia of Islam: "Faris Al-Shidyak,"* version 1.1, 2001, CD-ROM, Brill. Yet this entry makes no mention of a claim advanced by al-Sulh that two letters written by Shidyaq, indicate that he himself dated his birth to 1801. In error, Trablusi and al-Azmeh state that al-Sulh dates the birth to 1804—he clearly advances 1801 as the date that Shidyaq believed he was born (Sulh, *Ahmad Faris al-Shidyaq*, p. 23).

11 Indeed, even his grandfather suffered from politically motivated conflict within the community—al-Azmeh and Trablusi report that he committed suicide after losing his property to a local strongman.

12 As'ad's conversion and death are chronicled in detail in: Butrus ibn Bulus Bustani, *Qissa As'ad al-Shidyaq* (Bayrut: Dar al-Hamra, 1992). Also see: Ussama Makdisi, "Reclaiming the Land of the Bible: Missionaries, Secularism and Evangelical Modernity," *American Historical Review*, Vol. 102, No. 3 (1997): 680–713.

13 Al-Bustani's account of As'ad's death recounts that Faris escaped under threats from his own brothers, who were vehemently opposed to As'ad and Faris' skepticism.

14 His attacks on both Protestant and Catholic clergy punctuate *al-Saq* and take up entire chapters at a time. See in particular: Book 1, Chapter 5; Book 1, Chapter 15 and Chapter 16; Book 1, Chapter 20; Book 3, Chapter 20; Book 3, Chapter 19.

15 See especially the introduction to: Ahmad Faris al-Shidyaq, Fawwaz Trabulsi and Aziz al-Azmeh, *Silsilat al-a'mal al-majhula* (London: Riad El-Rayyes, 1995).

16 See: A.J. Arberry, "Fresh Light on Ahmad Faris al-Shidyaq," *Islamic Culture* (1952), pp. 155–68. for a better sense of the very high hopes al-Shidyaq held for the impact of *al-Saq*.

17 Jaroslav Stetkevytch dismisses the work as "a grotesque ode" (10) while Arberry terms this poem "an interesting example of the nineteenth century revival of classical norms" (A.J. Arberry, "Fresh Light," p. 157).

18 In a discussion of Shidyaq in her PhD dissertation, Janine Abboushi Dallal briefly compares some corresponding passages between *al-Saq* and *Kashf al-mukhabba* (Dallal, "The Beauty of Imperialism").

19 See especially the opening chapter of Book 1, which contains several digressions on the ignorance of religious clerics, especially of the Arabic language.

20 For more on the development of and competition between pan-Islamist and nationalist movements in Egypt, see: Israel Gershoni and James P. Jankowski, *Egypt, Islam, and the Arabs: The Search for Egyptian Nationhood, 1900–1930* (Oxford: Oxford University Press, 1987).

6 TRANSACTIONS AND TRANSLATIONS: *HAJJI BABA ISPAHANI'S* VALUE BETWEEN ENGLISH AND PERSIAN READERSHIPS

1 This popularity is as "enduring" among Persian readers as it has been among Anglophone readerships, if not more so. This is evinced by the continual reprintings of earlier editions. Also, the novelist and critic Ja'far Mudarris Sadeghi has edited a new edition that was printed in 2000, with an excellent critical introduction.

2 The introductions to two editions of *Hajji Baba* by and Richard Jennings (1949) and Richard Altick (1954) both display a similar kind of ambivalence concerning the relative literary value of the text.

3 "In this connection mention should also be made of the Persian translation made by the talented and unfortunate Hajji Shaykh Ahmad 'Ruhi' of Kerman of Morier's *Hajji Baba…*" (Browne, *Literary History*, p. 468).

4 These debates are described in detail by Huma Natiq, "Haji Morier va qissih-yi isti'mar." Also, it is no more than a curious coincidence, perhaps, that in recording the Ali Baba narrative from an Arab source for use in his edition of the Arabian Nights, Galland indicates in his extant notes that the original name for this famous character was "Hogia Baba" (Chraibi, "Galland's 'Ali Baba'," p. 160).

5 Useful biographical information on Mirza Habib may be also be found in the afore-mentioned edition of Hajji Baba prepared by Sadeghi (2000).

6 Muhammad Khan himself died under suspicious circumstances after he was exiled from Tehran to Mashhad by Nasir al-Din Shah in 1866 (Amanat, *Pivot of the Universe*, p. 398).

7 One such poem is contained in the collection: Khan Malak Sasani, *Yadbudha-yi sifarat-i Istanbul* (1966), p. 162.

8 This text has been recently published in a new edition: Mirza Habib Isfahani, *Khatt Va Khattatan* (Tihran: Kitabkhanih mustufi, 1991).

9 The portrait drawn of Mirza Habib by the Iranian travelogue writer Haji Pirzadeh confirms his less than refined habits and manners, which are subject to Pirzadeh's condemnation despite his admiration of Mirza Habib's literary skills. See: Pirzadeh, Muhammad Ali, *Safarnameh-yi Haji Pirzadeh* (Tihran: Intisharat-i babak, 1360/1981) Vol. 2, pp. 94–6. Mr Manuchehr Kasheff, an instructor of Persian at Columbia University, has informed me anecdotally that Mirza Habib was known to have created a remarkable body of obscene poetry as well, which was circulated in Iran as well as among émigrés abroad; I have found no published record of this legacy.

10 This is mentioned in Jamalzadeh's introduction to his edition of the text: James Justinian Morier, Mirza Habib Isfahani and Muhammad 'Ali Jamalzadih, *Sarguzasht-i Haji Baba-yi Isfahani* (Costa Mesa, CA: Mazda Publishers, 1996). Also, a 1952 edition of Hajji Baba in Persian, apparently the first edition to be published in Iran, states that it is "based on two written manuscripts and *two Calcutta editions*"—more evidence of a second edition that may have been contemporary to Phillott's (See: James Justinian Morier, *Sarguzasht-i Haji Baba-yi Isfahani* (Tihran: 1330 (1951/2)). Of note is also the fact that if the 1952 edition is the first Iranian printing of Hajji Baba, its timing is rather provocative, coinciding as it does with the nationalization of oil by Mossadeq and the exiling of Muhammad Reza Shah until his restating in the CIA-organized coup of 1952.

11 There is no indication that Mirza Habib knew English, and E.G. Browne reports that he did translate *Gil Blas* and plays by Moliere from French into Persian. It is likely that Mirza Habib worked from the 1824 translation by Defauconpret: James Justinian Morier, *Hajji Baba*, traduit de l'anglais par le traducteur des romans de sir Walter Scott, Auguste-Jean-Baptiste Defauconpret. Paris: Haut-Coeur et Gayet jeune, 1824. For more on Mirza Habib's translations from French literature see: Maryam B. Sanjabi, "Mardum-Guriz: An Early Persian Translation of Moliere's Le Misanthrope," *International Journal of Middle East Studies*, Vol. 30, No. 2 (May 1998): 251–70.

12 "Round" being a term appropriated from its use by Deidre Shauna Lynch, *The Economy of Character* (Chicago, IL: Chicago University Press, 1998). Of course, literary studies of character have made the distinction between "full"/"empty" characters and other similar configurations.

13 All further references to the English text of Hajji Baba will be to the following edition: James Justinian Morier, *The Adventures of Hajji Baba of Ispahan* (London: Cresset Press, 1949).

14 The reviewer includes gloating remarks about the irrationality of a female character in Hajji Baba as reminiscent of English girls "in every boarding school for five miles around London."

15 A curious embellishment on the notion of "the public" readership is hinted at in a letter from Morier to James Murray, his publisher, in negotiations for the terms of the publication of his latest work, *Zohrab, the Hostage.* Apparently, after giving a manuscript of the work to Frances Burney, and having met with her approval, Morier asked Murray to consider the fact that Burney "is an author herself and likely to know the tastes of her sex & *as they will form the greater part of my readers* I think her approbation valuable." (quoted in Henry McKenzie Johnston, *Ottoman and Persian Odysseys*, p. 218. Emphasis added). Unfortunately, this study cannot begin to tackle the complication this comment introduces to a notion of the "reading public" who would consume oriental settings in novels in 1824.

16 See, for example, the memoir: Murtiza Musfiq Kashani, *Ruzigarha va andishihha* (Tihran: Ibn Sina, 1962), p. 59. This memoir, includes descriptions of public readings of books and newspapers. Even though Kashani's memoir describes a period some fifteen years after Shaykh Ahmad's death, we may imagine that this practice was established previously, with public readings of Constitutional Revolution-era newspapers and books. Aryanpur also describes the manner in which expatriate publishers of reform literature such as pamphlets and newspapers would anonymously mail their publications to a variety of people, both sympathizers and not, in Iran through intermediary addresses in Paris or Berlin (Aryanpur, *Az Saba ta Nima*, Vol. 2, pp. 21–5).

CONCLUSION: TOWARD CRITICAL PHILOLOGY

1 I would like to acknowledge my debt to Elliott Colla for his suggestion of the term "critical philology" to describe the methodological framework I discuss here.

BIBLIOGRAPHY

N.B. All translated editions of "Alf layla wa layla" are listed by the name of the translator.

Periodicals cited (alphabetically by publication)

"Mirza Habib Isfahani," *Akhtar*, May 23, 1893, Vol. 19, no. 13: 206.

"The Arabian Nights Entertainments, carefully revised, and occasionally corrected from the Arabic," *The American Quarterly Review*, December 1829: 283–303.

"Hajji Baba of Ispahan," *Blackwood's Edinburgh Magazine*, LXXXIV(1824): 51.

"Athar adabiyya: Alf layla wa layla," *al-Dhiya*, Vol. 3(1900–1901): 564–5.

" 'Arabian Nights', Review of 'The Book of a Thousand Nights and a Night'," *Edinburgh Review*, 335(1885): 174–84.

"Alf layla wa layla," *al-Hilal*, October 1, 1894: 107.

Sharif, Hikmat Bey. "Alf layla wa layla," *al-Hilal*, June 15, 1895: 852.

"Alf layla wa layla," *al-Hilal*, December 1, 1895: 252–4.

"Alf layla wa layla," *al-Hilal*, May 1, 1901: 446.

"Alf Layla wa layla," *al-Muqtataf*, May 1901: 474–5.

"Tabi 'al-radd 'ala Rizqallah Hassun," *al-Jawa'ib*, April 28, 1868: 2.

al-Jawa'ib. April 21, 1868: 3.

Sigma. "Pantagruelism or Pornography?" *Pall Mall Gazette*, September 14, 1885.

"So'ali az herat hiresad," *Qanun*, n/d, no. 17: 3.

"Dar bab-i ettehad-i millal-i Islam," *Qanun*, n/d no. 18: 1.

"New Arabian Nights Entertainments," *The Times*, Thursday, May 4, 1826: 3.

"On Novel Writing," *The Western Monthly Magazine and Literary Journal*, April 1834, 3(16): 193–200.

Books, articles, and monographs

Abbott, Nabia. "A Ninth-Century Fragment of the 'Thousand Nights': New Light on the Early History of the Arabian Nights," *Journal of Near Eastern Studies*, Vol. 8 (1949): 129–64.

Abboushi-Dallal, Janine. "The Beauty of Imperialism," PhD Dissertation, Harvard University, 1991.

'Abbud, Marun. *Saqr Lubnan: Bahth fi al-nahda al-adabiyya al-haditha wa rajuliha al-awwal Ahmad Faris al-Shidyaq*, Bayrut: dar al-kashshaf, 1950.

Abdel-Malek, Kamal and Hallaq, Wael (eds). *Tradition, Modernity, and Postmodernity in Arabic Literature: Essays in Honor of Professor Issa J. Boullata*, Boston, MA: Brill, 2000.

Abrahamian, Ervand. *Iran between Two Revolutions*, Princeton, NJ: Princeton University Press, 1982.

Abu-Lughod, Ibrahim. *The Arab Rediscovery of Europe: A Study in Cultural Encounters*, Princeton, NJ: Princeton University Press, 1963.

Abu Talib Khan, Mirza. *Masir-i Talibi ya safarnamih-yi Mirza Abu Talib Khan*, Tihran: saziman-i intisharat va amuzish-i inqilab-i Islami, 1363 [1984].

Adonis, An Introduction to Arab poetics, Austin: University of Texas Press, 1990.

Ahmed, Leila. *Edward W. Lane*, London: Longman, 1978.

Alcalay, Ammiel. *After Jews and Arabs: Remaking Levantine Culture*, Minneapolis, MN: University of Minnesota Press, 1992.

Alf layla wa layla, 5 vols, Beirut: 1888–1890.

Algar, Hamid. *Mirza Malkum Khan: A Study in the History of Iranian Modernism*, Berkeley, CA: University of California Press, 1973.

Ali, Jassim. *Scheherazade in England*, Washington, DC: Three Continents Press, 1981.

Allam, ‘Abd al-Rahim. “al-Riwayya al-Maghribiyya al-maktuba bi al-Arabiyya: 1942–2003,” *al-Rabat*: Wizara al-Thaqafa, 2003.

Allen, Roger. “The Beginnings of the Arabic Novel,” in M.M. Badawi (ed.), *Modern Arabic Literature*, Cambridge: Cambridge University Press, 1992, pp. 180–92.

——. *An Introduction to Arabic Literature*, Cambridge: Cambridge University Press, 1984.

——. “Literary History and the Arabic Novel,” *World Literature Today*, Vol. 75, No. 2 (Spring 2004): 204.

——. *A Period of Time: A Study and Translation of Hadith ‘Isa Ibn Hisham*, London: Ithaca Press, 1992.

Altick, Richard. *The English Common Reader*, Chicago, IL: University of Chicago Press, 1957.

Alwan, Muhammad Bakir. “Ahmad Faris Shidyaq and the West,” PhD Dissertation, Indiana University, 1970.

Amanat, Abbas. “Hajji Baba of Ispahan,” *Encyclopedia Iranica*, Ehsan Yarshater (ed.), Columbia University Press: November 19, 2004. www.iranica.com/articles/v11f6/v11f6002.html

——. *Pivot of the Universe*, Berkeley, CA: University of California Press, 1997.

Anderson, Benedict. *Imagined Communities*, New York: Verso, 1991.

Aravamudan, Srinivas. *Tropicopolitans*, Durham, NC: Duke University Press, 1999.

Arberry, A.J. “Fresh Light on Ahmad Faris al-Shidyaq,” *Islamic Culture*, Vol. XXVI (1952): 155–68.

Aryanpur, Yahya. *Az Saba ta Nima: tarikh-i sad u panjah sal-i adab-i Farsi*, 2 vols, Tihran: intisharat-i zaddar, 1994.

Austen, Jane. *Persuasion*, London: Penguin Books, 1994.

‘Awad, Luis. *Dirasat fi adabna al-hadith*, Cairo: dar al-ma’rifa, 1963.

——. *Tarikh al-fikr al-misri al-hadith: min ‘asr Isma’il ila thaura 1919*, Cairo: maktaba madbuli, 1986.

al-Azmeh, Aziz, *Islams and Modernities*, New York: Verso, 1993.

Badawi, M.M. (ed.). *Modern Arabic Literature*, Cambridge: Cambridge University Press, 1992.

——. *Modern Arabic Literature and the West*, London: Ithaca Press for the Board of the Faculty of Oriental Studies, University of Oxford, 1985.

——. *Qadhiyyat al-hadatha, wa masa’il ukhra fi al-naqd al-adabi*, Cairo: dar al-sharqiyat, 1999.

Bakhash, Shaul. *Iran: Monarchy, Bureaucracy and Reform under the Qajars: 1858–1896*, London: Ithaca Press, 1978.

Balaghi, Shiva. "Constitutionalism and Islamic Law in Nineteenth-Century Iran: Mirza Malkom Khan and Qanun," in Andas Sajo (ed.), *Human Rights with Modesty: The Problem of Universalism*, Leiden: Brill, 2004.

Baron, Beth. *The Women's Awakening in Egypt: Culture, Society, and the Press*, New Haven, CT and London: Yale University Press, 1994.

Beaumont, Daniel. *Slave of Desire: Sex, Love and Death in The 1001 Nights*, London: Associated University Presses, 2002.

Berman, Marshall. *All That is Solid Melts into Air: The Experience of Modernity*, New York: Penguin Books, 1982.

Bhabha, Homi (ed.). *Nation and Narration*, London: Routledge, 1990.

Birkalan, Hande A. "The Thousand and One Nights in Turkish," *Fabula*, Vol. 45(2004): 221–36.

Boehmer, Elleke. *Empire, the National and the Postcolonial: Resistance in Interaction*, London: Oxford University Press, 2002.

Booth, Marilyn. "Woman in Islam: Men and the 'Womens Press'" in Turn-of-The-20th-Century Egypt," *International Journal of Middle East Studies*, Vol. 33(2001): 171–201.

Borujerdi, Mehrzad. *Iranian Intellectuals and the West*, Albany, NY: State University of New York Press, 1993.

Boullata, Issa J. and DeYoung, Terri (eds). *Tradition and Modernity in Modern Arabic Literature*, Fayetteville, AR: University of Arkansas Press, 1997.

Bourdieu, Pierre. *Distinction: A Social Critique of the Judgment of Taste*. Cambridge, MA: Harvard University Press, 1984.

——. *The Field of Cultural Production. European Perspectives*, Lawrence Kritzman (ed.), New York: Columbia University Press, 1993.

——. *Practical Reason*, Palo Alto, CA: Stanford Unversity Press, 1998.

——. *The Rules of Art: Genesis and Structure of the Literary Field*, Palo Alto, CA: Stanford University Press, 1992.

Brantlinger, Patrick. *The Reading Lesson: The Threat of Mass Literacy in Nineteenth-Century British Fiction*, Bloomington, IN: Indiana University Press, 1998.

——. *Rule of Darkness: British Literature and Imperialism, 1830–1914*, Ithaca, NY: Cornell University Press, 1988.

Brodie, Fawn M. *The Devil Drives: A Life of Sir Richard Burton*, New York: W.W. Norton, 1967.

Browne, Edward Granville. *A Literary History of Persia*, 4 vols, Cambridge: Cambridge University Press, 1959.

——. *The Persian Revolution of 1905–1909*, Abbas Amanat (ed.), Washington, DC: Mage Publishers, 1995.

Brugman, J. *An Introduction to the History of Modern Arabic Literature in Egypt*, Leiden: E.J. Brill, 1984.

Budayr, Hilmi. *al-Muathirat al-ajnabiyya fi adab al-'Arabi al-hadith*, Cairo: dar al-ma'arif, 1982.

Burton, Richard. *The Arabian Nights, Tales from a Thousand and One Nights*, New York: Modern Library, 2001.

——. *The Book of the Thousand Nights and a Night*, 12 vols, London: H.S. Nichols, 1897.

——. *Supplemental nights to the Book of the thousand and one nights / with notes, anthropological and explanatory*, 6 vols, Benares: Kamashastra Society, 1886–88.

al-Bustani, Butrus ibn Bulus. *Qissa As'ad al-Shidyaq*, Bayrut: dar al-hamra, 1992.

Cachia, Pierre. *An Overview of Modern Arabic Literature*, Edinburgh: Edinburgh University Press, 1990.

——. "Translations and Adaptations 1834–1914," in M.M. Badawi (ed.), *Modern Arabic Literature*, Cambridge: Cambridge University Press, 1992, pp. 23–35.

Chatterjee, Partha. *The Nation and Its Fragments: Colonial and Postcolonial Histories*, Princeton, NJ: Princeton University Press, 1993.

——. *Nationalist Thought and the Colonial World*, Minneapolis, MN: Minnesota University Press, 1986.

Chraibi, Aboubakr. "Galland's 'Ali Baba' and Other Arabic Versions," *Marvels & Tales*, Vol. 18, No. 2(2004): 159–69.

——. "Texts of the Arabian Nights and Ideological Variations," *Middle Eastern Literatures*, Vol. 7, No. 2(July 2004): 149–57.

Cioeta, Donald J. "Ottoman Censorship in Lebanon and Syria, 1876–1908," *International Journal of Middle East Studies*, Vol. 10, No. 2 (1979): 170–1.

Clark, S.H. *Travel Writing and Empire: Postcolonial Theory in Transit*, London: Zed Books, 1999.

Cronin, Michael. *Across the Lines: Travel, Language Translation*, Cork, Ireland: Cork University Press, 2000.

David, Deidre. *The Cambridge Companion to the Victorian Novel*, Cambridge: Cambridge University Press, 2001.

de Man, Paul. "Literary History and Literary Modernity," in Karen Newman *et al.* (eds), *Time and the Literary*, New York: Routledge, 2004.

Eliot, Simon. "The Business of Victorian Publishing," in *The Cambridge Companion to the Victorian Novel*, edited by Deirdre A. David, Cambridge: Cambridge University Press, 2000, pp. 37–60.

Fattah, Hala. "Representations of Self and Other in Two Iraqi Travelogues of the Ottoman Period," *International Journal of Middle East Studies*, Vol. 30 (1998): 51–76.

Feltes, Norman. *Literary Capital and the Late Victorian Novel*, Madison, WI: University of Wisconsin Press, 1993.

Ferdowsi, Ali. "Eating Corpse: The Deplorable Asylum of Hajj Sayyah at the US Legation in Tehran," *Annals of the Japan Association for Middle East Studies*, Vol. 11 (1996): 251–86.

——. "Hajj Sayyah," *Encyclopedia Iranica*, Ehsan Yarshater (ed.), Accessed November 19, 2004. Columbia University Press. www.iranica.com/articles/v11f5/v11f5046.html

Flaubert, Gustave. *Flaubert in Egypt: A Sensibility on Tour*, Francis Steegmuller (trans.), New York: Penguin Books, 1972.

Flint, Kate. *The Woman Reader (1837–1914)*, Oxford: Oxford University Press, 1993.

Franey, Laura. *Victorian Travel Writing and Imperial Violence: British Writing of Africa 1855–1902*, London: Palgrave Macmillan, 2004.

Galland, Antoine. *Les Mille et Une Nuits, contes arabes*, 3 vols, Paris: Classiques Garnier, 1955.

Gerhardt, Mia. *The Art of Storytelling: A Literary Study of The Thousand and One Nights*, Leiden: Brill, 1963.

Gershoni, Israel and Jankowski, James P. *Egypt, Islam, and the Arabs: The Search for Egyptian Nationhood, 1900–1930*, Oxford: Oxford University Press, 1987.

Ghanoonparvar, Mohammad R. *In a Persian Mirror: Images of the West and Westerners in Iranian Fiction*, Austin, TX: University of Texas Press, 1993.

Ghanoonparvar, Mohammad R. *Prophets of Doom: Literature as a Socio-political Phenomenon in Modern Iran*, Lanham, MD: University Press of America, 1984.

Ghazoul, Ferial. *The Arabian Nights: A Structural Analysis*, Cairo: Cairo Associated Institution, 1980.

——. *Nocturnal Poetics: The Arabian Nights in a Comparative Context*, Cairo: American University in Cairo Press, 1996.

Ghazoul, Ferial and Harlow, Barbara (eds). *The View from Within: Writers and Critics on Contemporary Arabic Literature*, Cairo: American University in Cairo Press, 1994.

Gheissari, Ali. *Iranian Intellectuals in the Twentieth Century*, Austin, TX: University of Texas Press, 1998.

Gilroy, Amanda (ed.). *Romantic Geographies: Discourses of Travel, 1775–1844*, Manchester: Manchester University Press, 2000.

Gilroy, Amanda and Verhoeven, W.M. (eds). *Epistolary Histories: Letters, Fiction, Culture*. University Press of Virginia, 2000.

Gran, Peter. *Islamic Roots of Capitalism: Egypt, 1760–1840*, Syracuse, NY: Syracuse University Press, 1998.

Gregory, Derek. "Scripting Egypt," in James Duncan and Derek Gregory (eds), *Writes of Passage: Reading Travel Writing*, London: Routledge, 1999.

Grewal, Indrepal. *Home and Harem: Nation, Gender, Empire, and the Cultures of Travel*, Durham, NC: Duke University Press, 1996.

Grotzfeld, Heinz. "Creativity, Random Selection, and pia fraus: Observations on Compilation and Transmission of the Arabian Nights," *Marvels & Tales*, Vol. 18, No. 2(2004): 218–28.

Haag-Higuchi, Roxane. "Touring the World, Classifying the World: The Iranian Hajj Sayyah and his Travel-Writing," in Roxane Haag-Highuchi and Christian Szyska (eds), *Erzählter Raum in Literaturen der islamischedn Welt.* Wiesbaden: Harrassowitz, 2001, pp. 149–60.

Haddawy, Husain. *The Arabian Nights: Based on the Text of the Fourteenth-Century Syrian Manuscript*, Muhsin al-Mahdi (ed.), New York: W.W. Norton & Co., 1990.

Hafez, Sabry. *The Genesis of Arabic Narrative Discourse: A Study in the Sociology of Modern Arabic Literature*, London: Saqi Books, 1993.

Haykal, Ahmad. *Mujaz al-adab al-hadith fi Misr (ila qiyam al-harb al-'alamiyah al-thaniyah)*, Cairo: maktabat al-shahab, 1989.

Haywood, John A. *Modern Arabic Literature 1800–1970*, London: Lund Humphries, 1971.

Hobsbawm, E.J. *Nations and Nationalism Since 1780: Programme, Myth, Reality*, Cambridge: Cambridge University Press, 1990.

Hole, Richard. *Remarks on the Arabian Nights Entertainments, in Which the Origins of Sindibad's Voyages and Other Oriental Fictions Is Particularly Considered*, London: T. Cadell, Jr and W. Davies, 1797.

Horkheimer, Max and Adorno, Theodore. "Odysseus or Myth and Enlightenment," Robert Hullot-Kentor (trans.), *New German Critique*, Vol. 56(1992): 109–141.

Hourani, Albert. *Arabic Thought in the Liberal Age*, London: Oxford University Press, 1970.

Hunter, J. Paul. *Before Novels*, New York: WW Norton & Co. 1994.

Hurley, Kelly and Beer, Gillian (eds). *The Gothic Body: Sexuality, Materialism and Degeneration at the Fin de Siécle*, Cambridge: Cambridge University Press, 2004.

Ilchi, Abu al-Hasan Khan. *A Persian at the Court of King George, 1809–10*, London: Barrie & Jenkins, 1988.

Irwin, Robert. *The Arabian Nights, a Companion*. London: Allen Lane. 1994.

Isfahani, Mirza Habib. *Khatt va khattatan*, Tihran: kitabkhanih-yi mustufi, 1991.

Jack, Ian. *British Literature 1815–1832*, Oxford: Oxford University Press, 1963.

Jameson, Frederick. *Late Marxism*, New York: Verso, 1990.

——. *A Singular Modernity: Essay on the Ontology of the Present*, New York: Verso Press, 2002.

Javadi, Hasan. *Persian Literary Influence on English Literature, With Special Reference to the Nineteenth Century*, Costa Mesa, CA: Mazda Publishers, 2005.

——. *Satire in Persian Literature*, London: Associated University Press, 1988.

Jay, Gregory. "Paul de Man: The Subject of Literary History," *MLN*, Vol. 103, No. 5(1988): 969–94.

Jayyusi, Salma (ed.). *Modern Arabic Poetry*, New York: Columbia University Press, 1987.

Johnson, Richard. *The Oriental Moralist or the Beauties of the Arabian Nights Entertainments*, London: E. Newbery, 1790.

Jusdanis, Gregory. *Belated Modernity and Aesthetic Culture: Inventing National Literature*, Minneapolis, MN: University of Minnesota Press, 1991.

Kamshad, Hassan. *Modern Persian Prose Literature*, Bethesda, MD: Ibex Press, 1996.

——. "New Light on the Translation of Hajji Baba Isfahani," *Persica*, Vol. 1(1964): 70–5.

Karam, A.G. *Encyclopedia of Islam: "Faris Al-Shidyak,"* version 1.1. 2001, CD-ROM. Brill.

Kashani, Morteza Mushfiq. *Ruzigarha va andishihha*, Tihran: intisharat-i Ibn Sina, 1962.

Kashani-Sabet, Firoozeh. *Frontier Fictions: Shaping the Iranian Nation, 1804–1946*, Princeton, NJ: Princeton University Press, 1999.

Kennedy, Dane. " 'Captain Burton's Oriental Muck Heap': The Book of the Thousand Nights and the Uses of Orientalism," *Journal of British Studies*, Vol. 39(July 2000): 317–39.

Khalidi, Tarif. *Arabic Historical Thought in the Classical Period*, Cambridge: Cambridge University Press, 1994.

Khorrami, Mohammad Mehdi. *Modern Reflections of Classical Traditions in Persian Fiction*, Lewiston, NY: Edwin Mellen Press, 2003.

Kilgore, Maggie. *The Rise of the Gothic Novel*, New York: Routledge, 1995.

Kirkpatrick, Hilary. *The Modern Egyptian Novel: A Study in Social Criticism*, London: Ithaca Press for the Middle East Centre, St. Antony's College, 1974.

LaCapra, Dominick. *History, Politics and the Novel*, Ithaca, NY: Cornell University Press, 1987.

Lamb, George (trans. and ed.). *New Arabian Nights' Entertainments (selected from the originial MS by Jos. von Hammer)*, 3 vols, London: H. Colburn, 1829.

Lane, Edward William. *The Arabian Nights' Entertainments*, New York: Tudor Publishing Co., 1927.

Laroui, Abdallah. *The Crisis of the Arab Intellectual: Traditionalism or Historicism?* Berkeley, CA: University of California Press, 1977.

Latour, Bruno. *We Have Never Been Modern*, Cambridge, MA: Harvard University Press, 1993.

Layoun, Mary N. *Travels of a Genre: The Modern Novel and Ideology*, Princeton, NJ: Princeton University Press, 1990.

Lukacs, Georg. *The Theory of the Novel*, Cambridge, MA: The MIT Press, 1999.

Lynch, Deidre Shauna. *The Economy of Character*, Chicago, IL: Chicago University Press, 1998.

Lynch, Deidre and Warner, William (eds). *Cultural Institutions of the Novel*, Raleigh NC: Duke University Press 1999.

McKenzie Johnston, Henry. "Hajji Baba and Mirza Abul Hasan Khan—A Conundrum," *Iran*, Vol. 33(1995): 93–6.

——. *Ottoman and Persian Odysseys: James Morier, Creator of Hajji Baba of Ispahan, and His Brothers*, London: British Academic Press, 1998.

McKeon, Michael. *The Origins of the English Novel, 1600–1740*, Baltimore, MD: Johns Hopkins University Press, 2002.

Mahdi, Muhsin. *The Thousand and One Nights*, Leiden: E. J. Brill, 1994.

Mahjub, Muhammad Ja'far. "Tarjumih-yi Farsi-yi Alf layla wa layla," *Sokhan*, Vol. 11, No. 1(1962): 34–53.

Makdisi, Saree. " 'Postcolonial' Literature in a Neocolonial World: Modern Arabic Culture and the End of Modernity," *Boundary 2*, Vol. 22, No. 1(1995): 85–115.

Makdisi, Ussama. "Reclaiming the Land of the Bible: Missionaries, Secularism and Evangelical Modernity," *American Historical Review*, Vol. 102, No. 3(1997): 680–713.

Malkum Khan, Mirza. *Ruznamih-yi Qanun*, Huma Natiq (ed.), Tihran: intisharat-i Amir Kabir, p. 2535.

Maraghihi, Zayn al-'Abedin. *Siyahatnamih-yi Ibrahim Bayk*, Vols 1–3, Istanbul: matba'ih-yi Abulziya, 1327.

——. *Siyahatnamih-yi Ibrahim Bayg*, M.A. Sipanlu (ed.), Tihran: intisharat-i agah, 2006.

——. *Siyahatnamih-yi Ibrahim Bayg, ya bala-yi ta'assub-i ou*, Tihran: nashr-i Sipidih, 1981.

Marzolph, Ulrich. "Narrative Strategies in Popular Literature: Ideology and Ethics in Tales from the Arabian Nights and Other Collections," *Middle Eastern Literatures*, Vol. 7, No. 2(July 2004): 171–82.

——. "The Persian Nights," *Fabula*, 45(2004): 275–93.

——. "Persian Popular Literature of the Qajar Period," *Asian Folklore Studies*, Vol. 60, No. 2(2001): 215–18.

——. "Persian Translations of the 1001 Nights," *Mipaku Anthropology Newsletter*, No. 16(2003).

Massad, Joseph. *Colonial Effects*, New York: Columbia University Press, 2001.

Matar, Nabil. *In the Lands of the Christians*, London: Routledge Press, 2003.

Mirabedini, Hassan. *Sad sal-i dastan nivisi-i Iran*, 3 vols, Tihran: nashr-i Chishmih, 1380/2001.

Mitchell, Timothy. *Colonising Egypt*, Berkeley, CA: University of California Press, 1991.

Moosa, Matti. *The Origins of Modern Arabic Fiction*, Boulder, CO: Lynne Rienner Publishers, Inc., 1997.

Moreh, S. "Blank Verse in Modern Arabic Literature," *Bulletin of the School of Oriental and African Studies*, Vol. XXIX, No. 3(1966): 483–92.

——. *Signs Taken for Wonders: Studies on the Sociology of Literary Form*, London: Verso, 1983.

——. *Studies in Modern Arabic Prose and Poetry*, Leiden: Brill, 1988.

Moretti, Franco. *Atlas of the European Novel, 1800–1900*, New York: Verso, 1998.

Morier, James Justinian. *The Adventures of Hajji Baba of Ispahan*, London: Cresset Press, 1949.

——. *The Adventures of Hajji Baba of Ispahan*, English Classics, Chicago, IL and London: Stone and Kimball Methuen and Co., 1895.

——. *Hajji Baba, traduit de l'anglais par le traducteur des romans de sir Walter Scott*, Auguste-Jean-Baptiste Defauconpret, Paris: Haut-Coeur et Gayet jeune, 1824.

——. *A Journey through Persia, Armenia, and Asia Minor, to Constantinople, in the Years 1808 and 1809 in Which Is Included, Some Account of the Proceedings of His Majesty's*

Mission, under Sir Harford Jones, Bart. K.C. to the Court of the King of Persia, microform, Philadelphia, PA: M. Carey, 1816.

——. *Sarguzasht-i Haji Baba-yi Isfahani* (a Persian Translation of Hajji-Baba of Ispahan), D.C. Phillott (ed.), Calcutta: Baptist Mission Press/Asiatic Text Society, 1905.

——. *Sarguzasht-i Haji Baba-yi Isfahani*, Tihran, 1330 [1951/2].

——. *Sarguzasht-i Haji Baba-yi Isfahani*, Mirza Habib Isfahani (trans.) and Muhammad 'Ali Jamalzadih (ed.), Costa Mesa, CA: Mazda Publishers, 1996.

Moss, Joss. *Word Crimes: Blasphemy, Culture and Literature in Nineteenth-Century England*, Chicago, IL: University of Chicago Press, 1998.

Mufti, Aamir. "The Aura of Authenticity," *Social Text*, Vol. 18, No. 3, (2000): 87–103.

al-Musawi, Muhsin Jassim. *al-Riwayya al-'Arabiyya: al-nasha' wa al-tahawwul*, Cairo: al-hayra al-Misriyya al-'amma lil kitab, 1988.

——. *The Postcolonial Arabic Novel: Debating Ambivalence*, Leiden: Brill, 2003.

al-Musili, Ilyas. *al-Dhahab wa al-'asifa: Awwal rihla sharqiyya ila al-'alam al-jadid (1683–1668)*, Nouri al-Jarrah (ed.), Bayrut: al-mu'assissa al-'Arabiyya lil-dirasat wa al-nashr, 2001.

Muwaylihi, Muhammad. *Hadith 'Isa ibn Hisham, aw fitra min al-zaman*, 7th edn, Cairo: dar al-ma'arif, 1947.

al-Nadim, Muhammad ibn Ishaq. *Fihrist*, Gustave Flugel (ed.), 2 vols, Bayrut: Khayats, 1964.

Natiq, Huma. *Az mast ke bar mast*, Tihran: intisharat-i aqa, 1978.

——. "Haji Morier va qissih-yi isti'mar," *Alefba*, (196?): 22.

——. "Mirza Aqa Khan, Sayyed Jamal al-Din et Malkom Khan à Istanbul (1860–1897)," in T. Zarcone and F. Zarinebaf-shahr (eds), *Les Iraniens d'Istanbul*, Paris: Institut Français de Recherches en Iran & Institute Français d'Etudes Anatoliennes, 1993, pp. 45–60.

Nicholls, Peter. *Modernisms: A Literary Guide*, Berkeley, CA: University of California Press, 1995.

Niranjana, Tejaswini. *Siting Translation: History, Post-Structuralism and the Colonial Context*, Berkeley, CA: University of California Press, 1992.

Ouyang, Wen-Chin. "Genres, Ideologies, Genre Ideologies and Narrative Transformation," *Middle Eastern Literatures*, Vol. 7, No. 2(July 2004): 125–9.

Pedersen, Johannes. *The Arabic Book*, Princeton, NJ: Princeton University Press, 1984.

Perera, Suvendrini. *The Reaches of Empire: The English Novel from Edgeword to Dickens*, New York: Columbia University Press, 1991.

Phegley, Jennifer. *Educating the Proper Woman Reader: Victorian Family Literary Magazines and the Cultural Health of the Nation*, Columbus, OH: Ohio State University Press, 2004.

Pinault, David. "Bulaq, Macnaughten and the New Leiden Edition Compared," *Journal of Semitic Studies*, Vol. 32. No. 1(1987): 125–57.

——. *Story-Telling Techniques in the Arabian Nights*, Leiden: Brill, 1992.

Poovey, Mary. *Uneven Developments: The Ideological Work of Gender in Mid-Victorian England*, Chicago, IL: University of Chicago Press, 1988.

Pratt, Mary Louise. *Imperial Eyes: Travel Writing and Transculturation*, London: Routledge, 1992.

Qazvini, M. "Wafiyat-i ma'asirin," *Yadgar*, Vol. 5, Nos. 8–9(1949): 69.

Ramos, Julio. *Divergent Modernities: Culture and Politics in Nineteenth-Century Latin America*, Durham, NC: Duke University Press, 2001.

Reynolds, Dwight. "Arabic Literature in the Post-Classical Period," in *Cambridge History of Arabic Literature*, Cambridge: Cambridge University Press, 2006, pp. 270–91.

Ringer, Monica. *Education, Religion and the Discourse of Cultural Reform in Qajar Iran*, Costa Mesa, CA: Mazda Publishers, 2001.

Roper, Geoffrey. "Ahmad Faris al-Shidyaq and the Libraries of Europe and the Ottoman Empire," *Libraries and Culture*, Vol. 33, No. 3(1998): 233–48.

Said, Edward W. *Culture and Imperialism*, New York: Vintage Classics, 1994.

——. *Humanism and Democratic Criticism*, New York: Columbia University Press, 2004.

——. *Orientalism*, New York: Vintage, 1994.

Sakkut, Hamdi. *al-Riwaya al-'Arabiyya, bibliyujrafiya wa madkhal naqdi, 1865–1995*, al-Cairo: qism al-nashr bi al-jami'a al-Amrikiyya, 1979.

——. *The Egyptian Novel and its Main Trends from 1913 to 1952*, Cairo: American University in Cairo Press, 1971.

Sallis, Eve. Sheherazade. *Looking through the Looking Glass: The Metamorphosis of the Thousand and One Nights*, Surrey: Curzon Press, 1999.

Sanders, Valerie. *Eve's Renegades: Victorian Anti-Feminist Women Novelists*, London: St. Martin's Press, 1996.

Sanjabi, Maryam B. "Mardum-Guriz: An Early Persian Translation of Moliere's Le Misanthrope," *International Journal of Middle East Studies*, Vol. 30, No. 2(May, 1998): 251–70.

Sasani, Khan Malak. *Yadbudha-yi sifarat-i Istanbul*, Tihran: 1966.

Sawaie, Mohammad. "Rifa'a Rafi' al-Tahtawi and his Contribution to the Lexical Development of Modern Literary Arabic," *International Journal of Middle East Studies*, Vol. 32(2000): 395–410.

Sayyah, Hajj Muhammad 'Ali. *Khatirat-i Hajj Sayyah ya durih-yi khawf va vahshat. ed. Hamid Sayyah va Sayf Allah Golkar*, Tihran: intisharat-i Ibn Sina, 1967.

——. *Safarnamih-yi Haji Sayyah bih farang*, Ali Dehbashi (ed.), Tehran: intisharat-i sukhan, 1999.

Scarcia, Gianroberto. "Quel Critere de Choix Dans La Traduction Persane du Hajji Baba?" in T. Zarcone and F. Zarinebaf-Shahr (eds), *Les Iraniens d'Istanbul*, Paris: Institut Français de Recherches en Iran & Institute Français d'Etudes Anatoliennes, 1993, pp. 187–91.

Schacker-Mill, Jennifer. "Otherness and Otherworldliness, Edward W. Lane's Ethnographic Treatment of The Arabian Nights," *Journal of American Folklore*, 113(448): 164–84.

Schmitt, Cannon. *Alien Nation: Nineteenth-Century Gothic Fictions and English Nationality*, Philadelphia, PA: University of Philadelphia Press, 1997.

Schwab, Raymond. *The Oriental Renaissance. Europe's Rediscovery of India and the East, 1680–1880*, New York: Columbia University Press, 1984.

Scott, Walter and Williams, Ioan M. *Sir Walter Scott on Novelists and Fiction*, London: Routledge & K. Paul, 1968.

Selim, Samah. *The Novel and the Rural Imaginary in Egypt, 1880–1985*, New York: Routledge, 2004.

Shafi'i Kadkani, Muhammad. *Shi'r-i mu'asir-i 'Arab*, Tihran: intisharat-i Tihran, 1977.

Shawabkeh, Mohammed Ali. *Arabs and the West: A Study in the Modern Arabic Novel, 1935–1985*, Amman: Mu'tah University, 1992.

Shaykhu, Abb Luwis. *Tarikh al-adab al-'Arabiyya fi al-qarn al-tasi'a 'ashr wa al-rub' al-awwal min al-qarn al-'ashrin*, Bayrut: dar al-mashriq, 1985.

al-Shidyaq, Ahmad Faris. *al-Saq 'ala al-saq fi ma hua al-faryaq; aw ayyam wa shuhur wa a'wam fi 'ajam al-'arab wa al-'ajam*, Shaykh Nasib Wahiba Khazen (ed.), Bayrut: dar maktaba al-hayat, 1965.

——. *I'tirafat al-Shidyaq fi kitab al-saq 'ala al-saq*, 'Imad Sulh (ed.), Bayrut: dar al-raid al-'Arabi, 1982.

——. *La Jambe Sur La Jambe: Roman*, René R. Khawam (trans.) Domaine Étranger, Paris: Phébus, 1991.

——. *Silsila al-a'mal al-majhula*, Fawwaz Trablusi and Aziz al-Azmeh (eds), London: Riad El-Rayyes, 1995.

Shirazi, Mirza Salih. *Guzarish-i Safar-i Mirza Salih Shirazi*, Humayun Shahidi (ed.), Tihran: intisharat-i rah-i nou, 1983.

Shukri, Ghali. *al-Riwaya al-'Arabiyya fi rihla al-'adhab*, Cairo: 'alam al-kutub, 1971.

——. *Marksiya wa al-Adab*, Bayrut: al-mu'assissa al-'Arabiyya lil-dirasat wa al-nashr, 1979.

——. *Thawra al-fikr fi adabna al-hadith*, Cairo: maktabat al-anjlu al-Misriya, 1965.

Siskin, Clifford. *The Historicity of Romantic Discourse*, Oxford: Oxford University Press, 1988.

——. "The Rise of Novelism," in Deidre Shauna and William Warner (eds), *Cultural Institutions of the Novel*, Durham: Duke University Press, 1996, pp. 423–40.

——. *The Work of Writing: Literature and Social Change in Britain, 1700–1830*, Baltimore, MD: Johns Hopkins University Press, 1999.

Smith, Charles D. "Love, Passion and Class in the Fiction of Muhammad Husayn Haykal," *Journal of the American Oriental Society*, Vol. 99, No. 2(1979): 249–61.

Sprachman, P. "Hajji Baba Meets the Westomaniac: The Convergence of Two Stereotyped Iranians," in Mehdi Marashi (ed.), *Persian Studies in North America: Studies in Honor of Mohammad Ali Jazayery*, Bethesda, MD: Iranbooks, 1994, pp. 289–306.

Stetkevytch, Jaroslav. "Some Observations on Arabic Poetry," *Journal of Near Eastern Studies*, Vol. 26, No. 1(1967): 1–12.

Stewart, Garrett. *Dear Reader: The Conscripted Reader in Nineteenth-Century British Fiction*, Baltimore, MD: Johns Hopkins University Press, 1996.

Strauss, Johann. "Who Read What in the Ottoman Empire (Nineteenth-Twentieth Centuries)," *Arabic Middle Eastern Literatures*, Vol. 6, No. 1(2003): 39–76.

Sulh, 'Imad. *Ahmad Faris al-Shidyaq: Atharahu wa 'asruhu*, Bayrut: dar al-nahhar lil-nashr, 1980.

Taha Badr, 'Abd al-Muhsin. *Tatawwur al-riwayya al-'arabiyya*, Cairo: dar al-ma'arif, 1968.

al-Tahtawi, Rifa'a Rafi'. *An Imam in Paris: An Account of a Stay in France by an Egyptian Cleric (Takhlis Al-Ibriz Fi Talkhis Baris)*, Daniel Newman (trans.), London: Saqi Books, 2004.

——. *Takhlis al-ibriz fi talkhis Bariz: min adab al-rihlat*, Cairo: maktaba al-kulliyya al-azhariyya, dar Ibn Zaydun, n/d.

Talattof, Kamran. *The Politics of Writing in Iran: A History of Modern Persian Literature*, Syracuse, NY: Syracuse University Press, 2000.

Talib, 'Umar. *al-Riwaya al-'Iraqiyya: dirasat naqdiyya*, Baghdad: dar al-shu'un al-thaqafiyya al-'amma: 1999.

Tarazi, Filib. *Tarikh al-sihafa al- 'Arabiyya*, Bayrut: al-matba'a al-adabiyya, 1913.

Tasuji, 'Abd al-Latif (trans.). *Hizar u yik shab*, 3 vols, Tihran: intisharat-i jami, 1379 [2000].

——. 'Abd al-Latif, Isfahani, Shams al-Shu'ar, and Ramazani, Mohammad (trans.). *Hizar u yik shab*, 3 vols, Tihran: kulal-i khadar, 1938.

Tavakoli-Targhi, Mohamad. *Refashioning Iran: Orientalism, Occidentalism and Historiography*, New York: Palgrave, 2001.

Thompson, Nicola Diane. *Reviewing Sex: Gender and the Reception of Victorian Novels*, New York University Press, 1996.

al-Tunisi, Khayr al-Din. *The Surest Path: The Political Treatise of a Nineteenth-Century Muslim Statesman*, Carl Leon Brown (trans.), Cambridge, MA: Center for Middle Eastern Studies, Harvard University, 1967.

Vincent, David. *Literacy and Popular Culture: England 1750–1914*, Cambridge: Cambridge University Press, 1989.

Viswanathan, Gauri. *Masks of Conquest: Literary Study and British Rule in India*, Delhi: Oxford University Press, 1998.

——. *Outside the Fold: Conversion, Modernity and Belief*, Princeton, NJ: Princeton University Press, 1998.

Watt, Ian. *Rise of the Novel*, Berkeley, CA: University of California Press, 1957.

Weber, Henry. *Tales of the East, Comprising the Most Popular Romances of Oriental Origin: And the Best Imitations of European Authors*, Edinburgh: James Ballantyne & Co., 1812.

Wesling, Donald. "Michel Serres, Bruno Latour and the Edges of Historical Periods," *CLIO*, Vol. 26 (1997): 189.

White, Hayden. "Literary History: The Point of it All," *New Literary History*, Vol. 2, No. 1 (1970): 173–85.

Williams, Raymond. *The Country and the City*, Oxford: Oxford University Press, 1973.

——. *Culture and Society: 1780–1950*, New York: Columbia University Press, 1983.

——. *The Politics of Modernism*, New York: Verso Press, 1989.

Wolfreys, Julian. *Victorian Hauntings: Spectrality, Gothic, the Uncanny and Literature*, Palgrave Macmillian, 2001.

Yarshater, Ehsan (ed.). *Persian Literature*, New York: Bibliotheca Persica, 1998.

Young, Robert. *Colonial Desire: Hybridity in Theory, Culture and Race*, London: Routledge, 1995.

Zaqarit, ʻAbd al-Majid Husayn. *Fi bina' al-riwayya al-Lubnaniyya (1972–1992)*, Bayrut: al-Jamiʻah al-Lubnaniyya, 1999.

Zarcone, T. and Zarinebaf-shahr, F. (eds). *Les Iraniens d'Istanbul*, Paris: Institut Français de Recherches en Iran & Institute Français d'Etudes Anatoliennes, 1993.

Zeidan, Joseph, T. *Arab Women Novelists: The Formative Years and Beyond*, New York: SUNY Press, 1995.

INDEX

For Product Safety Concerns and Information please contact our EU representative GPSR@taylorandfrancis.com
Taylor & Francis Verlag GmbH, Kaufingerstraße 24, 80331 München, Germany

www.ingramcontent.com/pod-product-compliance
Lightning Source LLC
Chambersburg PA
CBHW071515100726
47908CB00004B/1175

* 9 7 8 0 4 1 5 5 9 7 4 4 9 *

For Product Safety Concerns and Information please contact our EU representative GPSR@taylorandfrancis.com
Taylor & Francis Verlag GmbH, Kaufingerstraße 24, 80331 München, Germany

www.ingramcontent.com/pod-product-compliance
Lightning Source LLC
Chambersburg PA
CBHW071515100726
47908CB00004B/1175

* 9 7 8 0 4 1 5 5 9 7 4 4 9 *